The Canadian Family in Crisis

The Canadian Family in Crisis

Fifth Edition

John F. Conway

James Lorimer & Company Ltd., Publishers
Toronto 2003

James Lorimer & Company Ltd. acknowledges the support of the
Ontario Arts Council. We acknowledge the support of the
Government of Canada through the Book Publishing Industry
Development Program (BPIDP) for our publishing activities. We
acknowledge the support of the Canada Council for the Arts for our
publishing program. We acknowledge the support of the Government
of Ontario through the Ontario Media Development Corporation's
Ontario Book Initiative.

Cover photograph: Kids at playground in Hope, British Columbia.
Photo credit: Brian Milne, Firstlight.

Canadian Cataloguing in Publishing Data

Conway, John Frederick
    The Canadian family in crisis/John F. Conway. —5th ed.

Includes index.
ISBN 1-550028-798-2

1. Family — Canada. 2. Social change — Canada. 3. Family policy
— Canada. I. Title.

HQ560.C593 2003   306.85'0971   C2003-902791-0

James Lorimer & Company Ltd., Publishers
35 Britain Street
Toronto, Ontario M5A 1R7
www.lorimer.ca

Printed and bound in Canada

This book is dedicated to:

Geneviève Bergeron, 21,
Hélène Colgan, 23,
Natalie Croteau, 23,
Barbara Daigneault, 22,
Anne-Marie Edward, 21,
Maude Haviernick, 29,
Barbara Maria Klueznick, 31,
Maryse Lagonière, 25,
Maryse Leclaire, 23,
Anne-Marie Lemay, 27,
Sonia Pelletier, 28,
Michèle Richard, 21,
Annie Saint-Arneault, 23, and
Annie Turcotte, 21,

who were brutally murdered on 6 December 1989 at the École Polytechnique de Montréal.

May this book serve as a small candle to help illuminate the darkness of our understanding.

Contents

List of Tables and Figures

Acknowledgements

All or portions of the manuscript in its various editions were read by Curtis Fahey, Virginia Smith, Diane Young, Tara Tovell, Craig Saunders, and Kristen Pederson-Chew of James Lorimer & Company; and by Margaret and Sally Mahood. Their suggestions helped immeasurably. Copy editors Jane Fredemans and Dawn Hunter often rescued my prose from itself. It is impossible to list all my friends and colleagues who contributed over the years to shaping my ideas on the topic, but I thank them all. And I thank all those scholars cited in the endnotes whose work made this attempt at an overview possible. Leanne Sywanyk typed the manuscript, including my interminable revisions and insertions. Grants from the University of Regina President's Fund and from the office of the Dean of Graduate Studies helped defray some of the xeroxing and typing costs.

Finally, I have to acknowledge the help of my spouse, Sally Mahood, my three sons, Liam, Aidan, and Kieran, and my daughter, Meara. Writing this book and its revisions posed many mini-crises for our family, and their tolerance and good humour over the months were vital to seeing the task through to completion.

Author's Note for the 2003 Edition

This volume has been updated using the latest data available from Statistics Canada from the 2001 Census and Statistics Canada's projections to 2016. As in the 1997 edition, the assessment of the relevant social scientific literature on family and gender matters has been updated from 1987/88 to 1995/96. I have added an epilogue to assess both the major developments in the family in the new century, and whether we have transcended the "crisis" stage of family reconstruction and can now speak with certainty that the family forms of the future are now firmly established.

Although recent research results continue to confirm the basic arguments and analyses presented in previous editions of this book, there has been a significant shift in Canada's political culture that has changed the tone of my analysis. In previous editions, written during the early phase of the neo-conservative attack on Canada's system of public spending on health, education, and social welfare programs, the evidence seemed to suggest that strong public resistance would be successful in defeating that attack. As a variety of neo-conservative governments, both in Ottawa and in various provinces, faced defeat or imminent defeat because of promises from competing political parties to end the neo-conservative era, many were confident that new governments with fresh, popular mandates would return to the welfare state consensus that characterized Canadian political culture after the end of the Great Depression/World War II era. That proved to be a misguided assumption as formerly anti-neoconservative political parties formed governments and continued to implement the neoconservative agenda against the popular will. This new edition of *The Canadian Family in Crisis* attempts to address this harsh new reality facing Canadian families, especially those most vulnerable as a result of the crisis of the family.

One of the questions I am asked most frequently about earlier editions of the book is why I neglected to deal with the obvious regional, ethnic, and national differences that characterize families in Canada. The decision was deliberate and the reasons are two-fold. First, such differences are exceedingly complex. Families among the aboriginal nations vary significantly along a number of dimensions when compared to non-aboriginal families. So too do families in the Québécois nation vary when compared to those among English Canadians. First and second generation immigrant families, especially those from Third World cultures and those from traditional patriarchal European cultures, are also quite different from the families of Canadians into their third, fourth, and fifth generation in the country. The differences are exceedingly complex and sensitive and deserve a separate treatment.

Second, without the fullest development and analysis of data, superficial assertions about such differences lend themselves to misuse and do a disservice to our national debates on family policy. For example, apparently higher rates of wife abuse, child abuse, adolescent and youth suicide, and intra-family homicide among aboriginal families need to be probed more deeply. Is this a true "cultural" or "ethnic" or "national" difference? Or is it merely a reflection of higher rates of poverty, unemployment, and the stresses of life in a structurally racist society? Or is it a combination of economic injustice and the legacy of cultural genocide as has been recently argued? I suspect that if one controlled for socioeconomic status one would find that these alleged "cultural" differences would largely disappear, as such studies have shown in U.S. research on black and white families. After careful analysis, the data reveal that the rate of various family dysfunctions is not significantly different among blacks and whites in similar socio-economic circumstances. In short, such issues need to be carefully researched and not just reported as statistical counts. They not only require but deserve a book of their own.

As a result of these considerations, I decided to focus on the family in Canada as a national social structure, without attempting to address regional, ethnic, and sub-national variations.

Preface

The crisis of the family in Canada is one of monumental proportions, and it touches us all.

The figures are astonishing. In the first decade of the new millennium, one marriage in two may well end in divorce.[1] Between 1966 and 2001 the number of divorced Canadians increased by over 14 times as the divorce rate skyrocketed, and the duration of marriage before divorce fell dramatically.[2] More and more of us are declining to take the emotional risk of marriage. Single-parent and common-law families are growing faster than traditional "husband-wife" families.[3] Wife beating and child abuse, physical and sexual, are among the fastest growing crimes in the country. Each year tens of thousands of Canadian children suffer through a marriage break-down. More and more families are childless, and the Canadian fertility rate is dangerously below replacement levels. Nearly 100,000 children, aged 10 to 16, run away each year. Reports of the homelessness, hunger, poverty, violence, and sexual exploitation afflicting our children can be read daily in our newspapers.

What these facts tell us is that the traditional family no longer delivers emotional solace to a growing number of Canadian men and women. The family has also increasingly failed to provide many children with the minimal emotional and physical security necessary for shaping confident and emotionally healthy adults.

If the family serves any purpose in advanced urban industrial society, it is to provide emotional gratification for its members, while ensuring the birth, early care, and socialization of children. The crisis of the family has called into question these obligations. The traditional family is dying and new alternatives are emerging, but the transition involves pain, anguish, and uncertainty. While the sanctuary, the traditional family, is being dismantled around us, the new alternatives to deliver love and comfort and to socialize children have yet to receive the recognition and support so vital to their successful emergence. In recent years, even marginal supports of this transition have been cut and the rug has been pulled out from under the most vulnerable families.

This crisis is increasingly at the centre of political debate and public concern. Public support for an adequately funded and effective national daycare strategy has remained high, forcing politicians repeatedly to promise such a program. Yet upon election to government, political leaders have consistently refused to act, citing fiscal reasons. Meanwhile, conservative politicians, often in alliance with right-wing Christian fundamentalists, use the crisis of the family in a cynical, ideological game, claiming deep commitment to the old-fashioned, traditional family while attacking new family forms as promiscuous and "unnatural." Frequently, the defence of old-fashioned family values is used as a justification to attack what few publicly funded social supports are available to new, emerging family forms or to those hurt by family breakdown and upheaval. A withdrawal of support for impoverished, single-parent families headed by women is justified as a necessary measure to discourage promiscuity and to encourage young, single mothers to give their babies up for adoption. A refusal to act on a publicly funded daycare program is rationalized as a measure to keep the old-fashioned family intact, either by encouraging mothers to stay home or by encouraging informal "family" daycare alternatives. In Quebec, cash incentives are offered to women to have more babies, and new programs of cash payments for women who stay home and care for their kids, as proposed in Alberta, are devised. Such efforts to turn Canadians back to the traditional family cannot hope to succeed. But by focussing on such measures, governments appear to act, while the painful transformation of the family moves inexorably onward.

Some politicians genuinely believe that by resisting the new family forms and supporting the traditional family, they are doing the right thing. They remain supremely immune to the damage and pain they inflict upon victims of the family crisis. Others are convinced that only support for the old-fashioned family will sell on Main Street. Still others wonder how much intervention in the family, however beneficent, the public will accept. And the potential cost implications of effective family policies are enormous in the short term.

This poorly directed concern is understandable. As the crisis deepens, the ideological positions on the family harden. This is particularly true of the right wing. REAL Women (Realistic, Equal, Active and for Life) complains that the Supreme Court, the Charter of Rights and Freedoms, gay rights, abortion rights, and universal daycare are destroying the family as part of a feminist conspiracy and insists that more support must be forthcoming for the role of women as wives and mothers in the home. A new federal political party, The Family Coalition Party, was created based on opposition to abortion and support for the traditional family unit. The more successful Canadian Alliance has firmly staked out a very conservative position on the family, opposing feminism, reproductive choice, state family policies, universal daycare and public policy recognition of family forms other than the traditional patriarchal family. A central theme of the anti-choice movement is that the traditional family is being destroyed by the freedom of reproductive choice among women. Such attitudes are buttressed by more official opinions such as those expressed in a U.S. Presidential Task Force report, *The Family: Preserving America's Future*, which seriously argues that the crisis of the family has resulted from decades of "liberal social experiments, from no-fault divorce to permissive sex to the easy availability of welfare."[4]

On the other side, feminist groups ranging from the National Action Committee on the Status of Women to various pro-choice groups, joined by groups of trade unionists, social workers, social scientists, mental health workers, and day care advocates, have mounted a convincing lobby that insists that the crisis of the family must be confronted. The price of avoiding the issue is just too high: homeless and hungry children; child and teen suicide; battered women and abused children; enforced pregnancy and unwanted babies; and increasing economic injustice for growing numbers of women and children. The crisis of the family, they argue, has become a general social crisis and must be confronted with effective family policies.

The structural transformation of the family continues irresistibly, and those in power take half or quarter measures, or none at all. As the debate rages, the victims of the crisis of the family continue to grow in number.

Many years ago the famous American sociologist Robert S. Lynd wrote a provocative little book entitled *Knowledge for What?*[5] Lynd enjoined social scientists to accept as part of their scientific obligation to the community the urgent clarification and communication of the pressing problems of an epoch to the people. Some years later C. Wright Mills wrote *The Sociological Imagination.*[6] He appealed to social scientists to endeavour to make "personal troubles of milieu," where people try as best they can to adjust to crises individually, into "public issues of social structure," where the community, alerted to a problem that is in fact centrally social, can mobilize its collective resources to adjust to the problem while endeavouring to solve it. This book was inspired by these two imperatives.

In the past 40 years, there has been an enormous amount of research in Canada on the problems of women and the family. This book is deeply indebted to that work. One thing has been made crystal clear — the crisis of the family and the problems of women in achieving equality are intimately linked and cannot be solved separately.

PART I

The Changing Nature of the Family

Therefore shall a man leave his father and his mother, and shall cleave unto his wife and they shall be one flesh ...

And the Lord God said unto the woman ... I will greatly multiply thy sorrow and thy conception; in sorrow thou shalt bring forth children; and thy desire shall be subject to thy husband, and he shall rule over thee ...

And unto Adam he said ... cursed is the ground for thy sake; in sorrow shalt thou eat of it all the days of thy life ... In the sweat of thy face shalt thou eat bread ...

Therefore the Lord God sent him forth from the garden of Eden, to till the ground from whence he was taken.

Genesis

Introduction

Social scientists often get carried away with a definition of terms, discussing fine distinctions between "statistical families," "economic families," and "extended families." But the family in our experience is clear. It is the coming together of two adults, usually but not always a man and a woman, usually but not always legally married, to express their mutual love and commitment. If the relationship lasts, children are often produced, and then the family is made of mother, father, and children living together under one roof, developing a long-term economic, social, and emotional unit. Sometimes, as the years advance, the family expands to include aging grandparents.

The big things are commitment, obligation, responsibility. Recognizing that we all must age and that our sexual currency on the love market must decline, physical love is replaced by deeper bases of understanding and support and, often most importantly, the shared love and excitement of raising children. The establishment of the family is an effort to find assured meaning and solace, as well as to express our emotional selves in more fundamental and lasting ways. That was the family. That is the family. And that will be the family in the future. The human species has not yet produced an alternative as fulfilling or as rewarding.

That fundamental marriage, or common-law, relationship that brings two adults together sets the stage for the bearing and raising of children, for the care and comfort of the old and dying, and for emotional and financial support in our declining years. In the distant past, marriage and the family were *the* social structure of the species. And today they remain *the* central social experience of our day-to-day lives.

The family in this sense is in crisis. It has been in crisis before — when feudalism declined and collapsed; when industrial capitalism emerged; when war, famine, and plague swept a land. But the crisis today, just like previous crises, is specific and needs focussed attention, if only because new embryonic family forms are emerging and urgently appealing for midwives.

1 / Families Past

The Origin of the Family

We will probably never know for certain when, where, and how the human family emerged. Freud suggested that, prior to civilization, the human species probably lived in hordes much like those of our present primate relatives.[1] These hordes were characterized by a dominant male who enjoyed sexual access to all the females and denied sexual gratification to the younger, subordinate males. But, inevitably, the younger males conspired against the dominant male (father), rose up against him, and slew him. There followed a wanton sexual debauch with the females. Extending his metaphor, Freud speculated that the younger males were overcome by guilt for having slain the father, for their incestuous liaisons with the females, their mothers, and for the aggression it led to among themselves. Ultimately, the young males erected taboos against incest and aggression and realized that human social life, on which their collective survival depended, had to be rooted in the suppression of instinctual gratification.[2] The seeds of the human family were thereby sown: the suppression of sexuality within the group, controls on sexual gratification, the prescription to go outside the immediate group for sexual partners, and the subordination of the sexual and aggressive instincts to the tasks of survival and civilization.

While Marx might have conceded the outlines of Freud's metaphor, he argued not that our animal natures were merely repressed, therefore always threatening to burst through the fetters of civilization, but that as the human species emerged our very nature was transformed. Thus, members of the human species became human in the fullest sense, rather than just intelligent animals wisely controlling their more bestial tendencies in the interests of co-operation and survival. Marx never specifically wrote at length on the emergence of the family, but Engels did.

Taking off from Morgan's nineteenth-century classic *Ancient Society*, Engels attempted to relate forms of the emerging human family to Morgan's main stages in the history of human development.[3] Thus during the period of "savagery," when the human species took its survival directly from nature through hunting and gathering, the dominant family form was "group marriage," which was characterized by informal pairing and a simple division of labour based on age and sex. Dependence was mutual, as the food-gathering activities of women and children were as vital as the hunting activities of the men. During the period of "barbarism," after the invention of agriculture and the domestication of animals led to complex systems of food production and storage, the dominant family form was "pairing marriage." It required a more permanent household organization, but the division of labour remained mutual. There was still no clear dependence of women and children on men. As barbarism evolved into more complex forms of "civilization," a more strictly monogamous marriage emerged, laying the basis for the modern nuclear family. With civilization came private property and the state, as well as the more rigid patriarchal family based on male domination and the subordination and dependence of women and children. Monogamy was enforced on women (but not on men) in order to assure paternity and the orderly inheritance of property by the progeny of the dominant male. The emergence of the modern nuclear family form lies, therefore, for Engels, at the cradle of women's oppression with the establishment of a rigid patriarchy and a system of male privilege.

Certain themes are clear. How did forms of sexual regulation emerge? How did patriarchy reach ascendancy? How did the relationships of mutuality and reciprocity get transformed into relationships of domination and dependence? And these are important questions. Even today, biological determinists continue to assert that male domination and female subordination are "natural" and biologically inevitable. It is important, therefore, to understand how the human family came into being and developed, if only to remind ourselves of its *social construction* — that is to say, to remind ourselves that the species and its circumstances, not Nature, decreed the character and form of the human family.

It has been suggested that there appears to be a gradual move from sexual promiscuity to increasing exclusivity in moving from lower to higher non-human primates.[4] Some lower primates practise extreme sexual promiscuity when the female is in estrus. At the next stage there is a degree of exclusivity, since mating occurs mainly between estrus females and dominant males. Finally there's the gibbon, one of two anthropoid apes most closely related to the human species, whose social organization closely parallels a human, monogamous, nuclear family.

By and large, however, there are few clear indications of a nascent human family among the primates. Like humans, infants of non-human primates are dependent on their mothers for a long period of time. Unlike humans, non-human primate sexuality is clearly directed hormonally. Like humans, non-human primates live in groups and engage in complex social interaction. Unlike humans, non-human primates neither co-operate nor engage in systematic food sharing. The social life of non-human primates may be a step towards human social life, but only a very small step.

A number of crucial things evidently happened in the transition of the human species from its primate roots. Co-operation had to replace conflict. Year-round sexual interest had to establish itself. Systems of kinship had to replace hierarchies based on brute strength. More complex patterns of social life, including a division of labour, mutuality, and reciprocity, had to replace the simple primate social life of competitive sexual activity, grooming, random play, and protection from predators. Territorial hostility had to be replaced by mechanisms to assure harmony and mutual aid.

Early Families

All this and more was achieved by the remarkable human invention of the family. With the family came a division of labour, food sharing, long-term relationships of reciprocity and obligation, the regulation of sexual activity, harmony, and co-operation, elaborate kinship relationships binding disparate groups together, and the assurance (more or less) of survival for all members of the family group from birth to death. The human family was clearly the watershed that separated the human species from all others. The species could not have survived without it.

When they compare the highest non-human primate hordes and the simplest hunting and gathering human groups, cultural anthropologists point to the enormous discontinuous chasm that separates the two. Freed from the rigidity of biological adaptation, the human species has been able to survive in virtually every environment presented to it. Through cultural and technological innovations, humans can live underwater and in outer space, fly through the air, and race at dizzying speeds along the ground. Today this is so self-evident as to be hardly worth noting. But if we return to the contrast between our nearest primate cousins and our simplest human ancestors, what is most striking is just what was at first distinctively human.

There were three specifically human adaptations that marked the species off clearly from all other animals. These were the division of labour, food sharing, and the establishment of a new social role, that of "husband-father."[5] These three phenomena assured the species' survival and success. The division of labour — women gathering food and men hunting — provided the species with a more secure and balanced supply of food. The change from the anarchy of individual feeding to the systematic, reciprocal sharing of food characteristic of the human species in all times and places occurred. What was required was the establishment of the husband-father social role, "in which specific males relate to specific females and their young, taking on special responsibility for their welfare."[6] And this new social formation was cemented by emotional attachments resulting from continuous "year-round *sexual interest* under conscious control in both partners," made possible by "the suppression of estrus and the concealment of ovulation."

This more or less universal early human family form, defined by Gough as "a married couple or other group of adult kinfolk who co-operate economically and in the upbringing of children, and all or most of whom share a common dwelling,"[7] dominated and defined the experience of the species from perhaps two million years ago to 10 or 15,000 years ago, when agriculture and the domestication of animals began. If the life of the human species to this moment in time were 24 hours, this "primitive" family form existed for 23 hours and 46 minutes. The more modern family form, which culminates in today's nuclear family, emerged only 14 minutes ago. The specific content of the family form varied, but there were certain universals: some degree of taboo against incest; a sexual division of labour; group security; and forms of marriage defined as "a socially recognized, durable (although not necessarily lifelong) relationship between individual men and women." From this marriage relationship "springs social fatherhood, some kind of special bond between a man and the child of his wife, whether or not they are his own children physiologically."[8] And, finally, men generally enjoyed higher status and greater authority than women.

Perhaps this last point needs further attention. Women may not have had as much status or authority as men in hunting and gathering societies, but neither were they oppressed, nor were there elaborate systems of male privilege. If women's lesser status had any biological root it was because they bore and suckled children, and women in such societies would probably be pregnant or suckling an infant throughout their fertile years. Indeed, given life expectancy, it is doubtful many women lived beyond their fertile years. This fundamental biological fact meant that it was not practical for women to hunt and that it made more sense for them to gather food and carry out household tasks, things that could be easily reconciled with pregnancy and infant care. The practicality of the situation provides an explanation — we need not hypothesize some hormonal or instinctual basis for what was an eminently practical sexual division of labour.

Men's superior strength may also provide some explanation for their higher status as well as their possession of and knowledge of weapons. But the status differences between the sexes were not particularly marked. Women's food gathering activities were vital to survival as were their child bearing and rearing functions, since children were the group's future. Children were the old-age pension for those few to live to an old age. Furthermore, women performed crucial domestic tasks — food preparation and crafts of various kinds. Indeed, women probably invented agriculture

and domesticated the first animals. Therefore, women were highly regarded in the family as a system of survival and social life
between the sexes went forward on a roughly egalitarian basis.
Proponents of the subordination of women can find no support in
hunting and gathering families. Life for women, as for men, may
have been short, but it was neither nasty nor brutish.

Ironically, woman's greatest contribution to the species became
the source of her enslavement to male patriarchy and male privilege.
Agriculture and animal husbandry led to the need for more permanent settlements — the need for developed property and its defence
as well as to the emergence of the first fairly regular economic sur-
pluses. Such property had to be defended, and the surplus had to be
controlled and distributed. As more complex social systems were
elaborated on the more secure bases of wealth and survival, production and politics became increasingly separated from the
household. Women's sphere — child care and domestic work, supplemented always by labour in the fields — became increasingly
private and centred in the immediate nuclear family. Men's sphere
— hunting, now warfare and politics, and the supervision of property, production, and surplus — became more and more part of an
enlarged public sphere from which women were more or less systematically excluded. As civilization became ever more complex,
women became chattels, dominated by, and subordinated to, men.
Children, previously the assured collective future of the small
group, became private possessions of the father. Marriage became
increasingly an enforced and continuing monogamy on women, as
men strove to assure their paternity, the future of their property, and
their "line." As property, politics, and production became the public
sphere in which men exercised their expanding options and powers,
home, hearth, and heart became the private sphere in which women
exercised their narrowing options and powers under the diligent,
paternalistic supervision of father and then husband.

While women's work was still recognized as vital, it was
locked up in a narrow definition of womanhood, which idolized
the domestic virtues overlaid with obedience, and participation
of women in the public sphere was constricted if not outright forbidden. A woman could still have influence and find fulfillment,

but only if she accepted the narrow confines of the womanly virtues and if she were blessed with a kind and loving father and a gentle and loving husband. Otherwise, her life could be one of unrelieved suffering, hard work, and degradation.

The Industrial Nuclear Family

If, in our 24-hour life of the species, the monogamous, patriarchal family emerged 14 minutes ago, the Industrial Revolution, which ushered in the modern industrial nuclear family, occurred less than two minutes ago. The Industrial Revolution, which set in motion the social, political, and economic changes that were to lead to the beginnings of women's emancipation, at first more deeply enslaved them. Further, the Industrial Revolution, which was to transform the family into its modern form, at first threatened to destroy all vestiges of significant family life, at least for the industrial working class. The pre-industrial patriarchal family of rural cultivators was still a unit that combined production and consumption, life in the public sphere and life in the private sphere. The division of labour based on sex remained rigid, and women remained largely consigned to the hearth. But the distance between hearth and field was not that great, and though it occurred in the context of patriarchy and male privilege, social and economic life between the sexes, and between adults and children, continued to be importantly mutual and reciprocal. As the capitalist market emerged and commercial agriculture took hold, the separation between domestic life and production for the market increased. As capitalism and the market triumphed, the separation between the two areas became greater and greater, resulting in the public sphere dominated by men becoming increasingly central in importance, and the domestic sphere increasingly secondary.

The Industrial Revolution completed the process of separation between spheres of production external to the family and the spheres of consumption and reproduction internal to it. Work became something done outside the home to provide for the family's subsistence. The family's economic importance declined sharply as it was stripped of its productive economic functions.

For the first generation or two of the Industrial Revolution, the family almost ceased to exist for many among the new working class as every member — husband, wife, and children — was forced into the factory system to toil for subsistence. As the revolution continued to consume this industrial fodder at an alarming rate through accident, illness, and exhaustion, working class organizations, middle-class reformers, and enlightened capitalists began to present a compelling case for reform. For the working class, reform became a matter of life and death. For middle class reformers, humanitarian reform was the only way of preventing a disastrous decline in the collective morality, health, and vitality of the society. For enlightened capitalists, reform became essential to ensure that labour continue to be productive, healthy, and somewhat contented.

In this context the modern version of the industrial nuclear family emerged, a universal but poorer expression of a model of family life only the middle and upper classes could hope to afford to enjoy with any degree of security. The notion of motherhood emerged: the sacred and primary vocation of women, consigned to and subordinated in the domestic sphere while enjoying the benign and devoted economic support of men. The notion of fatherhood, and of the providing husband, was also born: a man must work out in the cruel world, but he did so in order to support a devoted wife and obedient children, who in turn waited to soothe, comfort, and refresh him for the next day's effort. So too emerged our romantic notion of childhood as an age of innocence, during which the necessary skills for adulthood would be lovingly if somewhat sternly imparted. Family life was private, and the home was the place where love, fulfillment and emotional meaning were sought. In many ways, it was a cruel vision that few could live in reality. Women and children continued to work in the wage labour force, in factory or in field, usually out of necessity, sometimes out of choice. But that vision of the family became the ideal to which many aspired, a dream of a heaven, or at least a haven, on earth. And as reforms were instituted, as real wages climbed, it became the reality for increasing numbers of ordinary people.

But this vision was based on the subjugation of women under

the autocratic control, benign or otherwise, of men. Women could not vote. Women could not own property. Women could not keep their wages. It was legal for a husband to beat his wife and take his sexual pleasure from her regardless of her consent. Women were, legally speaking, non-persons with few rights, no privileges, and only indirect power. A woman who could not, or would not, embrace her allotted place in the scheme of things was either outcast or sentenced to a life of enormous difficulty.

By the mid-nineteenth century, the industrial nuclear family had become the norm for virtually all Canadians regardless of class, including farmers producing for the market.[9] The husband/father worked outside the home to bring home a wage or salary (or profits, if he were a small or large capitalist). The wife/mother worked in the home, doing domestic labour (or supervising others doing it for her), bearing and raising children, and providing for the emotional needs of family members. No longer important in the social production process, the family had become the site for consumption and for the emotional fulfillment of its members. Sex roles were clearly defined and the lives of the sexes were separated clearly in the two spheres — private and public. The ideological glorification of the family, of childhood, of husband-fatherhood, and of wife-motherhood, ensured that the industrial nuclear family was the way all good, normal people lived. Men eventually became husbands and fathers, devoting their labouring time to securing the economic survival needs of wives and children. Women eventually became wives and mothers, devoting their lives to hearth, home, and husband. Good, normal men and women raised obedient, respectful children who would themselves leave the home of their family of birth and find fulfilment by establishing their own homes and families. This notion of the family, and indeed the reality of the family for most, was to continue until the post-World War II period when fundamental economic changes began undermining the traditional industrial-nuclear family and transforming it extremely rapidly.

The Industrial Revolution, though initially enslaving women more completely, had also set in motion a series of intellectual and economic changes that established the conditions necessary for the increasing emancipation of women. The great democratic agitations, most clearly epitomized by the American and French Revolutions in the eighteenth century, and the revolutions of the 1830s and 1840s in the nineteenth century, inevitably provoked a debate about the rights of women. The arguments in favour of rights for women were given their best articulation in Mary Wollstonecraft's *Vindication of the Rights of Women in 1792*, in William Thompson's *Appeal of One Half the Human Race against the Pretensions of the Other Half* in 1825, and in John Stuart Mill's *On the Subjection of Women* in 1869. The 1882 Married Women's Property Act in the United Kingdom was one of the first victories of this agitation for women's rights. With the turn of the century, the debate over women's suffrage dominated pre-World War I politics. Except in New Zealand and Finland, where the vote was won for women in 1893 and 1907 respectively, what finally won women the vote in places like Canada, Great Britain, and the United States was the role they played in the war effort during World War I. The contributions women made in factory, field, and the armed services gave irresistible material force to the intellectual, political, and philosophical arguments which had long since been won by the advocates of women's rights.

Two industrial developments, accelerated as a consequence of World War I, continued the process of women's material emancipation and the transformation of the nature of the family. If the early phase of the Industrial Revolution had more completely subjugated women by more clearly consigning them to the hearth, the later phases began to pull women away from the home and into the paid industrial labour force. The modern industrial economy needed women's labour, and women increasingly needed to, and wanted to, work. Women may have remained low paid, segregated into "women's work," and treated as a reserve army of labour; nevertheless their labour became increasingly necessary to the expanding industrial capitalist economy. At the turn of the century the female participation rate in the labour force was just under 20 per cent, after World War I it rose to just over 20 per cent, and thereafter it began a slow but steady climb to just over 30 per cent in 1961. Most of these women were single. Even as late as 1951, only just over 11 per cent of married women were working.[10] But the stage was set.

The other industrial development had to do with the industrialization of housework, as more and more labour- and time-saving inventions lightened the burdens of domestic labour. Until some technical alternatives to labour-intensive domestic drudgery were available and affordable, it was simply not feasible for a married woman with children to contemplate a significant commitment to work outside the home. Therefore, although members of the family of the 1940s and 1950s didn't realize it, the family as an institution was on the threshold of a dramatic transformation in its nature, a change that was to be so rapid as to create "a crisis of the family."

The Decline of the Industrial Nuclear Family

The traditional industrial nuclear family reached its apotheosis in the 1940s and 1950s. This was the era of the glorification of the family dad at work and mom at home with the kids imposed as the norm on society. And it was the norm. It was the family depicted in Dick and Jane readers and on television shows like *Father Knows Best*, *Life with Riley*, *Leave It to Beaver*, and *The Adventures of Ozzie and Harriet*. It was the family of the Dagwood and Blondie comic strip and movie series. This was the way people expected to live and the way they were taught to want to live.

This traditional family indeed existed for the overwhelming majority of Canadians in the 1940s and 1950s. In 1941 only 4.5 per cent of married women held a job outside the home.[11] The impact of World War II was evident in the 1951 rate when 11 per cent of married women were in the paid workforce. This changing reality of married women was the inevitable consequence of a general rise in overall female participation in the labour force. In 1941, 21 per cent of females over 15 years of age were in the labour force, by 1945 this grew to 33 per cent, falling back to 25 per cent the following year and further shrinking to 24 per cent in 1951.[12] But this post-war decline was short term.

Working women in 1951 were overwhelmingly single — 62 per cent — while 30 per cent were married, 7 per cent were widowed, and just over 1 per cent divorced. Most of these women worked in areas like services (personal, recreational, food, and lodging), health and welfare, education, and in certain types of factories, manufacturing textiles, foods and beverages, and leather and rubber products.[13] On a weekly basis, working women could expect to earn about 55 per cent of what men earned.[14] The pattern was clear: women who worked in the labour force did so until marriage, when most withdrew, re-entering it typically only under the compulsion of loss of husband through death or divorce. In fact, only a bare majority of single women 15 years of age and older worked in 1951 — 58 per cent. Men worked outside the home. Women — even 42 per cent of single women — did not, except, one suspects, out of the most extreme necessity.

And what of the home and the family of 1951? There were about 3.3 million families comprising over 87 per cent of Canada's 14 million people. Over nine in 10 were headed by married men and enjoyed a husband and wife at home. Such a family had in fact been dubbed the "normal" family in the 1941 census. Only just over 10,000 families were headed by a divorced person, overwhelmingly a woman. Divorce was so unusual that there were a scant 32,000 divorced people at the time the census was taken, but it was twice the number in 1941, a taste of things yet to come.

And what of children? The average family in 1951 had two children, but averages can often be deceiving, as in this case. In 1945, Gallup reported that 60 per cent of Canadians thought the ideal family should have four or more children.[15] By 1951, few had reached that goal: 32 per cent of families had no children, 24 per cent had one, 20 per cent had two, and another 24 per cent had three or more. Fertility rates among women remained high from 15 to 44 years of age.[16] Having babies, for many women in 1951, spanned a lifetime.

Childbirth was still a risky business in 1951; more than one mother of every 1,000 infants died in childbirth. Further, 39 out of every 1,000 infants died before reaching one year of age, and over 18 of every 1,000 births were stillbirths.[17] Women wanting to control their reproductive function faced criminal law and unforgiving public attitudes. Birth control and abortion were illegal; and a woman risked sterility or death if she sought an underground abortion.

The large, stable family of the 1940s and 1950s, in which I grew up, is in the minds of most conservative politicians today when they design family policies. It sounds idyllic. But that semblance of serenity and security was purchased at the enormous cost of consigning half our population to a life of domestic isolation and hard labour. On Mondays, laundry day in our house, my mother would spend 10 to 12 hours feeding the wash for eight people through a wringer washer and hanging it on the line to dry. The price for that appearance of stability was borne, usually silently, by women. Juxtaposed with the smell of freshly baked bread in my memory is my mother's quiet weeping some nights after she thought we were long asleep.

For women who wanted a choice, there was none, and the socialization process ensured that few wanted to be anything other than wives and mothers. Low wages, restricted jobs, no career future, hostile attitudes, and blatant sexual discrimination made the paid labour force an option of only very last resort. Today wife beating and child abuse are major public issues, but we have no reason to suspect these atrocities were any less epidemic in 1951. Indeed, they may have been more commonplace, if only because they were more hidden, and women in 1951 did not have even the few legal protections available today.

In other words, this traditional nuclear family was premised on the oppression and exploitation of women. And for every wife and mother who successfully practised her wiles on her husband in the television world, there were probably many others in the real world whose efforts were met with verbal abuse at best, or fists and boots at worst. Remember *Life with Riley*, the comedy television serial? Riley was a big, friendly buffoon, who was always successfully conned and manipulated by his wife and children. But the message was clear: buffoon or not, Riley was the head of the house, and his real power had to be dealt with.

When my mother re-entered the labour force at the age of 46 in 1957, a whole new world that had nothing to do with her motherly or wifely status opened up for her. At first she went out to work because the family needed the money, but she never wanted to return to live in domestic bliss. When she re-entered the workforce, she didn't realize that her new-found sense of self was a small part of a larger social transformation that was to rumble throughout the 1960s and erupt into an earthquake in the 1970s, 1980s, and 1990s.

Women's Liberation and the Decline of Patriarchy

The women's liberation movement of the 1960s again inserted feminism into our political, social, and economic discourse, something that had been largely absent since the suffrage movement of the turn of the century. Despite early efforts to dismiss the movement, the feminist agenda quickly established itself. Although it emerged hand in hand with movements for civil rights, peace, an end to the Vietnam war, student power, and a sensible approach to the environment, the movement has persisted to the present day, scoring a series of major victories.

The new feminism was new precisely because it was so thorough in its critique of the place of women in society. Whereas the suffragists had largely accepted that women were to be wives and mothers first, the new movement criticized these orthodoxies and the subordination of women they enforced. The movement criticized the place of women in marriage and the family, in factory and office, in field and parliament — indeed, in all the private and public spheres where women were confined by the old notions.

Two publishing events of the early 1960s epitomized the new feminism. One was the publication of Parshley's translation of Simone de Beauvoir's *The Second Sex* in 1961.[18] The other was the appearance of Betty Friedan's *The Feminine Mystique* in 1963.[19] Despite the obvious differences between the perspectives of the two authors, these books struck a chord among women of the 1960s, and provoked many men to begin a critical reassessment of relations between the sexes. Friedan's question "Is this all?" and de Beauvoir's call for an equal brotherhood with men both reflected and helped to clarify a deep dissatisfaction among women.

In Canada the women's movement won some significant victories. In 1968 a new Divorce Act established more lenient grounds for divorce, including physical and/or mental cruelty and a three-year separation (changed to one year in 1985). In 1969 birth control was legalized and limited access to safe, legal abortions granted. In 1967 a Royal Commission on the Status of Women in Canada was set up. Mandated to examine women's status in Canada with the widest possible latitude, the Commission reported in 1970.[20] Although a decade later the Canadian Advisory Council on the Status of Women complained that the *Report* and those recommendations ultimately implemented "had very little effect,"[21] the *Report* was in fact a monumental indictment of the second class situation faced by women in the society and the economy. Subsequently, laws were passed forbidding sexual or marital discrimination, improving women's legal status and granting women somewhat stronger rights to shares of property in the event of a marriage breakdown. Programs of affirmative action were begun to help overcome the legacy of inequality. It became very quickly clear that Canada, like other Western industrialized countries, had entered a new era.

What impact did this have on the family? Inevitably the family began to change more rapidly. But we have to be careful here lest we join the chorus on the far-right, which claims that the women's liberation movement somehow caused the good old family to change. Structural changes in the society and the economy affecting the family had already begun in the post-World War II period — more women were working, more married women were working, more women with children were working, the number of children per family was going down, divorces were increasing. What happened in the 1960s was the coming together of a set of material and ideological circumstances that made women's emancipation increasingly possible. Certainly some of this had to do with women's changing attitudes about themselves and their purpose in life. But choices can only be contemplated when they are available. The economy was changing so that women could more and more conceive of a life and an identity outside the home, since more and more jobs became available. Advances in household technology and declines in the birth rate meant less time each day and fewer years of a woman's lifetime had to be devoted to domestic labour and child rearing. The inability of a single wage to provide a family with all that it increasingly wanted and expected added a further pressure on women to seek remuneration outside the home.

Between 1966 and 1976, therefore, the family changed dramatically. In 1966, 92 per cent of families were still husband/wife families, and only 8 per cent were single parent families. By 1976, 90 per cent were husband/wife families while 10 per cent were single parent. Families were smaller and less stable. In 1966, there were 1.9 children per family; by 1976 this had fallen to 1.6 children. The fertility rate had fallen well below the replacement level of 2.1 children per woman. In 1970, Gallup reported that 34 per cent of Canadians believed the ideal family had only one or two children; by 1974, 52 per cent felt that way. In 1966, 29 per cent of families had no kids, 40 per cent had one or two, and 31 per cent had three or more. By 1976, 30 per cent had no kids, 48 per cent had one or two, and only 22 per cent had three or more. In 1966, only 2 per cent of families were headed by a separated spouse, while not half of 1 per cent were headed by a divorced spouse. By 1976 these figures had become 3 per cent and 2 per cent respectively. In 1966 less than half of 1 per cent of Canadians over 15 were divorced; in 1976 about 2 per cent were divorced.[22] In 1966 the divorce rate was 235 per 100,000 married women; by 1976 the rate was just over 1,000, an increase of almost five times.[23]

More and more married women were working outside the home. In 1966, 27 per cent of married women were working.[24] In 1976, 44 per cent of married women held down a job, including 37 per cent of those with children under the age of six. And the rate was highest among younger wives. Practice and attitudes were changing rapidly. For example, in 1960 Gallup found that only 5 per cent of Canadians approved of married women with young children working outside the home. By 1975, 18 per cent approved.[25]

Let's pause here to present a "snapshot" of the Canadian family at the end of the 1970s and the beginning of the 1980s.[26] Most families, 89 per cent, were still husband/wife families, and 57 per cent of them had children still at home. But 51 per cent of wives worked outside the home, including 45 per cent of those whose youngest child was under age three, 52 per cent of those whose youngest child was between the ages of three and five, and 61 per cent of those whose youngest child was between the ages of six and 15. Altogether, 55 per cent of wives with children under 16 years of age worked. These working wives and mothers could expect to earn, on the average, 64 per cent of what men earned and brought home 28 per cent of total family income. These husband/wife families had an average of 1.3 children. Not surprisingly, in 1981, 52 per cent of Canadian children were supervised, for part of the day, by a nursery school or kindergarten, a daycare centre, or a babysitter inside or outside the home. Only 48 per cent of children were cared for exclusively by parents in their own home.

The other 11 per cent of families were single parent, 83 per cent headed by women.[27] Almost one-third of these families headed by women resulted from bereavement, while 55 per cent resulted from divorce or separation, and 11 per cent were headed by women who had never married. These families had an average of 1.7 children. Families headed by women could expect to receive only 52 per cent of the family income enjoyed by families headed by men. Now the fastest growing family category, single-parent families headed by women increased 59 per cent from 1971 to 1981, while husband/wife families increased by only 22 per cent. But there was another rapidly growing "family" formation, that of the non-family household. In 1971, only 18 per cent of households were non-family; in 1981 this was true of one in four households. In 1971, only just over 6 per cent of women, and 4 per cent of men, lived alone. In 1981, over 10 per cent of women and almost 8 per cent of men lived alone. For many, then, marriage and the family were ceasing to be the centre of their existences, either as a result of circumstances or choice.

By the end of the 1970s and throughout the 1980s, it was clear that a variety of types of family formations was emerging; some of them had always characterized a minority of families in former times, some were quite new. Excluding childless couples and those living alone (two growing categories of households with great significance for our population figures in the future), there were at least six major categories or types of families as we exited the 1980s. There was the traditional family, with dad out at work and mom at home with the

1.3 kids. There was the dual-income family, with both spouses in the workforce. There was a "transitional" family in which the mother temporarily left the labour force for a child's younger years and then returned to work. There was the single-parent family headed by either a man or a woman. Such families would have to be further categorized as to the reasons for their formation: separation, divorce, death of spouse, or single (i.e., never married). Then there was the "blended" family, one of increasing consequence, in which divorced partners with children remarry, sometimes to someone with children from a previous marriage, sometimes to someone childless.[28]

The family of our myths, rooted in the isolated domestic enslavement of women, had ceased to exist. And there was no hope of going back since the trends so clear at the end of the 1970s accelerated even more rapidly throughout the 1980s and 1990s. But these new emerging family forms brought with them, for women, a new kind of enslavement, for men, a new sense of unease, and for children, a new vulnerability and uncertainty. Families were in crisis as the problem of transition and adjustment remained largely unaddressed and completely unsolved.

2 / Families Present

Let's survey the diversity of family forms in Canada at the beginning of the new millennium. All the developments noted from the 1960s to the 1990s have continued. The speed of change has been remarkable and the direction consistent.

The Husband/Wife Family

In 2001, more than 82 per cent of Canada's 31 million people lived in 8.3 million families. Of these, just over 7 million families, or 84.3 per cent, were husband/wife families (including common-law).[1] There was an average of 2.6 people in each household, including an average of 1.1 children per family. This is the only family type to have declined in its share of total families since 1981. Statistics Canada projects that in the year 2016, Canada's 37 million people will live in 10.4 million families. Husband/wife families will total 8.8 million, or 84.6 per cent of the population, with an average of one child. There are four significant variations of husband/wife families in Canada.

The husband/wife family with both spouses working

If there is a "typical" family in Canada, it is now what Statistics Canada calls the "dual-earner family."[2] By 2001, an estimated 65 per cent of all husband/wife families enjoyed two earners; over one-half of all families in Canada are now of this type (4.5 million). This reality is reflected in the enormous growth in labour force participation throughout the 1980s and 1990s among married women with children.[3] By 1999, 63 per cent of married women with children under six years were working, as were 69 per cent of those with children still at home. Overall, in 1999 more than 55 per cent of all women were in the labour force. The rates were highest among younger and better-educated women. Almost 74 per cent of women between the ages of 25 and 44 worked, while only just over 37 per cent of those 55 and older did so. Almost 75 per cent of married women with children aged 6 to 15 worked. This burst in job holding by married women with children resulted primarily from the serious declines in real family income that characterized the 1980s and 1990s and that hit young families hardest.[4]

Married women therefore increased their importance in maintaining family income, bringing in a record high of 32 per cent of the total family income of dual-earner families. As well, dual-income families were better off on the whole, with average incomes in 2000 of $78,524, compared to an average family income of $55,020 for families dependent solely on a husband's income.

Such families were almost as likely to have children as traditional husband-income families. But they tended to postpone having children longer and to have fewer children — 56 per cent of traditional-earner families had two or more children compared to only 36 per cent of dual-earner families.

Although dual-earner families are the most economically successful family type, they have serious stresses.[5] Adequate and affordable daycare, balancing two jobs and family obligations, reconciling conflicts in parental and career demands on husbands and wives, and meeting the rocketing costs of raising children all provoke what sometimes appear to be an endless series of daily crises.

The husband/wife family with only the husband working
The traditional nuclear family of the 1940s and 1950s now constitutes only 18 per cent of all husband/wife families in Canada. Less than 16 per cent of total families (1.31 million) are of this traditional sort. Husband/wife families with only the husband working tend to have lower incomes and a higher risk of experiencing poverty. Both spouses tend to be older than the spouses of dual-earner families and less well-educated. Such families tend to have more children, and wives in such families tend to have had children at a younger age than their dual-earner counterparts.

Analyses of the problems faced by women in such families constitute a major portion of the vast literature generated on women in the last four decades. Such women are typically economically dependent and socially and emotionally isolated. They strive to realize themselves largely through the traditional roles of wife and mother. Therefore, they tend to subordinate themselves to the needs of husband and children and face severe limitations on their personal growth. They often feel their role is devalued by society.

Men in such families face significant stresses as well. Since they tend to have a strong commitment to the traditional role of husband/provider, the increasing economic stress of maintaining family income weighs heavily on them, and they have more difficulty adapting to the threat of female competition for jobs and promotions. Like the traditional wife, such a man is experiencing the distressing disintegration of a way of life around him as he struggles to seek confirmation of the intrinsic value of traditional sex roles.

The husband/wife family with only the wife working and the husband/wife family with no earner

These two groups of families, together, constitute 17 per cent of husband/wife families in Canada. In 5 per cent of cases, the wife is the sole earner, and in 12 per cent of cases, neither the husband nor the wife is an earner. While clearly most of these families can be explained by retirement, early or otherwise, or by unemployment cycles, there are some other significant trends. In 1967, only 1 per cent of husband/wife families depended on the wife as the sole earner. Thus there has been a very sharp fivefold increase in such families. The most significant feature of both these family groups is that, while the majority of both spouses is over 55, the proportion of husbands over 55 years is much greater. The explanation for the growth in these types of family, particularly the family in which the wife is sole earner, can be partly found in the steep decline in the employment of men from ages 55 to 64 that occurred between 1975 and 1995, a trend that appears to be long-term and upward. While much of the increase is explained by early retirement and a sustained absence from the labour force (never worked, or a five-year absence), nearly half of this increase is the result of a loss of job or layoff. Obviously, one of the consequences of the growth in female participation in the labour force is this emerging long-term trend to higher rates of unemployment among older men. Evidently they are bearing the brunt of the trend since the 1960s to lower rates of participation in the labour force for all men 15 and over, while female rates have increased dramatically.[6]

The Single-Parent Family

In 2001, 15.7 per cent of Canada's families were single-parent families, making it the third-largest family type and reflecting a startling growth rate of 50 per cent since 1981.[7] Over 81 per cent of such families are headed by women, including 96 per cent of single-parent families with heads between the ages of 15 and 24, and 86 per cent of such heads between the ages of 25 and 44. Over 2 million, or 17.3 per cent, of Canada's children live in single-parent families, and it is estimated that over one in two Canadian children will live part of their lives in a single parent family.

The female single-parent family

The reasons for the formation of this family type have changed dramatically. In the 1960s, the overwhelming majority of female single-parent families resulted from the death of a spouse (63 per cent), the next largest group resulted from separation or divorce (35 per cent), and only 2 per cent were headed by single (never married) mothers. By 1996, 54 per cent of such families resulted from separation or divorce, 20 per cent from death of spouse, while 25 per cent were headed by single mothers. In the case of marriage breakdown, mothers get sole custody of the children in about 61 per cent of cases. In addition to the growth in marriage breakdown, the most dramatic change in the basis for the formation of female single-parent families is the growing trend among single women to have and keep babies born outside of a permanent relationship. This trend began in the 1970s and has continued to advance in the 1980s and 1990s when, for example, over 86 per cent of unmarried mothers in Alberta and over 88 per cent in Ontario kept their babies. The increase has been supplemented by a rise in the number of older single mothers, often professionals, aged 30 to 39, seeking to become mothers without being wives, and sometimes doing so through artificial insemination.[8]

Female single-parent families are in the most difficulty economically. In 1999, 52 per cent of them were below the official poverty line, and such families received less than half the family income of husband/wife families, while remaining the most dependent on forms of government assistance. There are enormous variations in poverty rates based on the number of children, ranging from a high of 79 per cent poor for single mothers with two children younger than 7 years old, to a low of 39 per cent poor for single mothers with one child aged 7 to 17 years. This can be partly explained by female single parents' lower participation rate in the labour force. In the 1990s, 60 per cent of such parents worked, compared to about 70 per cent of mothers in two-parent families. Female job ghettoes, low incomes, the lack of affordable daycare, and the absence of a spouse obviously make it more difficult for single-parent mothers to bring home incomes that make that work worthwhile. As a result, single-parent families headed by women languish in poverty. In 1999, over 1.3 million children in Canada, representing 19 per cent of all children under 18, lived in families below the official poverty line. Over 51 per cent of children in single mother families were poor, representing over 40 per cent of all poor children.[9]

There are those who argue that these families are going through a brief episode in their life cycles and that most will eventually return to a family based upon a husband/wife relationship. But the trend for this type of family formation continues to go upward — that is, at each census the group is larger and represents a larger share of the total number of families. This means that many Canadians, especially women, will experience episodes of single parenthood. The Statistics Canada Family History Survey studied 1.4 million women aged 18 to 65 who were or had been single parents, representing 18 per cent of all women in that age group and 26 per cent of all those who had borne children.[10] The end of the single-parent episode was defined as when the woman entered a new relationship or when parenting ceased as children left home. The study found that the average age of single mothers when the episode began was about 21 years with a duration of over four years, while the average age of divorced or separated mothers when the episode began was 32 years with a duration of almost six years. Average durations of such length are not brief, and 12 per cent of the women surveyed endured a second experience of single parenthood.

Female single parents are beset by problems. There are the obvious economic problems of low incomes, poverty, poor housing, and constant stress and insecurity. There are the emotional and psychological problems of endeavouring to raise young children without the support of a spouse. There are the loneliness and lack of emotional and sexual fulfillment resulting from the absence of a stable love relationship. Furthermore, single parent mothers face more sexual harassment, at work and socially, since many men view single-parent women as "fair game." As well, single-parent mothers still face discrimination in society. And separated or divorced single-parent mothers are often the targets of physical abuse by former spouses, experiencing a much higher rate of wife abuse than married women.[11]

The male single-parent family

The reasons for the formation of this family type have also changed dramatically. In the 1960s the overwhelming majority of male single-parent families resulted from the death of a spouse, followed distantly by marriage breakdown. By the 1980s, marriage breakdown accounted for the formation of 67 per cent of such families, and bereavement for about 30 per cent (interestingly, almost 4 per cent were never-married fathers).[12] About 19 per cent of Canada's 1.31 million single-parent families are headed by men. Significantly, Statistics Canada projects that male single-parent families will grow rapidly between now and 2016, reaching 320,000 families, or 20 per cent of the 1.6 million single parent families expected in 2016.

Single-parent fathers tend to be older than single-parent mothers and to be parenting older children.[13] Only 4 per cent of single-parent family heads between the ages of 15 and 24 and 14 per cent between the ages of 25 and 44 are male, while 23 per cent are 45 or older. Single-parent fathers have a higher probability of remarrying, and the duration of divorce tends to be about one-half of that faced by single-parent mothers.

Male single-parent families are considerably better off economically than female single-parent families. A study by Richardson
revealed that only 10 per cent of divorced men, compared to 58 per
cent of divorced women and their children, were below the poverty
line. Canada-wide figures are less generous. About 18 per cent of
male single-parent families, including 27 per cent of children in such
families, are officially poor.[14] This is significantly above national
averages, but well ahead of the situation of female single-parent families. Male single parents receive 154 per cent of the incomes received
by female single parents and 64 per cent of the incomes enjoyed by
husband/wife families with children.

Contrary to popular stereotypes, studies of single-parent fathers
suggest they are quite successful at parenting, and they express
more satisfaction than single-parent mothers.[15] This doubtless has
something to do with their greater economic security. It might also
have something to do with the fact that single-parent fathers tend
to be raising older children. But they do share with all parents
Canada's crisis in daycare. And, in common with single-parent
women, they face the problems of loneliness, social isolation, a
lack of satisfying sexual outlets, and the dilemmas of reconciling
the conflicting demands of work, domestic labour, and child care.
Then, too, since their remarriage rate is higher, and the duration of
divorce much shorter, on the average, single-parent fathers face
fewer years of being alone. Furthermore, such men express greater
happiness and higher levels of satisfaction after remarriage.

The Common-Law Family

Although it has long existed, the common-law family came into
official being only in 1981.[16] Prior to 1981, the census counted
common-law marriages in the single category of "married or living as married." In 1981 the census began collecting such data,
supplemented by Statistics Canada's Family History Survey. In
2001, almost 2.4 million Canadians were living in over 1.1 million
common-law families, representing about 14 per cent of total families, and the common-law family was one of the fastest-growing
family types.

Table 1: Trends in family forms into the new millennium

		1980s			2001				2016		
	Number	% Husband /Wife Families	% of All Families	% Poor	Number	% Husband /Wife Families	% of All Families	% Poor	Number	% Husband /Wife Families	% of All Families	% Poor
1. Husband/Wife Families (includes Common Law)	5.9 million	–	88	11	7.0 million	–	85.5	10	8.8 million	–	85	12
Both Spouses Working	3.6 million	61	54	4	4.5 million	65**	54	3	6.0 million	68**	58	5
Husband Only Working	1.6 million	27	24	13	1.31 million	18**	16	13**	1.2 million	14**	11.5	15
Wife Only Working	236,000	4	3	?	350,000	5**	4	?	528,000	6**	5	?
Neither Working	413,000	7	6	?	840,000	12**	10	?	1.05 million	12**	10	?
2. Single-Parent Families	870,000	–	13	52	1.31 million	–	16	47	1.6 million	–	15	55
Female Single Parent	714,000	82*	11	60	1.06 million	81*	13	53	1.3 million	79*	12	64
Male Single Parent	157,000	18*	2	20	245,825	19*	3	18	300,000	21*	3	22
3. Common-Law Families	(487,000)	(8)	(7)	(?)	(1.15 million)	(16)	(14)	(?)	(1.6 million)	(18)**	(15)	(?)
All Families	6.7 million	–	100	13	8.3 million	–	100	12	10.4 million	–	100	14
Average Number of Children per Family	1.4	–	–	–	1.1	–	–	–	>1 (?)	–	–	–

* percentage of all single parent families   ** estimates   NB: 70% of couples with children are dual income

The Family History Survey found that common-law marriages were quite commonplace, particularly among the young. Seventeen per cent of adults between the ages of 18 and 65 had lived common-law at one time in their lives, including 22 per cent of those in the 20 to 24 year age group, but only 1 per cent of those in their forties. Among total marriages in the 1990s, common-law unions accounted for 75 per cent of marriages among the 15 to 19 year age group, 43 per cent of those among those 20 to 24, and 22 per cent among those 25 to 29. In 1981, these figures were 49 per cent, 23 per cent and 11 per cent, respectively.

Common-law marriages are most typically one-time events; 75 per cent end in legal marriage after an average duration of 2.3 years. Usually, but not always, partners in common-law liaisons married each other. Common-law families have an average of 0.8 children each, and about 46 per cent of such families have children. (Families based on legal marriage have an average of 1.1 children, and 59 per cent of such marriages have children at home.) Common-law families, since they are so young, share all the economic problems of young families in general, like declines in real family income and declining real wages for younger workers.

The growing rate of common-law marriage has to do with the overall crisis of the traditional family since young men and women are increasingly reticent about taking the step to formal marriage, at least until after a trial period. Perhaps it reflects a growing determination on the part of younger women to ensure that they avoid the

---

Sources for Table 1

Sources: Statistics Canada, *Canadian Social Trends*, 1986–2003 and Census Reports, 1986, 1991, 1996 and 2001; National Council of Welfare, *Poverty Profile, 1990*, and *Poverty Profile, 1999*; Statistics Canada, *Projections of Households and Families for Canada, Provinces and Territories, 1994–2016*, Ottawa: Ministry of Industry, 1995, Catalogue No. 91-522; Statistics Canada, *Population Projections for Canada, Provinces and Territories*, Ottawa: Ministry of Industry, Science and Technology, 1994, Catalogue No. 91-520. All figures are approximate and percentages are rounded. Some figures are best estimates based on a variety of assumptions, only some of which involve Statistics Canada's projections. The poverty figures for the 1980s and 1990s, which fluctuated from year to year, are an effort to provide a rough estimate of the poverty level in those decades. The 2016 poverty figures are worst-case scenario estimates, which assume the continuing dismantling of Canada's social programs.

burdens of a long-term commitment until they see if their partners can adjust to women's growing sense of freedom and independence. Perhaps, too, it reflects a growing willingness among young men to seek relationships that are more egalitarian and flexible. Growing economic uncertainty and insecurity doubtless play a big role in postponing formal legal commitment.

The problems with traditional patterns of courtship are obvious. Both men and women are on their best behaviour, especially men, who compartmentalize their social selves between who they are and what they do with male friends, with women from whom they are seeking casual sexual gratification, and with women they have decided are desirable for marriage.

The case of Chantal Daigle and Jean-Guy Tremblay provides an excellent example. Tremblay began pursuing Daigle, and within weeks the couple were cohabiting. Two months into the union Tremblay suggested marriage and urged Daigle to stop using birth control; a few months later she was pregnant. Daigle said that Tremblay then became physically and verbally abusive. Tremblay insisted that he never hit her "hard enough to leave marks." Daigle finally left Tremblay and decided to have an abortion. Tremblay successfully sought a court injunction forbidding the abortion, a decision upheld by the Quebec Court of Appeal. First, he told the press that he himself would care for the baby, then decided his father would, and then suggested he would allow Daigle to keep and care for the child. In an interview, Tremblay revealed his dream — a traditional family with him out at work and Daigle at home with the child. Daigle's response was simple, "I don't even want to see that guy again." Happily, the Supreme Court of Canada unanimously found in her favour.[17]

A period of common-law marriage is no absolute insurance for a woman, or for a man, but it provides more insurance than traditional courtship ending in idyllic marriage to be followed by capital "R" reality. In the context of today's emotional and economic uncertainty, it will doubtless continue to be an important testing period for growing numbers of young Canadians, likely a majority of them in this millennium.

Other Significant Family Trends

Transitional families

This term has been selected to refer to those families in which the wife works until the birth of a child, stays home for a portion of the child's younger years, and then returns to work. The figures show that this is probably the family of choice for many Canadians, an effort to combine, both for women and the family, the benefits of work outside the home with the benefits and fulfillment to be found, for child and mother, in a period of full-time parenting. There are also a growing number of men who enjoy taking on a full-time parenting role for a time.

In 1981, 52 per cent of all married women with children stayed at home. By 1999, about 70 per cent were in the workforce. With the modest improvement in the economy after 1986, the participation rate of married women with children under six briefly dropped in 1988. The fall and rise in the percentage of women with children under six working suggests that many of them were reluctantly in the workforce out of economic necessity.

The fact is that increasingly women and their families simply have no choice but to shorten a mother's absence from the labour force. The transitional family is increasingly beyond the grasp of even middle-class families, and women who wish to take time out from work for babies are aware of the tremendous financial burden involved.

The days are largely over when a working woman had to make an almost total economic sacrifice in order to leave work to have a baby. Formerly, women typically lost their income as well as seniority and often the job itself. And a return to the labour force often meant starting over at the bottom rung. Today, working women enjoy, through collective agreements and labour laws, the right to maternity leave and some guarantee of a later return to work without loss of seniority or job. Still, they cannot expect anywhere near reasonable compensation for foregone income. All that women in Canada receive is the maternity benefit under the Employment Insurance program, which entitles them to a 55 per cent benefit level for 50 weeks' leave (15 weeks maternity and 35 weeks parental) with a weekly maximum in 2001 of $413. There is a certain irony that we have used our unemployment plan to grant maternity benefits to women: they are unemployed!

A study by economist Monica Townson reported that Canada ranked 22 out of a group of 23 industrialized nations surveyed on maternity leave benefit policies.[18] Most countries paid higher percentages of the woman's former earnings and allowed the leave to extend longer.[19] If, as a society, we want sufficient babies to be born to renew our population, while at the same time allowing existing families to retain some degree of economic security and supporting women in their desire to work outside of the home, then we will have to do much better than we are doing.

The blended family

The blended family (also called the reconstituted, melded or remarriage family) is increasingly common. In 1967 only 12 per cent of all marriages were remarriages, while by 1997 over one in four marriages were remarriages.[20] And although there are almost one-half the number of divorces as marriages each year, Canadians generally remarry after a divorce, many for a third and fourth time. With rates like these, combined with the rise in common-law unions, arguably a majority of families in Canada today are based on remarriage. Since it is such a recent phenomenon, we are only beginning to learn about this family type. But we do know that accelerating divorce rates have not led to the widely heralded death of the family; rather, high rates of divorce and remarriage indicate that divorce simply leads to the reorganization of the family.

Neumann reports that the biggest problem faced by a blended family is that it must face "inheriting leftovers," particularly ongoing emotional relationships.[21] The blended family feels a lot of pressure to succeed. The stress of the sense of competing with the previous spouse, particularly in relationships with the children from the first marriage, requires a great deal of concerted effort.

Indeed, most research suggests that the biggest problems concern the children of the former marriage, especially if they are early adolescents aged 11 to 14.[22] Stepfathers seem to provoke the most problems, particularly with stepdaughters, and there is a greater risk of incest. What Nett refers to as the "discrepancy between parental and spousal roles" is greater in such families. The reason is self-evident: each spouse may be the biological parent of some children and the step-parent of others. The complexities of the problems faced by all families with children — sibling rivalry, competition for love and attention, emotional manipulation, maintaining discipline, enforcing rules, and ensuring a minimum of order — can become overwhelming. Indeed, there is also evidence that in some cases children over 10 years of age set out to "sabotage" the remarriage. Hence such families are somewhat less stable, and the adjustment period can be rather long. One Vancouver psychologist and family counsellor reports that it takes four to seven years for members of a blended family to begin to feel in their hearts like a "real" family. And he claims that 40 per cent of remarriage families fail within the first four years if there are children involved.[23]

Fewer children

More families are having no children, and those that do, have fewer. Over 41 per cent of married couples in 2001 were childless, up from 29 per cent in 1961. Each Canadian woman today will, on average, have 1.5 children, down from about four in 1960, and childlessness is rising. The number of childless, ever-married women aged 35 to 39 has almost doubled over the last 30 years (7 per cent to 13 per cent), while almost tripling among those aged 25 to 29 (14 per cent to 38 per cent). Meanwhile, for the first time in history, the fertility rate of women aged 30 to 34 has surpassed that of women aged 20 to 24, as women who postponed having children are having them and as fertility among the formerly most fertile group of women continues to decline dramatically. In 1961, over 40 per cent of Canada's population was under the age of 19. By 2001, that had fallen to 26 per cent and it is projected to decline to 20 per cent by 2016. Meanwhile, Canadians over 65, who made up only 8 per cent of the population in 1961, increased their share to 13 per cent in 2001, and this number is expected to grow to 16 per cent by 2016.

These demographics have ominous portents for the future. Today those over the age of 65 constitute the fastest growing population

group, while those under 15, and those between 15 and 24, are the
slowest growing groups. When those now in the 40 to 50 age group,
the baby boom bulge, hit 65, the distortion in the society will be
very serious. Canada's population will peak in 2011 and begin an
absolute decline if present trends continue. With declining numbers
of young people in the labour force and a growing army of the
elderly, the economic and emotional strains will be potentially phenomenal. Will we be able to honour our pension plans? Will we be
able to afford the rising costs of health care in general, and chronic
care for the elderly in particular?

As demographer Karol Krotki put it, "there is no doubt that our
society is dying out in a statistical sense — what we need is another
baby boom."[24] Other experts agree, and there have been some political responses by governments. Quebec offers cash incentives to
encourage child-bearing: $500 for the first child and $1,000 for each
subsequent child to a maximum of $8,000. There are further induce-
ments: larger tax deductions for child care costs, a special tax
deduction for working parents, an interest-free loan for the first family home, and a universal, generously subsidized daycare program.[25]
Quebec, of course, has an even lower fertility rate than the rest of
Canada. Ottawa also responded by financing 26 population studies
commencing in May 1986. One of these studies, by Quebec economist Georges Mathews, recommended a child allowance of $200 per
month for every child after the first two, payable until the child is five
years old. Improved maternity leave benefits and more subsidized
daycare spaces would also help people decide to have more children,
he argued.[26] So far, governments other than Quebec's have refused to
listen to such advice and have cut deeply into publicly-funded supports for families throughout the 1980s and 1990s, and Quebec's
cash for babies program ended in 2002, having had little impact.

The point is that the new family forms have proven themselves
incapable of renewing the population. The issue therefore affects
the whole society. Simplistic solutions cannot deal with the problem in the long run. Women don't decide not to have children
solely on the basis of economic considerations, though those are of
critical importance. Certainly, if having children were economically easier for women and their families, then probably more children

would be born. But, as well, we have to ensure that the bearing of children does not entail unacceptable social and psychological costs for women and for their spouses.

Rise in non-family households

As the young postpone marriage and as the proportion of the elderly in the population increases, there has been an amazing growth in non-family households. Although most of this increase is the result of the growth in one-person households, it also reflects a growth in flexible living arrangements in general. In 1961 only 4 per cent of Canadians 15 and older lived alone, rising to 10 per cent in 2001, an increase of 30 per cent in the last decade. By 2001, 1 in 4 of all households were "non-family" households. The two largest groups in this category are elderly widowed women and younger people who are either single, divorced, or separated. If we take only the population under 65, the trend to single-person households grows as age advances. Among 15 to 24 year olds, only 3 per cent live in such households, 96 per cent of whom are single. In the 25 to 44 year age group, 9 per cent live in single-person households, 70 per cent of whom are single. In the 45 to 64 age category, 17 per cent of Canadians live alone, 43 per cent of whom are divorced or separated, 29 per cent of whom are single, and 28 per cent of whom are bereaved. Such figures suggest that many younger Canadians are postponing family formation and that the experience of family living for many may be episodic as it is interrupted by divorce, separation or death.

Finally, as more and more gay people affirm their sexual orientation publicly, the figures on non-family and single households conceal a new family form, the gay family, which will continue to be a source of policy controversy as such families demand recognition and access to state and trade union family programs and benefits. The federal law outlawed discrimination based on sexual orientation in 1996. Repeated court decisions and arbitration rulings have affirmed that, under the Charter, same-sex couples deserve the same treatment as heterosexual couples. With the 2001 census, the same-sex couple family was recognized — over 34,000 were counted, representing 0.5 per cent of all couples. The general public has accepted this reality quite quickly. The 2002 *Maclean's* poll found that 49 per cent support recognition of same-sex marriage, with 46 per cent opposed. A 1996 Gallup poll found that a majority of Canadians believe that heterosexual and homosexual couples who live as married have a right to the same tax and employment benefits. The same year, another poll found that 60 per cent of Canadians found homosexuality to be an acceptable lifestyle.[27]

The growing diversity of family forms is self-evident. New, "unorthodox" family forms, especially dual-earner and single parent families, have become the orthodox family forms of the present and future as they characterize the experience of a growing majority of Canadians. Families are smaller and less stable, and family life is more episodic as we marry later, as divorce and separation rates grow, and as remarriage touches more and more of our lives. Many more Canadians are opting for single lifestyles, and fewer are feeling it obligatory to have children. More women are choosing to have children as single mothers and to remain single for significant portions of their lives. Materially, people have more choices, and, ideologically, people are more willing to exercise them.

3 / Families Future

After the Industrial Revolution the family became primarily a psychological institution. It now has no productive economic functions, and domestic family labour is no longer important in the facilitation of consumption. Certainly the consumption entailed in the acquisition of the technology and services to diminish domestic labour is tremendously important to the economy. But, still, a man does not *need* a wife to do domestic labour. Nor does a woman *need* a husband to bring home a wage. The sexual division of labour is no longer essential to survival. Many of the family's child care obligations are also gone. Today, a family can assign a major portion of what child care responsibilities are left to public schools, daycare centres, and babysitters. In other words, a family does not *need* a full-time parent in the house.

What are left are the family's emotional functions: love, renewal, meaning, identity, confirmation, support, recognition, a sense of belonging. Marriage and the family still provide some degree of regulation of sexual intercourse and the procreation of children. But again, one no longer *needs* a spouse for sexual gratification, nor to have and raise children (though here women obviously have more options than men).

Marriage and the family, therefore, have become more and more matters of choice and decision. The family long ago ceased to be an economic necessity, though the dual-income family of today has certainly become an economic convenience. But we are increasingly unwilling to give up merely for convenience what we were formerly compelled to give up out of necessity. Wives and husbands have long since ceased being necessities to each other in the brutal material sense. Fewer and fewer people, men and women, are willing to compromise too extensively if a marriage or family relationship is fundamentally dissatisfying and unhappy. This is certainly more true of women. Two in three divorces are initiated by wives, and an Ontario study found that 36 per cent of such divorces involved violence and/or alcohol abuse by the husbands.[1] That's one extreme. Clearly women are less willing to put up with violence and drunkenness. But more and more of them are also leaving what many around them considered to be happy, stable, and successful marriages. Brenda Rabkin's study found that such women simply wanted more from the relationship.[2] They wanted a greater degree of emotional intimacy, a more equal partnership, and greater control over their lives. They were willing to "trade down" economically to leave what they saw as dead-end relationships. A clear pattern emerged: their husbands resisted their efforts to greater independence and refused to do a just share of domestic and child-care work. This trend is inescapable. No institution that relies on the exploitation and oppression of a particular group can hope to survive when that group begins to resist. The traditional family depended on the domestic enslavement of women. Women have not only decisively rejected that, but they are also increasingly refusing to tolerate lingering traditional male attitudes and behaviours in the new family forms. As Rabkin points out, women are increasingly willing to exercise their new options. For different reasons, the same pattern is emerging among men. Growing numbers are avoiding marriage and the family, instead choosing to live for an extended period as single men, unfettered by marital and parental obligations. As a result, there is a complementary phenomenon among men and women. Women are unwilling to put up with the constraints traditional marriage entails, and many men are postponing the commitment of becoming husbands and fathers.[3]

But the increasing choices available to men and women will not make the changes go forward naturally, spontaneously, and exultantly. In such a fundamental transformation of as central an aspect of our social structure as the family, the individuals swept up in the changes, whether through choice or circumstance, or a combination of both, must make basic readjustments. Old behaviours, attitudes, and core identities must change as people strive to live in a new social world which requires the adoption of new behaviours and attitudes and the establishment of new core identities.

When technology wipes out industrial or craft skills that people have spent a lifetime acquiring and perfecting, they feel bereft, without confirmation of who they are, as they seek a new niche in the work world. Similarly, when agricultural crises force farm families off the land, they must repair the bruised social and economic roots of their identities as they seek another, far different way of life. All such large social structural transformations exact a certain social and psychological cost from those experiencing them. Old identities, and their daily material and social confirmation, are torn apart, and new identities must be rebuilt. And it is never easy.

Structural Transformation

The same can be said of the current structural transformation of the family. However, since the family touches us all so intimately, the social and psychological costs exacted from this transition are far larger and the pain of readjustment far greater. As we are socialized to take our expected place in our culture, we acquire what one sociologist has called a "social-structural map."[4] It becomes a central part of our core identity, guiding us from "one social-emotional place to another." It tells us to whom we can go for love, in whom we can confide, how to behave appropriately in different interpersonal and social situations. Most importantly, the social-structural map provides us with a set of "problem-solving responses." It pinpoints how we are to deal with the problems that beset us and to whom we can turn for help, guidance, and support. By identifying our emotional connections, the map gives us a sense of rootedness, of place, of confidence in, and predictability about, the world around us. It links us to the social world through a web of relationships that constitutes our sense of identity and place and daily provides us with repeated confirmations of who we are. When those relationships are disrupted or poorly developed, our adjustment and functioning become impaired. Clearly our families form the central part of our social-structural maps. Therefore, disruptions of, and readjustments in, family relationships can be enormously difficult or even damaging.

This basic axiom has been repeatedly confirmed. Virtually all epidemiological studies of mental and emotional disturbance have consistently found a clear inverse relationship between poverty and low socioeconomic status and the risk of such disturbance.[5] But such studies have also found a clear relationship between disruptions in family relationships and mental disturbance. Sometimes the underlying factor for disruptions in family relationships is economic, such as poverty or unemployment. Sometimes the disruptions in family relationships, particularly in the case of women, lead to poverty, resulting in a double jeopardy: distress as a result of family breakdown, followed by stress as a result of poverty and economic insecurity.

The Midtown Manhattan study found an association between psychological impairment and divorce or separation. The Stirling County study in Nova Scotia found a relationship between levels of community disintegration and attendant personal difficulties, including marital and family problems and the risk of psychiatric difficulty. The Camberwell study of depression among women found that "traumatic life events or major ongoing difficulties" preceded the onset of depression in women. Among the provoking events were "separation from a key person," such as divorce or separation. The researchers further found that among the factors that increase a woman's vulnerability to depression was "the lack of an intimate relationship with someone in whom she could trust or confide, especially a husband or boyfriend." Fourteen studies of the relationship between marital status and rates of mental disturbance found that rates were higher among single, separated, divorced, and widowed people than among married people. A nine-year study of 7,000 Californians reported that people who lack supportive social relationships exhibit higher rates of mortality, depression, suicide, and failure to cope effectively with life stress.[6] The consensus in the literature is that single men have higher rates of mental illness than married men. Furthermore, those who are separated or divorced have higher rates of suicide and mental disturbance than both single and married populations. Finally, the escalating incidence of mental illness among children has been correlated to the growing rate of family breakdown.

Clearly family breakdown exacts an astonishing emotional toll on those affected. But does this mean we should act to save the traditional family and to reverse the trends that appear to afflict us so grievously? The traditional family itself is implicated in a great deal of emotional and psychological disturbance. In other words, the changes in the family are causing a great deal of distress. But so too do efforts to resist those changes.

For example, the Camberwell study found that one of the major ongoing causes of depression in women was a poor marriage, and included among the vulnerability factors were having three or more children under 14 and no job outside the home. Other studies have found that the risk of psychiatric disorder in women is increased when they are caring for small children in social isolation. As well, high rates of depression occur among traditional wives when the children grow up and leave home.[7] And some studies have found that, in general, rates of mental illness are higher in married than in unmarried women. In a study of the relationships between mental illness and the economy, it was found that in times of economic difficulty middle-aged married men are more at risk of mental illness than other groups of men.[8] There is thus clear evidence that negative psychological effects can result for both men and women if they cling desperately to traditional marriage and sex roles in an effort to find meaning, happiness and security.[9]

Yet remaining single appears to be an unsatisfying solution for most. A Toronto study found that single men and women are more likely to feel that life is worse than they had expected, to exhibit twice the rate of depression, to experience four times the rate of loneliness, and to be less sexually gratified than married men and women.[10] And it appears that economic limitations are a key source of frustration for single men and women, especially single women. Understandably, therefore, 73 per cent of single men and women in the study believed that being happily married was important. But, surprisingly, the study found that 70 per cent would rather stay single than lower their expectations of marriage. This increasing caution is reflected in recent Statistics Canada data. In 1997, the average age of first marriage for women shot up to 28 years old. For men, it increased to 30 years. Common-law marriage is increasingly the marriage of choice among Canadians aged 15 to 29 years. Yet a commitment to legal marriage remains. The overwhelming majority of Canadians get married and remarry if things don't work out. In 2001, over half of men and women getting married are trying for at least a second time, if common-law unions are counted.

It appears, then, both that the social structural changes involved in the changing nature of the family are causing stress and provoking emotional difficulty and that trying to return to the traditional family would cause just as many problems. The obvious solution is to support the new emerging family forms at both personal and policy levels. These changes will lead to the more complete emancipation of women, free men from the burden of traditional male role models, and provide children with a more enriched life. Still, the costs will be great, and some groups will be at higher risk. Can we make a painful transition less painful? Can we make a deeply disorienting experience less disorienting? Admitting that we have a crisis of the family on our collective hands and agreeing to move decisively to meet it requires a more complete accounting of the costs being exacted from the victims. First, the children.

PART II

Victims of the Crisis: Children

"My early childhood was a little rough, rocky and shaky ... After my parents got divorced the whole family structure in my mind got destroyed ... It was pretty traumatic ... It crushed me and I lost a real sense of hope."

David, a survivor of an
adolescent suicide attempt, 1997.

Introduction:
Who Cares for the Children?

In 1959 the General Assembly of the United Nations adopted *The U.N. Declaration of the Rights of the Child*, enumerating eleven specific principles as well as affirming a child's right to enjoy the fundamental rights and freedoms "specified in the Universal Declaration of Human Rights ... to the end that he may have a happy childhood and be enabled to grow up."[1] As we watch television reports of children damaged and destroyed by famine in Africa or by civil war in Bosnia, as we read reports of the sexual enslavement of children in Bangkok or Vancouver, or of the cruel exploitation of child labour around the world, we are moved and outraged. Less dramatically, certainly, but here in Canada too, growing numbers of children suffer from our society's incapacity to deliver adequate protection from physical harm, sufficient calories to fend off malnutrition, and the minimal emotional support and security necessary to ensure psychological health and happiness. For thousands of Canadian children, Canadian society has failed to honour principles of the U.N. Declaration, including:

2. The child shall be given the means necessary to enable him to develop physically, mentally, morally, spiritually and socially, in a healthy and normal manner and in conditions of freedom and dignity.

3. The child shall enjoy special protection by law and by other means ...

8. The child shall in all circumstances be the first to receive protection and relief ...

10. The child shall be protected against all forms of neglect, cruelty and exploitation ...

Thirty-six years later, in 1995, a U.N. advisor warned that Canada's cuts in social programs were violations of the U.N. Convention on the Rights of the Child since they were increasing child poverty and putting more children in circumstances where their basic needs were not being met. The U.N. was shocked that such a state of affairs existed in an industrialized country like Canada. Well, you could respond, no society can be perfect, and we can't hold the whole society to account for the failures of individual fathers and mothers to live up to their responsibilities. Perhaps that argument would be comforting if we could be assured that the victimization of children in Canada were caused by the actions of irresponsible individuals. Unfortunately, the evidence is otherwise and provides no such comfort. Much, perhaps most, of the victimization of children can be traced directly to the structural failure of the changing family to fulfill its obligations as an institution. And while it may be true that in particular tragic instances individual blame can be assigned, it is incumbent on us to try to understand the social context and the stresses and strains that may have increased the risk of such tragedies. In that way we can move from simply dealing with casualties and symptoms to dealing with causes and prevention.

The vital importance of childhood experiences in shaping the adult personality is widely known, and it has been estimated that about half of a child's full cognitive development is reached by the age of three or four.[2] The core self-concept and basic social-structural map are established primarily through interaction with parents and other adult caregivers in the child's immediate experience, the amount of time a child enjoys with them, their educational level, and the economic affluence of the household have positive associations with the child's development.[3] It is from these "significant others," as Mead put it, that the child acquires his or her sense of self and place, and anything that disrupts the security, stability, and quality of a child's early interactions with parents can have not only immediate negative consequences, but also long-term deleterious effects on later adjustment.

Our society expresses deeply ambivalent attitudes regarding children. One sociologist has suggested that children today are seen largely as "emotional assets" of parents.[4] Children bring no economic rewards to the family; indeed, they are a source of constant financial drain. Yet people continue to have children for the emotional gratification they bring. As families have fewer children, parents can indulge their children more than ever before. Designer clothes, expensive high-tech toys, and the latest computers all appeal to a growing market among affluent parents. Yet at the other end we can see children lining up at food banks and school meal programs. Most of us love and protect our children diligently, yet daily we read reports of abused children who die at the hands of those we expect to love them most. And the institutions we were taught to respect and to trust, from government and the church to residential schools and children's hockey leagues, seem to have been callously indifferent to the suffering of many children in their care. As a society we want and need mothers of children to work, yet we pay minimal wages to our daycare workers. There is something deeply wrong with a society that remains incapable of providing adequate quality care for all of its children, where some children enjoy love and security, others are repeatedly physically and sexually abused, and others are beaten to death.

Canada's daycare crisis reflects well this deep ambivalence toward children. Canadians are seriously divided on the question of increased government spending to provide subsidized daycare centres. In an August 1989 Gallup poll, 49 per cent favoured such increased spending while 43 per cent opposed it.[5] Predictably opinion follows age on the question. Those most likely to have young children heavily favour increased government spending for daycare, while those less likely to have young children tend to oppose it strongly.

As a result the crisis of care for young children of working parents remains chronic and worsens. Today, 75 per cent of women of child-bearing age are working. Over 50 per cent of the total Canadian workforce consists of families in which both parents work, and another 6 per cent of the workforce is comprised of working single parents. In other words, over half of Canada's total workforce requires daycare. Among women with children at home, those most likely to work are separated or divorced women between the ages of 35 and 44 years. Clearly their need for subsidized care is greatest.

Estimates vary about the number of children who require daycare and the number of available licensed spaces, but all studies agree that spaces lag far behind need.[6] A Special House of Commons Committee on daycare provided comprehensive figures based on 1986 data.[7] Fifty-six per cent of women with children under three, 62 per cent of women with children between three and five, and 68 per cent of women with children between six and 15 were in the labour force. This involved over 1.2 million preschool-age children. There were only just over 197,000 licensed daycare spaces available in that year. Among preschoolers cared for in non-parental arrangements, and requiring care, only 7 per cent of those aged up to 17 months, 14 per cent of those aged from 18 to 35 months, and 34 per cent of those from three to five years were served. The committee's report also provided estimates on the number of children aged six to 12 who were either unsupervised "latchkey" kids or received care from an older sibling — there were 360,000 such children in 1986, representing about 15 per cent of all Canadian children in that age group. By 2003, there were just under 400,000 licensed daycare spaces in Canada for an estimated 3.3 million eligible children (under 13) of parents requiring care due to work obligations.

Daycare, even poor daycare, is expensive. The average annual cost ranges between $6,000 and $8,400, though high-quality care can cost as much as $15,000. Clearly these costs represent an enormous drain on the incomes of working parents. Even so, a Decima poll found that 59 per cent of parents rated daycare quality as either fair or poor. The House of Commons committee's researchers found that even those administering and monitoring provincial systems believed that one in six licensed day care centres across the country were "poor" or "very poor," actually *below* minimal licensing standards. What about the conditions in unlicensed "family" daycare homes?

In 1987 the Health and Welfare Minister commented that parents, not daycare workers, are better qualified to raise children.[8] In response, the daycare lobby accused the minister of endangering children in unregulated, unlicensed daycare.[9] If working parents can't get good quality, regulated, licensed daycare, they will take what they can get. Nor does the minister's response provide solace to the estimated 6 per cent of young children who are left completely unattended by desperate working parents. This notion that parents, not daycare workers, ought to be caring for kids has become a consistent theme in the neoconservative resistance to public funding for adequate daycare, and has moved various provincial governments to implement support programs to encourage "stay-at-home" mothers.

The importance of adequate quality child care for working parents cannot be overstated. One major U.S. study of 30,000 employees in 30 corporations found that 40 per cent of women and 25 per cent of men with babies and toddlers claim that worries about child care reduce their productivity, and more than 50 per cent of both men and women felt stress as a result of work/family conflicts centring on child care problems. Those suffering such stress were more likely to be absent from work, to have trouble getting up in the morning, to believe their work performance suffered, and to have more health problems.[10] Another study found that the effect of working on a mother's sense of psychological well-being had most to do with the ease or difficulty of child-care arrangements. It found extremely high depression levels among employed mothers who had problems in arranging child care and who had the sole responsibility for child care.[11] The availability of adequate child care also clearly has a great deal to do with the decision of working parents to have children. Access to quality daycare for working parents increases psychological well-being, improves morale, increases productivity, and reduces absenteeism.

For the children of working parents, the importance of adequate, quality day care is self-evident. Low child/staff ratios, qualified staff, a low rate of staff turnover, and adequate resources for programming enhance a child's development, and the reverse has potentially negative effects.

The care issue is even more vital for children who are left unsupervised or supervised by an older sibling. American estimates vary on the number of such children: the U.S. census estimated that 2.1 million children under 13 are regularly left unsupervised by working parents before and after school. Others put the figure at between five and seven million children. In comparison, Canada has an estimated 360,000 such children. Market researchers have found that these children in many cases become the "brand managers" of the family and take on many household tasks: 37 per cent of children between six and 11 shop or do chores before dinner, 13 per cent of children aged six to 15 make dinner for themselves most of the time, and 8 per cent actually make dinner for the family. In response, marketing consultants have targeted for special attention syndicated children's television programs between three and five p.m. Spending on advertising in such shows went from nil in 1982 to $107 million in 1988 as more and more of the major consumer products manufacturers and their advertising agencies add "latchkey kids to the overall consumer mix." By the mid-1990s, each child was exposed to 48 minutes of commercials pushing as many as 192 products during a six-hour period on an average Saturday morning. Children's cable channels were promising advertisers that their channel "will give your product instant credibility with kids."[12]

The evidence is, then, overwhelming. The new family forms no longer provide adequate care for a growing number of our children. Such families require a community response in the form of a system of universally available quality child care. Perhaps the community has not acted because children are seen as the private "emotional assets" of their parents. Perhaps the public is reluctant to contemplate the levels of public spending necessary. Perhaps there remains nostalgia for the traditional family. An adequate system of publicly provided, universal child care would be an open admission that the traditional family is dead and that the increasingly dominant family forms require new community responses. Perhaps some are haunted by the obvious question: Just how many of the wives and mothers in Canada's traditional families would continue to embrace that role if quality child care were easily accessible and affordable?

Inadequate care is only one of the costs being exacted from our children as a result of the changing nature of the family, and perhaps it's the least important. Most working parents manage to muddle through their child care problems. And who is to say it is a bad thing for an 11- or 12-year-old to care for herself or himself after school or to prepare supper for the family? Indeed, as Mandell suggests, perhaps we are witnessing a transformation in our very notion of childhood as children contribute more and more to sustaining the household.

> [C]hildren are socially constructed as robust, independent and helpful individuals who are more involved in family economics ... Given then that couples are likely to continue to want and to bear children, it also follows that the role of children within families will alter to minimize parents' financial costs and maximize parents' emotional gains ... Rather than signalling a loss of childhood or a demise in children's innocence, these changes indicate the closer integration of children and women in a more egalitarian and interdependent family.[13]

While this argument has considerable merit, such a reconstruction of our notion of childhood, just like the reconstruction of the nature of the family itself, does not come easily. The transition costs, socially and psychologically, remain high. It is to these that we now turn.

4 / The Economic Insecurity of Children

Canada's distribution of income shares has been remarkably stable over time.[1] Attempts at income redistribution through an allegedly progressive income tax policy and a variety of income security policies designed to ensure a fairer access to income for lower-income Canadians have largely failed. The shares of total income, including social benefit payments, going to the poorest 20 per cent of Canadians in 1951 was 4 per cent, while the richest 20 per cent received 43 per cent. Forty years later the figures had changed little: the poorest 20 per cent received 5 per cent; the richest received 42 per cent. The real incomes of all Canadians have advanced considerably, and Canada remains an extremely privileged society, even for the poor, when compared to the lot of many in the Third World. But income levels and notions of poverty are relative to time and place. Though Canadians as an aggregate have improved their real levels of income, their shares of the pie have stayed relatively static. More than that, Canadians' expectations of a continuing advance in levels of real income, encouraged by the progress achieved in the 1960s and 1970s, have been dramatically dashed in the 1980s and 1990s, decades characterized by declines in real incomes.

Though shares of income have remained static for more than four decades, the nature of the income Canadians obtain has changed quite dramatically. Today more than 60 per cent of families have two or more earners, and over 70 per cent of wives work. In the 1950s, 60 per cent of families relied on one earner, and less than 15 per cent of wives worked. There has therefore been a dramatic rise in the real incomes of working married couples with young children, and the two-income family has become the dominant characteristic of high-earner families.

There has been another major change in the nature of the incomes of Canadians: their growing dependence on social benefits (including old-age pensions, income supplements, family allowances, employment insurance, and social assistance payments). In the 1950s, the lowest income group received 29 per cent of its income from social benefits. In the early 1990s, that proportion had about doubled to 57 per cent. (Middle-income families over the same period also about doubled the proportion of their incomes coming from social benefits: 5 per cent to 9 per cent). Therefore, although the share of income received by the lowest-income families remains small, increasingly that income is made up of social benefits. In 1951, 56 per cent of the income obtained by the poorest fifth of Canadians was *earned* income. By 1990, about 30 per cent was earned. What this means is that those who are most economically insecure today are those most dependent on state aid, rendering them even more vulnerable to the whims of politicians.

The cuts in social programs that continued and escalated throughout the 1980s and 1990s, and that have largely focussed on income supports like family allowances, unemployment insurance payments, and welfare benefits, have hit the most vulnerable and the least secure the hardest, leading to declining income shares for the poorest 40 per cent of the population. These social programs were necessary not to *redistribute* income but to ensure that the distribution remained about the same. In their absence, the poorest 20 per cent of Canadians would today be receiving less than 3 per cent of total income. As for the income tax system, the effects are marginal at best. In 1990, the highest income quintile saw its income share fall from 42 per cent before taxes to 37 per cent after taxes, while the lowest quintile gained 3 per cent. By 1994, government income supports to the poor had long since become their most important source of income, ranging from a low of around 50 per cent of income for single and childless men and women, to 73 per cent for single-parent mothers with kids under 18, and over 90 per cent for the poor aged 65 and over. Meanwhile, federal and provincial cuts in social welfare rates between 1986 and 1996 have dramatically reduced payments to the most needy Canadians, both in absolute dollars and in the failure to match inflation, particularly in Alberta and Ontario, where the reductions were savage (17 per cent in Alberta and 22 per cent in Ontario for a couple with two kids).[2]

Not surprisingly, Canada's poverty rates track rises and falls in real income levels. Poverty is controversial in a society like ours, which affirms egalitarian ideals. As a result, politicians in power tend to minimize the extent of poverty, while those in opposition tend to maximize it in order to attack the government's economic policies. Therefore, the level that is chosen to define official poverty is a source of considerable disagreement. Statistics Canada, for example, from time to time assesses what an average family spends, as a percentage of income, on such basic necessities as food, clothing, and shelter and then sets the official poverty line at 20 percentage points above that level.[3] In the 1970s, the Statistics Canada poverty line was set at 62 per cent — that is, families or individuals spending 62 per cent or more of their incomes on the basic necessities were deemed to be officially poor. This poverty line was again revised in the 1990s and set at 56.2 per cent, down from the 1980s cut-off of 58.5 per cent.[4] The Canadian Council on Social Development (CCSD) argues that the poverty line ought to be set to include all families who earn 50 per cent or less of the average family income, and the 1971 Special Senate Committee on Poverty set the poverty level at about 56 per cent or less of the average family income. All poverty lines make adjustments to account for size of family, region, and rural/urban differences. In terms of the politics of poverty, it is important to realize that official poverty figures always understate its real extent. Nevertheless, this has not deterred politically motivated neo-conservative politicians and intellectuals — like Canadian Alliance MPs and Fraser Institute "experts" — from attacking official poverty figures as gross overstatements, insisting that a true poverty rate should include only those in the most dire straits. By waving this statistical magic wand, Canada could "solve" the political problem of poverty overnight by simply defining it out of existence. Despite such efforts, most published data and poverty studies use the Statistics Canada poverty line, the one used in the formulation of government policy.

A related issue is the question of a poverty line, or a low-income cut-off, to measure poverty. For example, in 1998, Statistics Canada declared that in communities with populations of 500,000 or more, all families of three with incomes at $28,405 or less were "poor." Those who earned $28,406 were officially "not poor." Obviously, this declaration makes no social or economic sense. When we talk therefore of the official "poor," we exclude a significant group of the "near poor," who are almost equal in numbers and face the same problems as the "official poor." Only once, in 1969, did Statistics Canada study this group, concluding that they were more similar in many ways to the official "poor" than to the official "non-poor."

There is a third issue in the politics of poverty. Many of the poor are very poor, falling far below the official poverty line. One Montreal study found that about half of the official poor receive 60 per cent or less of the Statistics Canada poverty line income.[5] We know that Canadians on welfare in 1995 received benefits ranging from 48 to 69 per cent of the official poverty line, depending on the generosity of the province of residence.[6] Furthermore, full-time workers at the minimum wage cannot expect to earn much more than 68 per cent of the poverty line. And things have been getting worse very quickly. In 1975, a worker on the minimum wage could earn a poverty line income with 50 hours of work each week. In 1986, a worker on the minimum wage had to put in 87 hours to reach the poverty line.[7] In 1994, it took 100 hours of work each week for a minimum-wage earner to support a family of three at the poverty line. That helps explain why in 1967, 62 per cent of the poorest Canadians still managed to own their own homes, no matter how modest. That figure fell to 23 per cent by the early 1990s. It also explains why the heads of most poor families (55 per cent) are active in the labour force, yet remain officially poor.

With these three *caveats* in mind — official figures tend to understate the real extent of poverty, arbitrary official poverty lines ignore an almost equal number of "near poor," and many of the official poor are very, very poor — we can examine the extent of poverty among Canada's children.

Child Poverty

Child poverty is deeply unsettling. As John Sargo said in *The Bitter Cry of the Children* in 1906,

> Poverty ... is always ugly, repellent and terrible either to see or to experience; but when it assails the cradle, it assumes its most hideous form.[8]

Even for the roughest minded, children are not seen as the authors of their own misfortune. When a Tory backbencher once commented that many people were "poor by choice," many probably agreed, but it cannot be argued that children make that choice. Their deprivation closes a lifetime of doors of opportunity. The "feminization" of poverty, which I will address in Chapter 8, is acknowledged but there is also a "juvenescence" of poverty — a larger and larger portion of the poor in Canada are children, many of whom are young children in families headed by young parents.

In 1971, 1.7 million of Canada's 6.8 million children were poor — one in four,[9] and children accounted for about 39 per cent of all poor Canadians.[10] Over the next decade, Canada scored some considerable success in its commitment to reduce poverty. By 1980, 984,000 of Canada's 6.6 million children were poor, representing 15 per cent of all children, or about 27 per cent of all poor Canadians. Therefore, in a decade, the absolute number of poor children had been cut in half, and the proportion of poor Canadians who were children had been dramatically reduced. This was part of the more general success story in reducing Canada's official poverty. Indeed, in 1980 the poverty rates for all Canadians, and for children, were the same at 15 per cent. But the long recession of the 1980s and the successful neoconservative attack on the social security net changed all that. Poverty rates began to move up again, 16 per cent in 1999, but the poverty rate among children went up much more dramatically. In 1999, Canadian children still made up 27 per cent of the poor; but one child in five, 1.3 million, was officially poor, and as many as half of these were "very poor." There were perhaps another million "near poor."

There has, in fact, been a clear trend in the last 25 years — the greatest risk of poverty has shifted from the old to children and young families. In 1969 elderly families (head over 65) suffered a poverty rate of over 42 per cent. In 1999, that rate was under 9 per cent. On the other hand, in 1972 families headed by persons under 25 years suffered a 16 per cent poverty rate. In 1999, that had increased by almost three times to almost 47 per cent. Now the risk of poverty in Canada is greatest for families with children, for single parent families, and for families with only one earner. That was clearly partly the result of the trend towards poorly paid jobs for young workers in the 1980s and 1990s. For example, 16 per cent of workers aged 16 to 24 earned the lowest wages in 1981; this figure more than doubled to 33 per cent by 1986, and fluctuated between 50 and 60 per cent in the 1990s. Even as we move towards a marginal economic recovery, women and children remain the most likely to be left out.

As a result, during the past decade Canada witnessed levels of hunger and homelessness unprecedented since the Great Depression.[11] In Atlantic Canada, 150,000 people routinely rely on food banks, as do 81,000 in Toronto alone.[12] In B.C. there are over 50 food banks, the most in any province. In 1986, over 1.2 million meals were served in soup kitchens and homeless shelters. In 1987, the CCSD estimated there were as many as 250,000 homeless in Canada, including many children, as the "new homeless" made up of whole families began to grow. Hungry children, including, for example, hundreds in Vancouver's 17 inner city schools, have become commonplace across the country. One can view this deterioration as symptomatic of a growing general social crisis resulting from the erosion of the social welfare system, as Graham Riches argues in his book, *Food Banks and the Welfare Crisis.*[13] Or, with neoconservative politicians, one can believe that hungry children exist only because they do not have parents who love them enough, lazing in bed rather than preparing school lunches for their children, or rushing off to work without feeding them.[14]

The negative impact of poverty is well-documented.[15] A massive health survey carried out jointly by Statistics Canada and Health and Welfare Canada found that low-income Canadians tend to be less educated and less happy and to have poorer health and shorter lives than more prosperous Canadians. There was a clear inverse relationship between mortality rates and social class that remained "durable" over time. These findings were confirmed by an Ontario health survey: those with higher incomes lived longer and healthier lives than those with lower incomes. If the lowest income and highest income quintiles are compared, the lowest had almost three times the rate of mental disorders, more than twice the rate of negative feelings, and seven times the rate of anxiety and depression. Men at the top of the income scale live 6.3 years longer and enjoy 14 more years of good health than men at the bottom. Further confirmation of this pattern was provided by a McMaster University Health Status Index (HSI) Survey. The Survey found a direct relationship between health and income, and between health and unemployment. Those with the lowest incomes and those who experience unemployment are at greater risk of ill health than those with higher incomes and those with paid employment. A Statistics Canada National Health Survey found that low-income Canadians were twice as likely to rate their health as poor in comparison to high-income Canadians. Another study found that poor women suffer three times the frequency of depression of middle-class women.

The National Council of Welfare's comprehensive report, *Poor Kids*,[16] pointed out that poor kids are more likely to be sick and to suffer retarded development, more at risk to fail or drop out of school, more likely to live in crowded and unhealthy homes, and more likely to be labelled delinquent than better-off children. The Ontario health survey found that children in lower socioeconomic groups are more likely to suffer from chronic health problems, more at risk to develop psychiatric disorders, and more prone to poor school performance than more affluent children. Indeed, a more recent study found that poor children have twice the school dropout rate of non-poor children. A Statistics Canada study found that poor children in urban Canada are much more likely to die than the children of the better-off. This pattern was found to be the case for child deaths as a result of accidents among older children and for child deaths as a result of illness among infants. The poorest 20 per cent of Canadians in urban Canada had a child death rate up to the age of 19 years of 90.6 per 100,000, while the wealthiest 20 per cent had a rate of 58.1 per 100,000. Recent data on the increases in low-weight babies and in infant mortality rates confirm that low-weight babies (who are less likely to survive, more likely to have serious health problems, and more likely to suffer growth retardation) are 30 to 50 per cent more likely to be associated with low-income families. Furthermore, babies born to the lowest income Canadian families have 1.7 times the mortality rate of those born to the highest income families.

Children raised in poverty are more likely to be poor later in life and in turn to raise children in poverty. They very quickly lose any hope for the future. June Callwood captures well the downward spiral in the psyches of poor children.

> Until about the age of 8, children born to someone poor do not believe that the bad times will last ... Ten-year-olds already are wiser and know that being poor will be endless. They protest unbecomingly, some with rage, some with cunning, some by withdrawing.[17]

Imagine that you are one of Canada's more than one million officially poor children. You live in a tiny house that is cold in spring, autumn, and winter. You share a double bed with three siblings, and during the winter it is pushed so close to the space heater there's a constant risk of fire. When the cold comes, the rats come in. You are almost always hungry; three mornings a week there is a hot breakfast at school, and near the end of the month you go with your mother to the food bank. Some days you take food from your school room's "sharing shelves." You miss a lot of school because you are often sick, and sometimes there are no clean clothes to wear. Often there's no place at home to do homework. Your parents can't afford the extra charges for many of the school's programs. Every now and then on payday dad doesn't come right home and mom gets worried and then angry. Finally, dad comes home, and there's a big argument. Sometimes they hit you after they've quarrelled if you get in their way. You feel things will never get better and that there must be something terribly wrong with you and your parents because you are so poor. Though you are unaware of it, you are almost twice as likely to die young, three to four times as likely to become seriously ill repeatedly, and twenty times as likely to fail academically and socioeconomically as your wealthier peers. Not only are you not aware of it, there is very little you can do about it. Though this portrait is fictionalized, it was drawn from the *Poor Kids* report and accurately reflects child poverty. In 1996, a report by the Canadian Council on Social Development stated that the number of poor children was increasing and the circumstances of poor children were deteriorating, while kids who were not poor were doing quite well.

Child Poverty and the Family Crisis

To what extent is child poverty in Canada a result of the crisis of the family? Divorce typically leads to a precipitous fall in the material standards of living for women and a dramatically higher poverty rate for women and children. The transition to new family forms has thus increased the poverty, and general economic insecurity, of many children (see Table 2).[18]

In 1971 there were about 1.7 million officially poor children, representing almost 25 per cent of all children in Canada. Over 79 per cent of these children lived in husband/wife families, just about 18 per cent lived in single-parent families headed by women, and just under 3 per cent lived in single-parent families headed by men. If we look at it another way, over 69 per cent of children in single-parent families headed by women and almost 34 per cent of children in those headed by men were officially poor. Thus, children in single-parent families headed by women faced over *three times* the risk of being poor compared to children in husband/wife families, while children in single-parent families headed by men faced almost *one-and-one-half times* the risk. Clearly, these 1971 figures tell us that the absence of a husband/wife family was a significant factor in poverty for over one in five poor children.

Table 2: Poor children under 16 by family status, 1971 and 1998

	1971 Number	%	1998 Number	%
All poor children	1,657,017	100	1,327,000	100
Husband/wife families	1,314,576	79	668,000	50
Female single parents	296,298	18	546,000	41
Male single parents	46,028	3	113,000	8.5
Estimate of number affected by marriage breakdown	147,000	9	386,000	29

Sources: National Council of Welfare, *Poverty Profile 1988*, *Poverty Profile 1990*, *Poverty Profile 1998*; National Council of Welfare, *Poor Kids* (Ottawa, 1975); Mary Anne Burke, "Diversity: The New Norm," Statistics Canada, *Canadian Social Trends* (Summer 1986); Jillian Oderkirk and Clarence Lochhead, "Lone Parenthood: Gender Differences," Statistics Canada, *Canadian Social Trends* (Winter 1992); Garnett Picot and John Myles, "Children in Low-Income Families," Statistics Canada, *Canadian Social Trends*, (Autumn 1996).

By 1998 things had changed dramatically. Over 1.3 million children, representing 19 per cent of all children, were poor. That improvement, however, involved a significant redistribution of poverty as children were negatively affected by changes in the family. In 1998, just over 50 per cent of all poor children lived in husband/wife families, a sharp decrease from 1971. Only a little under 12 per cent of all children in husband/wife families were poor that year, a considerable improvement over the 21 per cent figure of 1971. Children in single-parent families headed by women accounted for about 41 per cent of all poor children in 1998, more than twice the share in 1971. And children in single-parent families headed by men accounted for over 8 per cent, again a substantial rise. By 1998, children in female single-parent families faced *five times* the risk of poverty compared to children in husband/wife families, while children in male single-parent families faced over *twice* the risk.

By the 1990s, about 60 per cent of female single-parent families, and 70 per cent of male single-parent families, resulted from
divorce or separation. These figures suggest that for as many as
386,000, or over 29 per cent, of all officially poor children in
Canada, marriage breakdown was a factor of some significance in
precipitating a fall below the poverty line. A similar estimate for
1971 suggests that was true for only about 147,000, or about 9 per
cent, of all poor children. In other words, even as the total number
of poor children declined, the proportion of all poor children for
whom family breakdown was a significant factor in precipitating
poverty increased *by over three times*. In 1998, 19 per cent of all
children in Canada were poor, and for over one in four of them
marriage breakdown was implicated in the fall into poverty.

This brings us to a fourth issue — the duration of episodes of
poverty. The statistics reported above describe the occurrence
and distribution of poverty and identify those groups which experience a higher risk. But they tell us nothing about how persistent
poverty is for a particular individual over time. Some will argue
that episodes of poverty are brief in an individual's or family's
total life experience. Many university students, for example, are
officially poor for a time, but go on to comfortable incomes after
graduation. And if children, and their parent or parents, suffer
only brief episodes of poverty, the problem is hardly as pressing
as the statistical snapshot suggests. But if, on the other hand,
poverty remains a chronic condition for large numbers of people
over a number of years, then the consequences are much more
disastrous.

Just as Statistics Canada has not devoted much attention to the
"near poor," so it has neglected the *persistence* of poverty over
time. Ross reports three Canadian studies on the question.[19] The
1969 Statistics Canada survey reported that three in four of poor
unattached individuals and two in three poor families were poor in
1968 and in 1969, suggesting a high level of persistence. A similar
survey done by Canada Health and Welfare for 1972 and 1973
found that three in four of the poorest households remained poor,
while over one in two of the "near poor" did so. A third study done
by the Institute of Public Affairs at Dalhousie University studied a

sample of "welfare households" that went on to find employment between 1973 and 1976. Most jobs hovered at the minimum wage level, and three in four lasted six months or less, suggesting a high degree of persistence of poverty. All three studies suggest, therefore, a significant degree of persistence of poverty episodes over some considerable time. As Ross says, "What we do know ... suggests that probably between 50 and 75 per cent of the poverty group is stable over a two-to-three-year period and probably much longer."

In 1993, as part of a longitudinal study of labour and income, Statistics Canada finally began measuring the duration of poverty over six-year cycles. The first report was released in 1998.[20] Between 1993 and 1998, 7 million, or almost 30 per cent, of all Canadians were touched by poverty, confirming that for many poverty is episodic. The study also confirmed the known population groups at highest risk of poverty: women, children, single-parent families, young families, visible minorities, aboriginal Canadians, the disabled and recent immigrants (after 1979). The highest duration of poverty by age was for children: one in three Canadian children experience poverty for one of the six years, 16 per cent for three or more years, and 10 per cent for all six years. The highest duration by family status was for female single-parent families: 76 per cent tasted poverty for one year, 57 per cent for three or more years, and 42 per cent for all six years. Such figures suggest that for a significant percentage of high-risk groups in Canada, poverty is grinding and chronic, not episodic. For the chronically poor the risk factors were again confirmed. Those experiencing the longest duration of poverty tended to be children, women, the elderly, single parents, young families, visible minorities, aboriginal Canadians, the disabled and recent immigrants.

The studies therefore show that a large proportion of poor people suffer fairly long episodes of poverty. The high rates of poverty among female single-parent families, and the evidence of a persistence of poverty over time, confirm that many childhood poverty episodes are of considerable duration. Given that the average durations of single parenthood for Canadian women are quite long, and the evidence of chronic poverty for a large number of children during their more formative years, the crisis of the family lies at the root of much of this poverty.

The relationships between poverty and family breakdown are intimate and complex. Frequently, family breakdown precipitates a fall into poverty, particularly for single-parent mothers and their children. Men are often able to escape court-ordered obligations to their former wives and children. One Status of Women study reported that the national average of men who default on mainte- nance payments ranges between 50 and 85 per cent across the country.[21] For some of the few men who obtain custody of the chil- dren, the loss of the second income can lead to a period of family poverty, although the duration is typically about half of that faced by women in similar circumstances. On the other hand, economic stress and difficulty can help precipitate a family's disintegration, leading inevitably to a worse economic situation, again especially for women and children. For example, during the recession of the late 1970s and the early 1980s, some areas of Ontario's golden horseshoe suffered elevated levels of unemployment (up to 20 per cent in Windsor, for example). Social service agencies there report- ed an increase in family problem caseloads of from 25 to 377 per cent as families began to fall apart under the economic stress. Increased unemployment led to a rash of mortgage defaults, rates of alcohol and drug problems spiralled, child and wife abuse became epidemic, and separation and divorce rates marched upward.[22] In other words, while family breakdown often leads to poverty, unexpected unemployment and episodes of poverty some- times lead to family breakups.

The economic consequences of family breakdown can be extreme. For example, a study probed the backgrounds of 142 young homeless in Montreal aged 18 to 30 years. Most came from broken families and lived on the very precipice of daily survival. They tended to have serious mental health disorders, exacerbated by the routine abuse of drugs and alcohol.[23] Another Montreal study tried to obtain a more complete characterization of the poor. It was found that in 1981, 23 per cent of all Montrealers were offi- cially poor, but half of these were "very poor." One in three of these "very poor" were found to be aged 18 or less, and half of them lived in single parent families, amounting to nearly 44,000 children.[24] There are also the new emerging episodically homeless, often single-parent mothers with small children, who have been described as the "peripatetic poor," living on inadequate welfare payments and moving from temporary home to temporary home.

Furthermore, the problems of economic stress often result in serious family disruption as a prelude to family breakdown. Children of unemployed parents can suffer enormous mental stress that is psychologically worse than that of a parent losing a job. Such children quickly lose any sense of expansive optimism about the future, tend to see the world as a disordered place in which they are unneeded and unwanted burdens, and tend to suffer elevated risks of clinical depression. They also more frequently experience physical abuse.

On the more positive side, a stable and secure family is vital in establishing a child's sense of self-esteem and in fostering a sense of personal control over one's world.[25] Not surprisingly, it has been found that well-adjusted adolescents tend to come from families with higher levels of socioeconomic status. They have experienced no physical abuse. They can count on a more comprehensive system of social supports. Their parents tend to be more loving and caring. Their lives contain fewer stressful events, such as family breakdown. And, in general, they tend to have very positive concepts of themselves.[26]

Obviously, the increased levels of economic insecurity for many children resulting from the crisis of the family cannot be separated easily or clearly from the attendant increase in emotional and physical insecurity.

5 / The Emotional Insecurity of Children

Opinion on the emotional impact of family breakdown on children is divided.[1] One sociologist can talk confidently about "the *lack* of a clear-cut impact of divorce on children," insisting "it is unclear exactly *what effect* divorce has on children."[2] Others assert, "few children are untouched by divorce, but ... over 50 per cent are indistinguishable from others five years later,"[3] which suggests a considerable, prolonged negative impact. Psychiatrists and psychologists are much less divided: they flatly insist that divorce and/or separation have enormous negative emotional consequences for children. Why this divided opinion?

Part of the explanation can be found in the sad limitations of social science. Divorce or separation is the end of an often long and stressful process. And, of course, it continues to plague the separated spouses and their children. Further, the economic consequences are often disastrous. Therefore, separating cause and effect is virtually impossible. Are the problems of the children of divorce the result of the years of conflict and unhappiness that led up to divorce? Or of the divorce itself? Or of a precipitous fall into poverty? There is no way of knowing with precision.

When we talk about the emotional consequences of marriage breakdown for children, we are not just talking about the singular event of divorce or of the final signing of a legal separation document. We are clearly talking about a process that involves a variety of surrendered hopes, shattered dreams, violated expectations, economic strains, and unfulfilled cravings, often over many years. And how people work these through, or collapse under the stress, will be as unique and varied as their personalities and circumstances.

Sociologists quickly reject the evidence of individual cases because they do not allow us to make general statements about the consequences for children of parent loss. Indeed, one sociologist has argued that sociological findings on the emotional consequences of divorce for children tend to be much less negative and pessimistic than psychiatric findings. It is alleged that psychiatric findings will be more negative because psychiatrists will obviously be approached by those seeking help, not by those adjusting nicely. On the other hand, sociologists tend to try to base their conclusions on samples of all those affected by divorce or separation, scientifically drawn to assure some approximation of representativeness. But this argument tends to ignore the fact that many psychiatric studies do impose rigorous scientific controls and engage in careful comparisons between affected and unaffected groups.

Besides these scientific problems, there are ideological reasons why opinions on the emotional consequences of divorce or separation for children remain at variance.[4] Attitudes to divorce and separation have changed dramatically in less than a generation. Prior to the 1968 divorce reform, if an average person entered into an unhappy marriage, then by and large he or she was expected to put up with it. The breakup of the family was considered to be an overwhelming evil, especially for the children. Remember all those James Cagney gangster movies? Invariably the gangster had suffered the early trauma of parental divorce, separation or desertion. Children of divorce were on the slippery slope that led to the reformatory or the penitentiary. Divorcing parents were seen to be criminally self-indulgent, emotionally truncated, monumentally insensitive, or socially irresponsible, perhaps all four. The submessage was clear: you may have a bitterly unhappy marriage, but think of the children ... And again, the message was particularly aimed at women: do everything, accept everything, sacrifice everything, but, above all, keep the family together.

The new feminism contributed to a decline in such attitudes, attitudes that oppressed women with domestic slavery, subordination to the needs of husbands and children, and large doses of guilt. One of the early responses to the burgeoning women's movement was the amendment of the divorce law. Subsequently, in the 1970s and early 1980s there was, Richardson notes, "a tendency to romanticize divorce as a creative, rehabilitative, and liberating process."[5] And so it obviously was for those in unhappy marriages. Whenever the issue of the emotional consequences of divorce for children was raised, it was repeatedly confirmed that it is infinitely worse for all members of the family to remain in conflict-riven, unloving, and unhappy family situations. But to concede that does not therefore justify ignoring the negative emotional consequences of divorce for children. Children in unhappy families suffer the most; next come children of divorce who suffer a great deal.

Divorce or separation may be necessary and even good, but it is emotionally costly. Just as the new right tends to blame feminism and the women's liberation movement for the decline of the traditional family, so they assign similar blame for the emotional difficulties generated by family breakdown. It would not be surprising, therefore, to expect supporters of the rights of women to minimize or overlook the negative consequences of marriage breakdown. A far better response is to admit that great social changes often involve emotional suffering. Let us, therefore, assess the emotional consequences, bad and good, of divorce and separation and address them through policies and programs. After all, more than one in two children will spend part of their lives in a single-parent family. Richardson estimates that as many as 100,000 children each year are affected by divorce and separation.[6] Therefore in the over 30 years since the changes in the divorce law were made, it can be conservatively argued that between one and two million Canadian children have been touched by some form of marriage breakdown.

Experts have noted a dramatic increase in recent decades of children with emotional problems serious enough to require professional intervention.[7] According to one child psychiatrist, in the 1960s about one child in 10 suffered from an emotional or mental illness serious enough to require professional help. In the 1970s, that figure grew to about one child in 6.5.[8] In 1983 the Ontario Health Survey studied a sample of 3,000 children aged four to 16 and found the prevalence of psychiatric disorder to average over one in five. This figure was confirmed by the 1992 Ontario Health Survey and by a survey of research into the prevalence of mental disorders among children and adolescents.[9] Between the 1950s and the 1990s, teenage suicide and suicide-attempt rates have risen by more than 300 per cent in Canada.[10]

Since social support systems are crucial to emotional well-being, the collapse of such systems is typically implicated in the onset of psychiatric disorders.[11] As a result, psychiatrists have not hesitated in pointing the finger at family breakdown as a major reason for the rising rates of emotional distress among children. One child psychiatrist said, "the nuclear family is disintegrating and children have fewer support mechanisms to help them through difficult times,"[12] and another drew a larger portrait of the choice before us:

> Prostitution, child abuse, alcoholism, vandalism, suicide and depression are symptomatic of social malaise. Escalating divorce rates, increased mobility, changing social conventions, the erosion of institutional supports of church and school, all contribute to a sense of rootlessness and anomie.[13]

One study reported that from 15 to 25 per cent of the children touched by divorce require psychiatric treatment. Though most divorced spouses with children remarry within three to five years, 20 per cent experience another separation, compounding the earlier emotional problems. From 50 to 80 per cent of the patients treated by Canadian mental health clinics are from separated families.[14] And the negative emotional effects of parental loss through divorce or separation or death do not end with the end of childhood. Rather, it has been found that parental loss is the "single most powerful predictor of adult psychopathology."[15] And if parents divorce, the chances are much greater that the child will.[16] A study of families of almost 8,000 U.S. women aged 15 to 44 found that women who spent part of their childhood in a single-parent family, when compared to those from two-parent families, are more likely to marry and have children at a younger age, more likely to have children before marrying, and more likely to experience the breakdown of their own marriages. The authors concluded, "Parental role models and parental supervision are the major factors in determining an offspring's future family-formation orientation."[17]

Emotional Impacts

Though sociological studies are sometimes hesitant to draw firm conclusions about the specific emotional impacts of divorce, none deny they are serious. Very large scale studies show clear negative patterns among children from broken homes. One study of 18,000 U.S. children showed that children from broken homes exhibited significantly greater tendencies to demonstrate delinquent behaviour, to leave school before completion, to suffer from various illnesses, and to attempt or commit suicide. Another researcher reported that children of divorce are more isolated and withdrawn; act out more often; exhibit more absent-mindedness, moodiness, and inattentiveness; and present more physical symptoms of illness. A study of over 2,000 suicide-attempting children aged six-and-a-half to 17 found that the rate of such incidents went up by almost four times in five years and that the "pathogenic family influences" included family conflict and separation or divorce.[18] As well, it has been long-noted in North America that separation and divorce are the single most striking characteristics associated with attempted adolescent suicide.[19] Such persisting patterns of emotional distress among children affected by family breakdown have been repeatedly confirmed, and they stand as monumental evidence of the emotional burden imposed on children as a result of the transition from traditional to new family forms.

Additionally, clinical studies are beginning to give more details about specific impacts. One study of 100 adolescents consecutively discharged from a provincial psychiatric hospital found that at the time of admission 84 per cent either lived apart from their parents or with only one parent.[20] Seventy-four per cent were diagnosed as having a conduct disorder associated with an emotional disturbance, usually further complicated by an overlying depression. Another study of 51 families referred to various agencies for assessment in custody and access disputes assessed the adjustments of the children involved.[21] Older children demonstrated more disturbance than younger children, perhaps because older children had faced an average of four years of parental loss, while younger children had faced an average of two years. More optimistically, the study suggested that only one in 10 of the affected children studied manifested maladjustment serious enough to warrant clinical intervention.

Probably the best clinical studies have been done by E.M. Hetherington and her associates.[22] The researchers reported evidence of extreme stress during the first year following breakup. Children of divorce were found to exhibit more negative behaviour, to express more dependency, to be less affectionate and obedient, and generally to whine and nag more. One year after divorce, both boys and girls were still highly dependent, made excessive demands for help, acted out a great deal, and were resistant to parental authority. Boys seemed to manifest more problems than girls. In a six-year follow-up of 60 children of divorce, Hetherington confirmed the negative behaviour scenario, but she found that the problems were more persistent for boys and actually increased in boys after remarriage, but other studies have failed to find such a clear difference between the behaviour reactions of boys and girls.[23]

Furthermore, it has been shown that the responses of children affected by divorce differ by age.[24] Preschool and kindergarten kids, aged two to five, tend to regress at first, expressing fear of being deserted ultimately by both parents. They also express guilt feelings, believing somehow that they were responsible for the divorce. They also complain of nightmares and sleeplessness and are often afraid to sleep alone. They frequently complain of headaches and stomach aches. Early school-age children still suffer from some of these complaints, but they also tend to begin to deny the separation and to claim that they are experiencing no problems. But further clinical probing uncovers a sense of profound and lingering loss. Among older school-age children, those aged five to eight, clinicians report great sadness and explicit grieving. As well, about half of the children in this age group exhibit learning problems. By the pre-adolescent age of nine to 12 children tend to express a more thoughtful response to the divorce, yet they feel it necessary to assign blame to one parent and to view the other as the victim. Children in this age group still report some somatic symptoms — like headaches and stomach upsets — but of a more mild sort. When such children do express negative symptoms they are usually indirect, such as acting out, rebellion, running away, and stealing.

Adolescents, those aged 13 to 18, suffer the most. They express greater worries about sex, future marriage, degrees of intimacy, and the nature and extent of emotional commitment. They reveal a profound sense of anger and loss and are torn by conflicting loyalties. All this leads to a greater risk of serious delays in their normal psychosocial development and maturation. These adolescents also present more problems on parental remarriage, including more open grieving about the lost parent and anger that the divorce is now irrevocable.[25]

These negative effects of divorce tend to persist into young adulthood. Studies have suggested that young adults with divorced parents tend to be explicitly anxious about their marital futures, less likely to want to have and raise children, and more prone to postpone marriage. Young women tend to find parental divorce more stressful than young men, manifesting a longer delay in adjustment to the breakup. Furthermore, young women are more split in their post-divorce relationships with parents, tending to side with their mothers while experiencing an erosion in their relationships with their fathers. About two in three such young men and women express anger directed at one or both parents and worry about their parents' future adjustment and happiness, especially about the mother's ability to cope.

There is, therefore, actually very little disagreement about the negative consequences of divorce for children. In general, most children suffer varying magnitudes of serious sadness, grieving, anxiety, and depression during at least the first year after divorce. About two in three of such children return to a reasonably satisfactory normal adjustment, but a third continues to exhibit significant problems. One five-year follow-up study found that these children were still quite distressed and unhappy. But to reiterate another constant theme throughout the literature:

> Living with parents who have lost feelings for each other is infinitely worse.

One team of psychiatrists put it this way:

> If we accept that there is good evidence of the deleterious effects of divorce, how might we attempt to mitigate these effects? One answer would be to make divorce much more difficult to obtain. This certainly would change the statistics, but it is unlikely that it would improve the lot of the individuals affected. Indeed, at least for the child, the effects might be even more negative than being involved in the divorce; ... children in intact high-tension families are worse off than those whose parents have gone the route of separation and divorce.[26]

In the 1990s our perspective on the impact of divorce and separation on children matured. Clearly, a negative marriage full of conflict is emotionally damaging. Couples unable or unwilling to repair their relationships ought to separate and divorce, not just for themselves, but also for the children. Nevertheless, divorce is traumatic for children and divorcing parents must take tender care of the children affected in order to achieve a healthy readjustment, something that can only be reached with emotional devotion.

Children are, then, among the more serious emotional casualties of the collapse of the traditional family and the transition to new family forms. Men and women usually divorce for a variety of good and sensible reasons. Some women seek divorces because of a spouse's verbal and/or physical abuse or excessive consumption of alcohol. Some women seek divorce because their husbands refuse to support them in breaking out of the confinement of traditional roles. Some working women divorce because their husbands resist taking on a fair share of the domestic work and emotional burdens of home and family. As women become more and more economically independent, the former economic constraints tying them to an unhappy marriage are loosened. It is not surprising that among those most at risk of divorce are married couples where both spouses have independent incomes. Among those at a much lower risk are very high-income couples, dependent primarily on the husband's salary. Some men divorce because they wish to recapture the roaming freedom of their youth. Some because they cannot accept being replaced by a baby as the main focus of their wives' emotional attention. Some because they can't accept their wives' assertion of independence, others because they can't accept their wives' tendency to cling to traditional, dependent roles. Some men and women divorce because they fall out of love, but more usually because they fall into a new, more satisfying love. Usually men and women divorce reluctantly after many efforts to salvage a relationship. The typical divorce happens after about nine years of marriage, a lengthy emotional investment by any standard. Therefore, when a decision to divorce is made it is not impulsive: it is a considered, deliberate, and painful act.

Children cannot fully understand or accept this. For them, the divorce shatters the centres of their lives. Studies cited by Richardson are instructive.[27] Children of divorce are confused, shocked, and disbelieving. Even when there had been spousal violence and quarrelling, such children felt "their family life was basically happy" and that their parents' conflicts did not justify divorce. For them almost anything is preferable. And we should not expect children, even older children, to accept the ebbs and flows of emotional events in adult love relationships. A man or a woman wants love and fulfillment, sexual and otherwise, emotional meaning, and happiness out of a marriage relationship. From their parents children want love, protection, serenity, and security ... above all that the world as they have known it should go on in the future as it has in the past. To trade that for a search for personal happiness seems out of proportion for children. After all, it is a father or a mother being lost, not just a husband, wife, and lover. Husbands, wives, and lovers can, with some pain and difficulty certainly, ultimately be satisfactorily, perhaps even more happily, replaced. "Real" mothers and "real" fathers can never be replaced, and such a loss remains a lingering blot on many children's experience even into adulthood.

These psychological and emotional costs must be entered into the ledger recording historical change. And in the section of the ledger that records the costs of the transition of the family, there are many pages to be filled with those borne by our children. But there are even more to be recorded. The transition to new family forms also threatens the physical security of many of our children. These are often the permanent, forever irretrievable casualties.

6 / The Physical Insecurity of Children

When we read reports that 40,000 of the world's children die of starvation and/or disease each day, we can perhaps be forgiven for being thankful that a wealthy nation like Canada remains immune to tragedies of such magnitudes. The Canadian family still retains the institutional responsibility for the primary care, protection, and socialization of children. And the care we lavish on our children makes them among the world's most fortunate. But there is also a darker side. The Kid's Help toll-free nationwide phone line in Toronto receives over 4,000 calls from distressed children each day, but operators can handle only up to 1,500; the rest get busy signals. The callers range in age from three to 19, and counsellors estimate that 10 per cent of calls come from physically and/or sexually abused children and that 3 per cent are from children contemplating suicide.[1] Experts estimate that one in eight Canadian children suffer emotional or physical abuse.[2] For many children the family promises only terror, cruelty, and suffering, and it is estimated that between 60,000 and 100,000 Canadian children aged 10 to 16 run away from home each year. Studies have shown that such children are fleeing from homes in which 73 per cent suffered physical beatings and 73 per cent of girls and 38 per cent of boys suffered sexual abuse.[3] A growing proportion of Canadian children are thus physically at risk. Like all linkages between social causes and effects, the one between the physical insecurity of children and the problems involved in the transition to new family forms is difficult to prove. Sometimes the evidence is abundant, clear, and irrefutable. Other times, it is indirect, suggestive, and tangential, but convincing because of its preponderance.

We have already considered the relationship between child poverty and the family's transition. Clearly many of the negative consequences of poverty for children are the direct result of poverty *per se*, yet when poverty is itself a consequence of family breakdown or family change, the causal chain is more complex. We know that poverty for many women and children follows from family breakdown. Therefore, when we say that child abuse, for example, is caused by neglectful and emotionally uncontrolled parents, ought we not to ask what circumstances generate such parents? Or when we say that a child commits suicide because he or she feels bereft of hope and support, ought we not to ask how the child came to such a stark conclusion?

In what follows we will be examining the growing physical insecurity of children — health and mortality, suicide rates, child abuse, child and adolescent homicide, and the proportion of our children in formal state agencies of care. Only a small minority of our children face such appalling situations, but it is a much larger minority than people generally believe. If many children are suffering avoidable injury and death, then clearly the family is somehow tragically failing them.

The facts can be clearly stated. More of our children are being injured, many fatally, as a result of avoidable accidents.[4] More are committing suicide. More are suffering physical and/or sexual abuse. More are the victims of homicide. And more are being taken into forms of state care. This growing physical insecurity of our children can only be understood in the context of the transition from traditional to new family forms, and must be seen as part of the costs of this social change.

Child and Adolescent Mortality

In the early 1970s so-called "social injuries" passed illness as the leading cause of child death in Canada.[5] "Social injuries" result from situational circumstances and might have been prevented had there been greater care or more attention paid to the child's environment. Typically in these fatal injuries no individual blame is assigned. Canada had one of the worst records among industrialized nations for child deaths as the result of accidents. Among boys aged one to 14, Canada was third from the bottom, and among girls

of the same age, second from the bottom, in a group of 24 industrialized nations. A survey of 17,000 injured children who annually
went through Toronto's Hospital for Sick Children over a five-year
period found that the injuries resulted from 5,000 falls and 3,000
"bumps and blows," while the others were the result of violence,
burns, poisoning, either self-inflicted or inflicted by others. It is
estimated that about one in 10 pediatric injuries results from deliberate abuse, while another one in 10 results from neglect. A British
Columbia study found that violence was the leading reason for
hospital admission among the province's children. Another study
reported that children under five years of age are more likely to be
run down and killed in parking lots or by parents backing out of a
driveway than they are in street traffic. Those over five are more
likely to be killed by running unexpectedly out into oncoming traffic.[6] More recently, for the first time in history Canada's infant
mortality rate in 1993 increased over that in the previous year,
leading some to conclude that the cuts in Canada's health care and
social security systems were responsible for a deterioration in
many pregnant women's social circumstances and access to health
care. Infant mortality rates are a leading index by which the quality of life is assessed throughout the world. The increase in infant
mortality rates, if they indicate a trend, suggest that we are inflict-
ing the ultimate "social injury" on many of Canada's babies.[7]

Who is responsible for such "social injuries?" Clearly, more adequate care and closer supervision by adults would dramatically
reduce them. Why is such care not available to many of our children? Is single parenthood a factor? Are two working parents a
factor? Are kids being left unattended more often?

The pattern is quite general, and more disturbing because of its
generality. In 1961, the three leading causes of death among boys
aged 15 to 19 years were, in order of frequency: 1) traffic accidents; cancer; 3) diseases of the circulatory system and suicide
(tied). Of these, traffic accidents and suicide can be considered as
"social injuries." In the same year, the three leading causes of
death among girls the same age were: 1) traffic accidents; 2) cancer; 3) diseases of the circulatory system. Of these, only traffic
accidents are "social injuries." Thirty-two years later, in 1993, the

situation was disturbingly different. Among boys *and* girls the three leading causes of death were: 1) traffic accidents; 2) suicide; 3) cancer.[8] Therefore, two of the three leading causes of death among our adolescents are now in the "social injury" category.

How do we explain this? At one level, such statistics are a commentary on our medical successes in defeating disease and illness among children and adolescents. But now we face the daunting fact that most child and adolescent deaths are caused by "social injuries." Why has society not committed the kind of public resources to combat these social causes of child death that have for generations been committed to combatting illness and disease? How can traffic deaths be related to the crisis of the family? If children had better supervision, many such accidents would not occur. For adolescents what one might view as the sad price of greater independence — the unsupervised use of automobiles — is somewhat tempered by the contention by some child psychiatrists that many adolescent traffic fatalities are really cases of disguised suicide. At least part of the explanation of these changing patterns of mortality must be sought in the changing nature of the family.

A much less dramatic spotlight on the relationship between children's health risks and changing family forms was provided by a U.S. study of children in the eighth grade in Los Angeles and San Diego, which found that "latchkey" children, regardless of their parents' wealth or marital status, were more likely to smoke, to drink alcohol, and to experiment with marijuana.[9] Clearly the risk of greater rates of more serious misadventurous behaviour is also higher among such children in what is euphemistically called "self-care."

Parents find it harder and harder to provide appropriate levels of care for their children, and the question, "Who's minding the children?" takes on greater and greater urgency.

Child and Adolescent Suicide

Suicide is the ultimate act of despair and hopelessness. Rates of child and adolescent suicide have escalated since 1961, going up by a factor of four times between 1960 and 1994 among 15- to 19-year-old boys (from 5.3/100,000 to 20.4/100,000 population).[10] The overall suicide rate in 1994 (12.8) was nearly double the rate from the 1920s to the early 1960s (7.5) and has even far outstripped the rate during the dark decade of the Great Depression (10). But the most dramatic age-specific rate increase has occurred among adolescents. And it is estimated that there are from 30 to 40 suicide attempts for every one that is successful. In response to this suicide epidemic, the University of Toronto devoted $2 million in 1996 to establish the first university chair in suicide studies.[11]

Child suicide, suicides among those under 15, is still rare but increasing.[12] In 1966, there were 19 suicides among children and 68 suicides among adolescents representing, respectively, 1 per cent and 4 per cent of all officially recorded suicides. In 1986 there were 25 child suicides and 241 adolescent suicides representing, respectively, 1 per cent and 7 per cent of all suicides. In 1994 there were 49 child suicides and 252 adolescent suicides, representing over 1 per cent and 7 per cent of all suicides. It is not unusual to find at least one case each year of a child between five and nine years of age taking his or her own life.[13] For example, in Saskatchewan the 35 youth suicides in 1996 included one child of nine.

The fact that child suicides remained constant for 20 years and then increased sharply between 1986 and 1994 suggests that the number of deeply troubled children is growing. Further, the rate of suicides each year among children has been upwards, because the total number of children in the age groups in question has declined steeply. Furthermore, all experts agree that official suicide rates are far below the actual, since many apparently accidental deaths, or deaths by misadventure, are in reality hidden suicide. Suicides are often covered up by families, aided by sympathetic physicians and officials, particularly in the case of child suicide, which devastates a family beyond imagining. Although the favoured suicide technique among children is hanging, many ingest lethal overdoses of drugs. In the absence of clear evidence to the contrary, either event can be easily construed as accidental death.

In the case of adolescent suicide the evidence requires very little supplementary explanation. Despite probable underreporting, despite the declining number of adolescents as a whole, despite the rising overall suicide rate, adolescent suicide has skyrocketed in absolute numbers, as a proportion of all suicides, and as rates per 100,000 population.

Again, it is possible that in the 1960s there was a greater tendency to cover up adolescent suicides. However, the increase has been so great that a decline in the willingness to cover up suicides is simply an insufficient explanation of the steep rise. While data will never finally become available, adolescent suicides are much less easy to cover up because of the typical means used and of the ages of the victims. Adolescents are more likely to use guns or motor vehicle exhaust fumes, which are more difficult to interpret as accidents. Hanging and drugs are also more difficult to interpret as misadventures in this age group. Furthermore, adolescents frequently engage in elaborate pre-suicide behavioural rituals and often leave notes declaring their intentions.

The facts, then, are harrowing. More and more of our children and adolescents prefer suicide to continued existence. Why? In *Growing Up Dead: A Hard Look at Why Adolescents Commit Suicide*, Brenda Rabkin surveyed a variety of troubled backgrounds and individual coping responses. Her final judgement says it well:

> Young people commit suicide because of unbearable pain and a conviction that life is without hope, that new tomorrows are just miserable repeats of old yesterdays; so to continue living is pointless ... Each act of suicide is as idiosyncratic as the individual committing it. To view suicide solely in terms of theories and statistics is to ignore the human agony that prompts the act.[14]

Although it is difficult to disagree, if there are larger social patterns in child and adolescent suicide, they ought to be sought. Some studies have discerned significant patterns in child and adolescent suicide, particularly the psychosocial risk factors.[15] Among them are a number that are not particularly surprising — higher risk groups include those who had previously sought psychiatric or psychological help; those who had experienced the suicide of a member of the family or a friend; those with parents requiring psychiatric help; those who had attempted or threatened suicide in the past; those who had experienced a recent breakup with a boyfriend or girlfriend; those who abused alcohol or drugs; those who had lost a parent or parents through separation, divorce, or death; and those who had been physically and/or sexually abused by a parent or parents. Other risk factors include problems with the police, academic difficulties in school, and unemployment. Many of these factors are intertwined and many child and adolescent suicides are characterized by multiple risk factors. As Thompson says, after studying all completed child and adolescent suicides in Manitoba in one decade (190 cases):

> The most common risk factors for the population as a whole were alcohol abuse, a recent breakup with a boyfriend or girlfriend and a recent marital or family dispute ... Alcohol abuse is related to a recent breakup in a relationship and to a recent death among family or friends. Previous attempts were associated with psychiatric contact and suicidal ideation. Unemployment was associated with a history of drug abuse and school problems. A suicide note was found statistically more often when there was a history of parental separation and divorce.

And there are a series of significant overall relationships among the identified risk factors:

> Alcohol is the leading risk factor overall, agreeing with previous studies ... The association of this drinking with a recent breakup or death of a loved one suggests that these teenagers turn to alcohol in times of emotional stress ... The association between previous attempts, psychiatric contact and suicidal ideation probably stems from attempts leading to psychiatric contact. When a suicide is completed the psychiatrist is contacted and ideation reported. Many previous studies agree with our finding that this cluster occurs more often in females. That it occurs in both gen-

ders in the 18–20 year range likely indicates increasing duration of pathology with increasing age.

Finding a suicide note after a parental separation or divorce is more common in the 15–17 year range, as are school problems. One wonders if the notes left behind, which often apologized for what they were about to do, are not apologizing for a sense of responsibility for the breakup of the parents' marriage.[16]

The extent to which the intertwining of these risk factors dovetails with the emotional consequences of divorce or separation for affected children is remarkable. Indeed, the pattern of the relationship between family breakdown, the negative emotional consequences for affected children, and the emergence of risk factors for suicide among children and adolescents has been confirmed and reconfirmed. A related risk factor is ongoing family conflict, which may or may not lead to ultimate divorce, and it is again hard to separate the emotional consequences of an unhappy family experience over some years and the final breakup.

Indeed, family dysfunction or family breakdown remains among the most common risk factors in the background of children and adolescents who commit suicide. Psychological consequences of family problems and family breakdown, like low self-esteem, depression, anger, social isolation, school problems, acting-out behaviour, and excessive moodiness and absent-mindedness, parallel quite closely the psychological profiles of suicidal children and adolescents. Epidemiologically, suicide rates among children and adolescents affected by family breakdown range all the way from two times the rate among children with only one parent present in the home to four times the rate in homes where both parents are absent.

Epidemiological patterns do not *prove* a direct causal link; rather they are merely strongly suggestive that a causal connection between two associated phenomena is more probable. Reproduced below are two graphs, one charting the divorce rate in Canada between 1951 and 1996, the other charting the rate of suicide among adolescent males (the pattern for females is similar, but the rate is much lower).

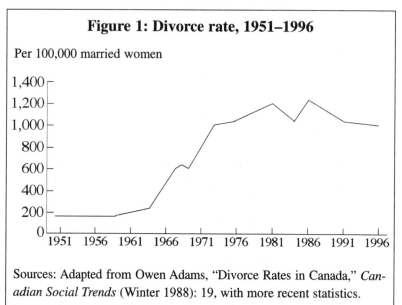

Figure 1: Divorce rate, 1951–1996

Per 100,000 married women

Sources: Adapted from Owen Adams, "Divorce Rates in Canada," *Canadian Social Trends* (Winter 1988): 19, with more recent statistics.

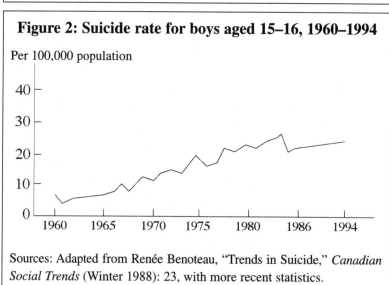

Figure 2: Suicide rate for boys aged 15–16, 1960–1994

Per 100,000 population

Sources: Adapted from Renée Benoteau, "Trends in Suicide," *Canadian Social Trends* (Winter 1988): 23, with more recent statistics.

What does this suggest? We can fairly safely say that the crisis of the family, as manifested in divorce and separation, is strongly associated with the rise in rates of suicide among adolescents.

Let us be crystal clear about what is and what is not being said. Divorce does not *cause* suicide in children. Indeed, many children from particularly unhappy families might have been more likely to attempt or commit suicide had the divorce not intervened. For many children, divorce leads to a happier future. Nor is every child in an intact family immune from suicide. What is being said emphatically is that separation and divorce, and the whole complex of subsequent emotional consequences of the family's breakup, place the affected children and adolescents *more at risk* of suicide.

Child Abuse

The case that first galvanized public opinion and spotlighted the problem of child abuse in Canada was that of 19-month-old Kim Ann Popen, who was brutally beaten to death in 1976. The immediate cause of death was fatal injuries to the head, but the autopsy revealed a litany of sexual and physical torture: bruised and cut genitals; a torn hymen; broken ribs; and an anus three times the normal size. Baby Kim had been subjected to repeated beatings and was under the care and protection of the Sarnia Lambton Children's Aid Society when the fatal decision was made to return her to her home. As a result, County Court Judge H. Ward Allen conducted an inquiry into the death and concluded that the following persons and agencies had failed to protect Baby Kim: the Social Services Ministry; the police; the Crown Attorney; the Lambton Health Unit; individual social workers; and all those family members and friends who knew of her plight. But the judge most strongly condemned the Children's Aid Society, insisting that the child would not have perished had the agency lived up to its responsibility to protect her.

Twenty years later the situation appears to have worsened. Scandals regularly rock the child protection system from coast to coast. In May 1994, John Ryan Turner's battered, bruised, and starved body was found in his bedroom in his parents' home on the Chatam Canadian Forces base in New Brunswick. He was three months shy of his fourth birthday. He had spent the last weeks of his life bound to a bed and gagged by a sock. Not only had he been systematically beaten, but the cause of death was starvation. His parents, Steve and Lorelei Turner, were charged with manslaughter, convicted and sentenced to 16 years in prison. Though alerted a year before the death by an anonymous tip, New Brunswick social services officials were exonerated despite having failed to act.

In September 1996, the parents of six-month-old Sara Podniewicz of Toronto, who died of pneumonia after severe neglect and savage physical abuse, were sentenced to life imprisonment for second-degree murder. Though alerted to the fact that the father, Michael Podniewicz, had pled guilty to aggravated assault against his 10-month-old son in 1989 (the infant suffered permanent brain injury caused by violent shaking), and had served five years in prison, the Toronto Children's Aid Society failed to monitor the family, relying on information supplied by the parents. In 1996, the Ontario Coroner's Office began a six-month investigation into why Ontario's child protection system had failed to prevent the killing of 128 children over a five-year period.

In Manitoba, the 1996 death of nine-month-old Sophia Schmidt led to the conviction of her stepmother for manslaughter and father for criminal negligence causing death. Sophia's death had been particularly agonizing — an autopsy found the infant covered with bruises, three broken ribs, a broken arm and leg, a human bite mark on her leg, cuts to her nose and toes, and a tear between her lower lip and gum. The judge denounced the social services agencies for a failure to act despite reasonable evidence of abuse and for "slavishly following the principles" of the Tory government's laws and regulations to give primacy to keeping families together. The agency had placed Sophia with the family in the first place. The case led to a public outcry for a thorough inquiry into Manitoba's system of child protection.

The 1992 death of five-year-old Matthew Vaudreuil in Vancouver resulted in the manslaughter conviction of his mother and a major judicial inquiry into an attempted cover-up by social services officials. The judge, in his 1995 report, concluded, "I regret to report that even as the ministry failed Matthew in life, it failed him in death." The judge concluded that there was just no excuse for the failure of the child protection service to act in Matthew's case which included: over 75 visits to 24 different doctors; the involvement of 25 different social workers and supervisors over the course of his short life; a mother already long identified by the agencies as a serious problem (she was young, mentally disabled, had herself been rotated through a series of foster homes and was a childhood victim of physical and sexual abuse). At the autopsy after his death, caused when his mother held her hand over his mouth and nose to punish him, Matthew's body told a terrifying story. He weighed under 37 pounds, and his body showed signs of prolonged torture and abuse: there was a footprint on his back; his body was covered in bruises; his teeth had punctured his inner lips; he had broken ribs and wrists, and had rope burns. Provincial Court judge Thomas Gove noted that the NDP government's policy of giving priority to keeping the family unit intact had led inevitably to a neglect of the child's welfare and security. He also noted that 19 children in the ministry's care had died from 1992 to 1995. A year later, in 1996, the B.C. minister responsible confirmed that 49 children involved with the ministry from November 1995 to July 1996 had died. The minister launched an external review, and in September 1996 the B.C. government established a Children's Commissioner with sweeping powers and a new Ministry for Children and Families with a $1 billion budget.[17]

Hardly a week goes by without another gruesome tale of starvation, crushed skulls, biting and beating infants to death, ruptured stomachs, broken bones at different stages of healing, or blindings, or burnings. And often it is reported that the authorities knew of the abuse. No purpose will be served here by an endless repetition of such horror stories — the social scientific and medical literature are full of them. Much more important are the questions: just how extensive is child abuse in Canada and what appear to be the factors that precipitate such abuse? Just what leads a parent or another adult to physically or sexually abuse his or her charge? Since the early to mid-1970s, when national attention focussed on the problem, there have been many studies and inquiries documenting this distressing phenomenon. The most recent and thorough was conducted by Health Canada's Laboratory Centre for Disease Control in 1991 and 1992, and published in 1994 by Statistics Canada. It provided an endless chronicle of the intentional injuries suffered by children at three urban pediatric hospitals in different provinces.[18]

Estimates vary on how extensive child abuse is. Partly, that is a matter of definition. When we speak of abuse, are we talking about physical and sexual abuse, psychological and emotional abuse, or abuse resulting from deliberate neglect and depriva-tion? A Decima poll found that one in three Canadian parents admit to slapping or spanking, and parents of young children under six are twice as likely to use physical punishment as par-ents of older children.[19] Is this abuse? The law says no, since the Criminal Code permits adults in charge of children to use "rea-sonable force ... by way of correction" of children. But experts worry about where the line is drawn. The 1980 Senate Report, Child at Risk, estimated that there are between 5,000 and 9,000 Canadian children suffering potentially damaging or fatal abuse. The Badgley Report estimated that one in three males and one in two females in Canada have been victims of unwanted sexual acts — with about 80 per cent of these acts occurring during childhood or adolescence. Statistics from the Metro Toronto Police for 1994–96, released in 1997, suggest that either the figures from the 1970s and 1980s were serious underestimates, or, as many suggest, child abuse has increased dramatically in recent years. Over the three-year period in Toronto alone there were 10,000 cases of abuse of children 15 years old or younger *reported* to Toronto police. More than half of them were cases of physical and sexual abuse. These figures include 10 child murders, 6 attempted murders, and about 600 cases involving the use of a weapon to inflict bodily harm.

Perhaps a firmer estimate is provided by a 1991 Gallup poll which found that one in six Canadians (17 per cent) say that they have "*personal* awareness of a *serious* instance of physical abuse of children by a parent," a much higher estimate than even the most impassioned anti-abuse activist has ever dared suggest.[20] Even more worrisome is that about 37 per cent took no action whatsoever to intervene. Further, when compared to a Gallup poll on the same question taken in 1982, the 1991 results suggest a significantly increased awareness of serious child abuse. In

1982, Gallup found that only 11 per cent of their sample admitted personal awareness of a serious case of child abuse.

The doctrine in the literature is that there is no reason to believe that child abuse is any more prevalent now than it ever was. Indeed, it is often argued, the apparent increase is merely an artifact of increased reporting of actions that in former times were hidden and even tolerated. But two arguments qualify an uncritical acceptance of this view. First, it is remarkable that child abuse has persisted and apparently increased at a time when it is almost universally condemned and when serious interventions, including legal sanctions, are for the first time being more or less systematically applied. This persistence is much more remarkable than the fact that hidden and more or less tolerated abuse of children went on systematically in the past. Even more significant, however, is the emerging evidence of the stressors that seem to be associated with child abuse. Clearly if they can be related to the current crisis of the family, then we can argue not only that child abuse might be increasing, but also that its causes are shifting and becoming more and more rooted in the problems associated with the transition to new family forms.

Throughout the literature on child abuse, especially feminist literature, there is a centrally recurring theme that child abuse, as well as other forms of family violence, must be viewed in the context of male domination and the patriarchal family. Males are socialized to be more prepared to use violence to defend and assert their power, authority, and position. Males are socialized to have a limited emotional repertory, and they are therefore more quick to see violence as an effective means of resolving conflicts. Therefore, when children intrude on men's spaces, resist their authority, or behave vexatiously, males are more likely to use physical punishment. Furthermore, we live in a society that celebrates violence and the macho male in sports, in politics, in war. As well, in our political culture those with power and authority routinely defend themselves from challenges through legitimate violence.

A Montreal case is a horrifying example of the implication of traditional patriarchal attitudes in instances of child abuse. The story was movingly told by Janet Bagnall in the 21 October 1989 edition of the Montreal *Gazette*.

It was December 28, 1987, three days after Christmas. In a small, fourth-storey apartment in north Montreal, an 8-year-old boy broke a household object. His social worker won't say what he broke, but she said it was neither valuable nor important.

In the child's mind, though, that wasn't the point. The point was that he would get another beating from his father. But this time, he panicked. He just couldn't face his father's belt across his back one more time.

He opened the door which led to the apartment's balcony, climbed up on the railing and jumped, intending to die.

Fortunately, the child lived, suffering only a badly sprained ankle thanks to a heavy groundcover of snow. In the aftermath, the child was taken into protection and placed in a foster home where he was reported to have done well. The boy was repeatedly beaten, and burned with lit cigarettes, by his father. Social workers approached the father to see if he would co-operate in dealing with the problem and cease his abuse. As the boy's social worker said, "Over the next few months I tried and tried and tried with the father, but it was no good. As far as he is concerned the child is his property and he can do what he wants with him. It is not safe for the child to return home."

Patriarchy is therefore a crucial factor in child abuse. Indeed, the overwhelming majority of child abusers are male, upwards of 85 to 95 per cent. But if we accept this general argument, then we ought to be able to argue further that today such a causal pattern might lead to more child abuse, or at least to changing patterns of such abuse. Today the dominant male patriarch is threatened on all sides — women are more assertive, attitudes more disapproving of the traditional male role are more widely shared, even children are more assertive. A traditional husband and father, who 30 years ago was able to rule the home with benign authoritarianism backed up always by the ultimate threat of force, might now lash out emotionally and physically more often to defend his position.

What does the literature tell us about the stressors commonly associated with child abuse? Is the threatened patriarchal male the major perpetrator? Or is it a more pathetic figure? Does the crisis of the family provoke child abuse in other ways? The literature fails to confirm clearly that child abuse can be largely explained as the result of the desperate efforts by threatened patriarchs to salvage their prerogatives and privileges. The child abusing male is a much less looming and tragic historical figure. Child abuse is much more complex.

Poverty, unemployment, and economic stress have been frequently associated with child abuse. Despite its repeated confirmation, some experts simply reject its meaningfulness and argue that child abuse cuts across all classes and income groups. An Ontario nurse, who deals with child abuse in her work, testified before an all-party committee of the province's legislature examining child abuse that the poor are more prone to physical child abuse because they suffer more stress and have fewer supports and resources to cope with problems and crises. Wealthier parents who abuse their children are more likely to engage in forms of emotional abuse and neglect, she alleged.[21] Both a Tory and an NDP member of the committee attacked this notion. The Tory argued, "Child abuse crosses all economic stratas [sic]. You just can't say that upper classes are more negligent and lower classes use physical abuse." The New Democrat argued that lower class abuse tends to get reported, while upper class abuse tends to be underreported, saying, "I think we have some stereotypic views of the working-class family where the father rules the family with an iron fist and that everything is calm and smooth in the upper-class family."

The resistance to admitting poverty as a major stressor in precipitating child abuse seems to come from two sources. Some feminist writers dislike any argument that deflects central attention away from the patriarchal family, and male supremacy in the family hierarchy, as the major background factor in child abuse. Poverty, unemployment, and economic stress as factors do just that. Others feel that an association between lower economic status and child abuse unfairly attacks working class and poor men and women, heaping emotional insult on economic injury. It is easy to understand the concerns. We ought not to lose sight of the power relationships in the traditional patriarchal family as a context conducive to child abuse, nor should we overlook the fact that wealthier people tend to be more immune from intervention by authorities and less likely therefore to be reported as abusers, particularly in cases where the evidence is marginal. But, and it is an important "but," again and again the association between poverty, unemployment, economic stress, and economic failure on the one hand, and child abuse on the other, has been found.

Marital conflict is also strongly associated with the incidence of child abuse. For example, it tends to be more frequent in families with young parents, families headed by single-parent mothers, families affected by strife and conflict, and families on the threshold of parental separation and/or divorce. Furthermore, husbands who abuse their wives also tend to abuse their children. And abused women often, in turn, abuse their own children.[22] Children in families that are socially isolated from family and friends are also more at risk of suffering abuse. Studies in Britain have found that battering mothers tend to be young, poorly educated and victims of abuse themselves, while battering fathers tend to be poorly educated and former victims of child abuse. The typical abusing couple, for child abuse is often a form of *folie à deux*, particularly in the collusion to cover up the crime, tended to have married young in defiance of their parents, to have few or no friends, to live a great distance from their families in increasing economic misery, and to have children who were frequently unplanned and premature.

Just these two — poverty and marital discord and breakdown — are repeatedly associated with child abuse, and they are closely related to the problems provoked by the family's transition. Typically there is a cluster of multiple stressors afflicting families at greater risk of child abuse: family instability and breakdown; poverty and/or unemployment; and other forms of social and economic stress. As well, there is a series of characteristics of the child which tend to put him or her at greater risk of abuse. Premature infants, for example, are more at risk of abuse. Experts speculate that because such infants spend weeks and sometimes months in hospital, emotional bonding fails to occur with the parents. Furthermore, they frequently continue to present the family with medical difficulties. Other children who are handicapped, or who present the family with ongoing medical and behavioural problems, are also more at risk of abuse. The "problem" or "difficult" child, medically or emotionally, is in general more at risk, because of the added stresses on the parents.

Such stressors do not, of course, alone explain child abuse. There are some crucial parental psychological characteristics that alone, or in combination with serious stress, set the stage for child abuse. The most commonly associated factor in child abuse is that child abusers suffered abuse themselves when they were children. They themselves grew up in situations of emotional deprivation, physical abuse, parental rejection, and family conflict. Child abusers tend to be young and unprepared for parenthood, and with unrealistic expectations about appropriate behaviour in children. Typically, female abusers have exaggerated dependency needs, while male abusers often possess sociopathic and/or psychopathic personality characteristics and have criminal backgrounds. Further, child abusers often have a high level of dependence on alcohol or other drugs. Abusers are frequently described as inadequate personalities with low self-esteem and high levels of psychological insecurity.

Child Homicide

The end result of child abuse is sometimes murder. Researchers at Johns Hopkins University reported in the late 1980s that murder had become the leading cause of death by injury among U.S. infants under one year of age.[23] One in three of these infants died of child abuse or as a battered child. Others died of suffocation, strangulation, deliberate drowning, stabbing, and gunshot wounds. Another large category died of "neglect-abandonment" — defined as deliberate neglect "with intent to injure or kill." In Canada, from 1985 to 1994 there was an annual average of 20 infants under one year of age murdered. In 1993 and 1994, the age of greatest risk of homicide was less than one year. Thankfully, this pattern did not hold in 1995, as infant homicides fell to eight.

Child murder is still quite rare, though it is more commonplace than in the 1960s. In 1966 there were 48 murders of children up to the age of 14, and 13 murders of adolescents aged 15 to 19. In 1986 the figures were 58 and 35, respectively; and in 1994, 45 and 51. Murders of babies up to the age of four remained fairly static — 34 in 1966, 32 in 1986, and 26 in 1994 — but we must recall the sharp decline in the total population of infants between 1966 and 1994. The most disturbing increase is that of adolescent homicide, which has grown incredibly in absolute numbers despite the decline in the total adolescent population. Again, we have no idea how accurate these official figures are, but if they err, they err on the side of underreporting.

The murder of a newborn is typically done by the parents, most often the mother. One psychiatric study reports that such mothers are usually young, single, and immature. Yet they are not clinically mentally disturbed; rather they tend to be passive and unable to cope.[24] Such acts are clearly acts of desperation on the part of a young, frightened, unwilling mother. A recent Canadian case history confirms the pattern, reporting the attempted murder of her newly born infant by a 16-year-old high school student. She had hidden the pregnancy from her mother and had the baby alone in the bathtub.[25]

Statistics Canada surveys of solved homicides show no dramatic upward trend in domestic homicides.[26] But the figures remain deeply disturbing nevertheless. Of those surveyed for 1986, 11 per cent were cases of fathers and 9 per cent were cases of mothers killing their children. In the single year of 1986, 55 of 191 domestic homicide cases were children killed by their parents.[27] For the years 1994 and 1995, of 363 domestic homicides (representing 38 per cent of all solved homicides), 88 cases involved children killed by their parents (59 by the father and 29 by the mother).[28] Parents who murder their children tend to be young. About half of mothers who killed their children were under 25 years of age, and one in five were teenage mothers. Similarly, about half of fathers who murdered their children were under the age of 30.

Clearly, for the domestic victims of child homicide the family was neither sanctuary, nor haven, nor a place of love and happiness. And for those many victims of child homicide whose deaths were the final episode of repeated abuse and neglect, the thought of the months, weeks, and days preceding death is too devastating for words to express.

State Care

The family systematically fails about one in every 100 Canadian children who, for a time, live in forms of state care.[29] Of these children, 60 per cent live in foster homes, 20 per cent in group homes, and another 20 per cent in juvenile institutions and treatment centres. About two in three come from officially poor families. Similarly, about two in three are taken into care as a result of "parental neglect or incapacity."[30] Up-to-date national figures are hard to come by, since the area is one of provincial jurisdiction, and provinces use different criteria and categories for "care." But experts in the area suggest that one in 100 remains an adequate estimate,[31] and there is some indication that the figures may be rising.

But such figures do not begin to reveal the total number of children placed in forms of emergency or exceptional care. Many families in distress rely upon networks of relatives and friends to take over the care of threatened children, turning to official agencies only when authorities intervene. Furthermore, many child-care workers are constrained by government policy to take children into care only in the most extreme of circumstances, and workers are encouraged to reunite children in care with their natural families, often without much regard for the risk to the child. Additionally, many child care workers are reluctant to take children who are at risk into care simply because the official state care system is so bad.

The appalling situations in many of our state-sponsored or supported foster homes, group homes, and institutions have regularly made headlines. The allegations have included numerous serious assaults and other forms of abuse and maltreatment,[32] including the use of behaviour modification and aversive therapy techniques on children incarcerated.[33] Treatment meted out in some foster homes is often not much better. The recent exposure of the case of Dereck O'Brien's treatment in a foster home in Mount Pearl, Newfoundland, in the 1960s shocked most. O'Brien alleges that his state-approved foster parents forced him and his brothers "to scrounge through garbage for food, to drink water off a basement floor, to use a dump as a bathroom."[34] I can recall a television documentary exposing the child-rearing practices of foster parents who adhered to fundamentalist Christian doctrine that instructed them that systematic beatings of children were necessary for a good Christian upbringing. In 1986, David Tickell, then the Saskatchewan Ombudsman, released a report indicting the province's child protection system for permitting, frequently knowingly, the widespread physical and sexual abuse of children under the care of the system, sometimes in foster homes, sometimes by failing to act quickly enough in a known case of abuse or neglect, other times by returning the child to the original home prematurely.[35] Similar criticisms were made in the 1990s following investigations in B.C., Manitoba, Ontario, and New Brunswick, suggesting that the traditional conservative family lobby has successfully intimidated governments and public servants enough to prevent them from carrying out self-evidently necessary and timely interventions in dysfunctional families to rescue children at risk.[36]

The nation was reminded again in 1989 of the serious deficiencies in the state-sponsored child protection and care system. Revelations of repeated physical and sexual abuse of children at the Mount Cashel Orphanage in St. John's, Newfoundland, and allegations of physical abuse at the Bosco Homes in Saskatchewan shocked many. The Mount Cashel and Bosco Homes revelations were followed throughout the 1990s by a flood of scandals, investigations, and court cases from coast to coast as decades of ugly truths about physical and sexual abuse and emotional maltreatment of children in the state-sponsored care system — orphanages, reformatories, and residential schools for aboriginal children — were exposed to public view.[37]

Quebec's Commission de Protection des Droits de la Jeunesse

reported that even those young people (aged 12 to 17) who expressed positive feelings about the benefits of stays at provincial rehabilitation centres face a "bleak, barren future." Camille Messier described the kinds of children in such centres:

> More than a third had broken with their parents, close to a third were the victims of an abusive home life; 19 per cent were 16 and 17-year-old boys who were facing criminal charges under the Young Offenders Act and whose parents consequently had washed their hands of them; and a last group — about 15 per cent of the total — were the children whom the youth-protection system had failed.[38]

These children, who reach legal adulthood at 18 and therefore must leave the state's care system, unrealistically dreamed about returning to their family homes or of setting up house on their own. Instead, they typically face isolation, unemployment, and poverty, with no network of support. These children are the most prominent victims of our failing family system — the "official" and reluctantly recognized victims. Yet too often the system designed to rescue and protect them fails, and all too frequently places them at risk.

Although there is clearly significant overlap among the categories, evidence shows that over 1.3 million Canadian children flounder in poverty; upwards of one million suffer from forms of physical and sexual abuse, and for thousands such abuse is life-threatening; another 1.5 million experience some form of emotional or psychiatric disorder; many thousands are injured or killed each year by forms of "social injury"; hundreds commit suicide, while more dozens are murdered each year; and finally tens of thousands languish in forms of state care. This situation reflects not only a tragic failure on the part of our whole society, but, more specifically, a growing incapacity of our changing family forms to fulfill the family's primary institutional obligation to provide care, comfort, love, security, and protection. Children are among the front-line victims bearing the costs and consequences of the family's social transition. They are the first casualties. Their innocence and helpless vulnerability make their plight particularly horrifying, but their parents are also victims bearing the costs of these changes in the family's massive transformation. We must recognize that parents too must cope with and adapt to social forces beyond their personal control. It may be true that Canadian men and women are not completely innocent of the plight of many of their children. Yet neither are they completely guilty.

PART III

Victims of the Crisis: Women

"Equal with men? Yes, the law says we must be. And we also have to be equal with horses to get the strength."

Tatyana Geoshvili,
working Russian wife and mother.

Introduction:
The Oppression of Women

The oppression of women in Canada remains a fact of daily life, apparently remarkably resistant to all our efforts to the contrary. Oppression — defined eloquently and simply by the *Shorter Oxford English Dictionary* as "the imposition of unjust burdens" — afflicts women in virtually every social, emotional, political, and economic aspect of their lives. Whether they are CN crew dispatchers subjected to "sexual touching, bum patting and ... sexual molestation;" or rape victims whose complaints are dismissed as "unfounded;"[1] or a vocational school student stripped of her office as student president when she became pregnant out of wedlock;[2] or the Lyndhurst Hospital social worker fired after she complained about unwanted sexual touching by her supervisor; or the female athletes forced into sexual intercourse by coaches;[3] they are constantly reminded that they are sexual objects. Patriarchy may not be entirely well after the last 40 years of assault by the new feminism, but it remains unmistakably alive and frequently even robust.

On paper and in theory, laws, regulations, and official promulgations make gains for women look and sound impressive. But the practical reality is something else. Laws are only good if they are systematically enforced. Declarations and promulgations are not worth the paper they are written on if no serious action is taken to realize even the most eloquently stated goals. The two young women at CN, for example, were obliged to go through a degrading arbitration process before being vindicated. And the Lyndhurst Hospital social worker was fired in 1993 but the hearing of her case was delayed by employer tactics until January 1997. In 1974 the RCMP began hiring women officers, about 800 by 1986, but these women officers exhibited five times the resignation rate as a result of "sexual harassment and rampant sexism." Ten years later, though their numbers had doubled to 1,600 officers, and their resignation rate had been reduced to "only" twice that of male officers, the sexism had continued: an internal RCMP study found 6 in 10 female officers had experienced sexual harassment, including 1 in 10 involving unwanted sexual touching.[4] Canadian women won another victory in 1980, when 52 women were finally admitted to Canada's military colleges, but five years later a confidential Department of National Defence report obtained by *The Globe and Mail* justified the exclusion of women from combat and near-combat jobs on the grounds that women lacked the necessary endurance and strength, and that the presence of women would lead to sexual and romantic hanky-panky. Nevertheless, a human rights tribunal in 1990 directed Canada's military to achieve the full integration of women in all roles, including combat, by 1999. Despite this directive, women in the military, particularly those aspiring to combat roles, have been subjected to ongoing verbal and physical sexual harassment, as well as brutal hazing in some cases. Canada's first female infantry officer, Sandra Perron, was subjected to an excessively rough training exercise at combat school, which included being tied to a tree barefoot in the snow and being slapped during a mock interrogation. Ms. Perron left the military when she recognized that her superiors had deliberately stalled her career by giving her trivial assignments. Another female combat officer resigned "in disgust" as a result of the harassing, degrading, and insulting sexist treatment received at officer training school.[5]

There has been a grand deception going on and the gap between our rhetoric and our actions regarding the situation of women in Canada has never been greater. And women have been required to fight for modest real gains through a sort of trench warfare, almost on a case-by-case basis, fighting to gain ground inch by reluctant inch. Victories are frequently won at great cost, financial and emotional. And they are often Pyrrhic victories — victories that too often have all the taste of defeat. What women can win in public is often stolen in private as they are subjected to sexual harassment, perhaps less overt career discrimination, and personal hostility. In a sense then, women, as they escape old oppressions, confront new ones.

This is particularly true when the impact of the crisis of the family on women is examined. While the traditional family relied on the largely silent oppression of women in the home, the new family forms frequently impose even greater unjust burdens. Women are still assumed to be primarily responsible for child care and for keeping the family unit running smoothly, even as they take on equal burdens in the work world. Women therefore carry the major burden of the current family crisis — whether it's earning that all-important second income while continuing to meet most of the old domestic expectations, or picking up the pieces and putting them back together with the children after separation or divorce, or managing the many tensions of a reconstituted family, or putting up tolerantly with male angst in response to rapidly changing sex roles.

One of the best-documented aspects of women's new oppression is the price exacted from working women if they wish to establish a family and have children.[6] Inevitably, they put less time and energy into education, career training, and advancement. Even those who make it into high-paying professional or business jobs find it necessary to severely scale down career aspirations if they wish to marry and to have children. Therefore, while women have fought to gain equality in the world of work with men, they have found many of the fruits of such gains snatched from their grasp because of their continuing child-bearing and -rearing tasks.

This is not a new insight. In 1976, Dorothy Dinnerstein argued forcefully that the new feminism can never achieve full equality for women as long as women continue to be primarily responsible for child care.[7] A decade later, Sylvia Hewlett went further, arguing that the U.S. feminist movement had made a strategic error by fighting for strict equality with men while ignoring the costs to women of bearing and raising children.[8] By pursuing an abiological notion of equality with men, such as is embodied in the Equal Rights Amendment, the U.S. women's movement failed to fight for and secure a system of family supports. Meanwhile, the European feminist movement struggled for equal rights in tandem with demands for programs to help working women deal with family

obligations. Consequently, women in Europe have not only succeeded in more significantly narrowing the pay gap with men, but
also in winning generous full-pay maternity leave benefits and high
levels of state aid to daycare.

In Canada the situation is similar. Precious little action has been
taken on issues like maternity leave, daycare, and other kinds of family support programs. As a result, the women's movement in North
America is moving increasingly from ideological issues to very
practical ones. Increasingly, men are asked more practical questions
— do you support state aid to daycare? do you support effective
affirmative action programs for women? do you support equal pay
for work of equal value? do you support programs of full-pay maternity leave? do you support women's right to choice on reproductive
matters? Increasingly, the focus of the women's movement has
moved to the concrete issues of pay equity, child-care support,
reproductive choice, and the fair sharing of domestic work.

That such a practical focus has become pre-eminent is understandable. A 1985 world survey of the situation of women
concluded that the changes in the status of women in the world
since World War II have been "modest."[9] The survey concluded
that there is no place on earth where women enjoy wage parity with
men. Furthermore, as a result of un- and underemployment, low
pay, job ghettoes, and residual responsibility for the children after
family breakdown, women are facing an accelerating process of the
feminization of poverty.[10] A group of Commonwealth experts
reported in 1989 that "the recession of the early 1980s and subsequent budget cuts by governments around the world have been
particularly damaging to women and issues that concern them."
The report goes so far as to assert that recent government policies
"have halted and even reversed the progress ... which women
enjoyed in the preceding three decades." The U.N.'s Fourth World
Conference on Women, held in 1995 in Beijing, China, repeatedly
documented the deteriorating status of women throughout the
world, including the advanced, industrial societies. This is a result
of the dismantling of social programs and reductions in social
spending brought about by a decade of neoconservatism and tri-
umphant free-market doctrines.[11]

A 1993 Gallup poll revealed just how far Canadians believe women have come.[12] Asked if they believed that women in Canada "get as good a break as men," 41 per cent answered yes, while 56 per cent said no. In 1971, the figures were 64 per cent and 36 per cent, respectively. In other words, Canadians believe that the situation has worsened. Revealing the public's level of cynicism, 57 per cent agreed that "men are willing to let women get ahead but only if women still do all the housework at home." Another 46 per cent agreed that "a woman who takes years out of her career for child care can never make up for it on the job." Meanwhile, fully 74 per cent of Canadians oppose employment equity programs at the same time as 60 per cent support the goals of the feminist movement. Interwoven with these conflicting attitudes and perceptions — some of which perhaps conceal a degree of hostility to women's aspirations — lies women's albatross: the primary responsibility for raising the children. Fifty-three per cent of Canadians still believe that married women with families impose a "harmful effect on family life" if they work outside the home.

Such attitudes and opinions are sustained by and reflect the structural reality of patriarchy and the continuing oppression of women. They are the result of a continuing sexist socialization on the one hand, and a neglectful miseducation of the young on the other. Sociology and social psychology have long known that in the socialization process children absorb norms, values, behaviours, and attitudes much more from what they observe than from direct instruction. Therefore, if our children still have sexist attitudes, it is because we still live our daily lives in a sexist and stereotypical manner.

Sexual stereotypes still bombard us in the media. We know that children from the age of two to 11 watch an average of about 19 hours of television each week and are relentlessly bombarded by many hundreds of commercial messages as well as the stereotypical content of most shows. The media — especially television — play a big role in the socialization process, impacting on aspirations, future hopes, and basic achievement orientation and thereby helping shape styles of life, educational choices, and occupational selection as well as marital and sex role behaviour. The Canadian Radio-television and Telecommunications Commission (CRTC) has exerted pressures for self-regulation, but progress has been very slow.

The reading materials in our schools, after more than two decades of study and critical assessment, are still blatantly sexist and biased against women. A study commissioned by the Ontario Federation of Women Teachers' Associations concluded that the reading material used in grades four through six still present children with "a male-dominated world in which women's place is limited and specific."[13] Male characters — men and boys — were "vastly over-represented," and women's occupations were frequently family-based. The tasks performed by men and boys differed greatly from those performed by women and girls. In one reader, "boys handled equipment, played piano, danced, argued, collected stickers and protected mussels," while "girls became afflicted with 'the vanity of city girls,' abandoned a ballet recital, went on a diet, dreamed sad dreams and cried."

The results of such miseducation and missocialization has shown up in studies done on the aspirations and expectations of adolescent girls.[14] Research in the 1950s and 1960s suggested that adolescent girls saw their wage work as only temporary, while boys contemplated vocations and careers. But despite the great changes throughout the 1960s and 1970s, studies in the 1970s reported "that adolescent girls still plan to stay home with their children until the last child is in school, even though they also expect to have paid employment." As well, studies in the 1970s and even up to the 1980s "indicated that adolescent girls still see their lives in very traditional and romanticized terms."[15] Furthermore, girls often begin to scale back their career aspirations to meet the sexist expectations and limited opportunities they confront:

> While male students concentrate on putting more effort into getting into university or establishing themselves in a trade, female students are dreaming of marriage. The heavy emphasis on appearance and relationships channels girls' energies away from career planning at the very time it is most important.

In the 1980s, Baker studied adolescent girls and adolescent boys across Canada, and the results were deeply disturbing. Most girls expected to attend university, and those who mentioned specific jobs anticipated professional or managerial posts. About three in four expected to get married and almost the same number expected to have children, but few expected divorce, or if they saw divorce as a possibility, thought that it would not have much of an impact on their lives. Most saw marriage in highly romantic terms: relaxed evenings with their husbands while untroublesome children slept contentedly.

One of the most distressing findings has to do with sexuality and unplanned pregnancy. Only nine of the 122 girls said such a pregnancy would not happen because they would use birth control or would not indulge in sexual intercourse. Among the others, 34 would seek an abortion, five would put the baby up for adoption, while 14 didn't know what they would do. Almost half, 60 girls, said they would keep the baby, either alone or in a marriage or common-law relationship. They were quite oblivious to the stark implications of such a decision. There were six teenage mothers in the study and their lives were bleak and hopeless compared to those of the other adolescent girls.

> The unmarried mothers ... who usually had about Grade 10 education and generally came from lower SES [socioeconomic status] families, spent much of their time watching television or reading romantic novels when they were not caring for their child. Their child-rearing took so much of their time and energy that most had little desire or opportunity to look for work outside the home or to improve their educational qualifications ... However, they seemed uncertain how to improve their lives. They saw their lives improving when their child grew older and they could get out more often.[16]

During the 1990s the problems of adolescent girls appear to have worsened. Ironically, the successes of the women's movement appear to have increased the stress on adolescent girls as pressure leads them to become, in some ways, more unrealistic about themselves and their expectations. Despite the fact that adolescent girls outperformed boys in all school subjects, including maths and sciences, a real reversal from the 1970s and 1980s, levels of stress increased leading to a dramatic growth in risky behaviour like drinking, smoking, and excessive dieting. For example, a 1993–94 comparative study of girls aged 11, 13, and 15 found increased stress levels over the 1980s, resulting from peer pressure and performance expectations at home and school, causing feelings of low self-esteem and elevated self-doubt. Further, studies in the 1990s have found a dramatic increase in serious eating disorders, anorexia nervosa and bulimia nervosa, among adolescent girls. Even girls as young as nine are engaging in obsessive dieting to achieve the perfect body. Mary Pipher, in *Reviving Ophelia: Saving the Selves of Adolescent Girls*, tries to explain the dilemmas of adolescent girls in the following terms:

> Why are so many girls in therapy in the 1990s? Why are there more self-mutilators? What is the meaning of lip, nose and eyebrow piercings? How do I help thirteen-year-olds deal with herpes or genital warts? Why are drugs and alcohol so common in the stories of seventh-graders? Why do so many girls hate their parents? … At first blush, it seems things should be better now. After all, we have the women's movement. Hasn't that helped? The answer … is yes and no. Many [women today] are entitled in ways few women have been since the beginning of time. Many … are doing things [their mothers] never dreamed of doing. But girls today are much more oppressed. They are coming of age in a more dangerous, sexualized and media-saturated culture. They face incredible pressures to be beautiful and sophisticated, which in junior high means using chemicals and being sexual. As they navigate a more dangerous world, girls are less protected … Adolescent girls today … face a problem with no name. They know that something is very wrong, but they tend to look for the source within themselves or their families rather than … in the context of larger cultural forces.[17]

Perhaps this lack of realism, this romanticization of sex and relationships, this low self-esteem and high level of self-doubt, and an almost fatalistic approach to the future on the part of adolescent girls explains the continuing growth of teenage pregnancy. Trends indicate that the pregnancy rate is dropping among every other age group of fertile women.[18] Adolescent girls who keep their children add over 17,000 single-parent families to the rolls in Canada each year. A 1983 Ontario study reported that such mothers often live in deep and abject poverty, have little education and no job skills, and suffer from "quashed hopes" and deep discouragement.[19] One study found that adolescent mothers were less happy with the pregnancy, have a weaker network of social support to assist them through problems, and far less support from the father.[20] In the 1990s, poverty figures make it clear that the poorest families are single-parent families headed by adolescent girls and that the children of such families are the most at risk. This phenomenon of children having children is another dimension of the crisis of Canadian families.

Clearly the women's movement faces the difficult problem of reconquering the psychological terrain among each new generation of women in a milieu that continues to foster traditional attitudes in both boys and girls. While the structural oppression of women is relatively easy to document, this internalized oppression — "like a garrison in a conquered city" after Freud[21] — is more difficult to overcome. Externally imposed unjust burdens may anger, but self-imposed burdens merely eliminate options. Susan Brownmiller says, "Femininity, in essence, is a romantic sentiment ... of imposed limitations ... but while the extremes of masculinity can harm others (rape, wife beating, street crime, warfare and a related inability to concede or admit defeat), the extremes of femininity are harmful only — only! — to women themselves in the form of a self-imposed masochism (restraint, inhibition, self-denial, wasteful use of thought and time)."[22] One thinks immediately of the adolescent girl who cannot separate spontaneous romantic love and sex and therefore fails to plan birth control. Or of the girl swept away in the romantic vision of traditional marriage and children. Only later will they come to realize the full consequences of the burdens they have embraced with naive enthusiasm.

The crisis of the family cannot be separated from the oppression of women. Just as women bore the major economic, physical, and emotional burdens of maintaining the traditional family, today they bear the major burden — with the children — of the transition to new family forms. The more closely the situation is examined, the more clear it becomes that women will never achieve full liberation until the family's crisis has been resolved. And it will not be resolved until women's fullest liberation has been realized. In the meantime a heavy toll is being exacted.

7 / The Double Burden

Women's work in the home has typically been endless, invisible, unrecognized, and taken for granted.[1] No wages are paid and there's no discernible product that goes on the market. And because such work carries no recognition in the larger society, full-time housewives receive little prestige or attention from most social scientists who study work. Increased attention to the phenomenal growth in the paid work women do outside the home has served to downplay the continuing significance of the unpaid domestic work women do in the home. As Armstrong and Armstrong note in *The Double Ghetto*, "[T]he increasing visibility of women outside the home and the emphasis on female attainment of jobs at the top ... have camouflaged the lack of basic change in most women's work. In fact the division of labour by sex has changed little over the last 40 years. In Canada today, there is still men's work and women's work. If anyone works full-time in the home, it is almost always a woman, and women who work for pay still do most of the household chores."[2] But in the last two decades, feminist social scientists have documented the nature of housework and the time women traditionally have had and continue to have to devote to it. The Armstrongs usefully categorize women's domestic labour into five task areas: housework; reproduction and child care; care of the elderly and disabled; tension management; and sexual relations. The last two will be more appropriately considered in the chapter on emotional oppression. For now, the focus will be on housework and child-bearing and -rearing.

All the research on domestic labour suggests it was (and is) clearly the work of women. When sharing occurred, men tended to take on the more interesting tasks — entertaining the kids with games or a book — while women cooked, cleaned, ironed and so on. Men often argued that they did the regular "men's work" around the home — home repairs, painting, etc. — *and* brought home the bacon, so it was only a fair and reasonable division of labour that women should take the major responsibility for housework and child care. Most traditional wives in the past probably agreed. Indeed, men would often point to the fact that women significantly outlived men, presumably because they lived sheltered lives, free of the stress and competition out there in the market jungle.

All this changed as more women moved into the paid labour force and as the women's movement began its sustained critique of women's oppression both inside and outside the home. The palpable reality of working wives and mothers has confronted many men with the formerly "invisible" work of the housewife. And women who have remained full-time housewives at least now enjoy more recognition for the work they do, if not much more prestige. In 1989 the Canadian Advisory Council on the Status of Women asserted that women's unpaid domestic work accounts for 37 per cent of the total working hours of all Canadians and that full-time housewives put in 50-hour weeks. A 1996 analysis of data from Statistics Canada's General Social Survey found that the average Canadian adult spends 22 hours a week in unpaid domestic work. For women, the average was almost 29 hours; for men, 16 hours. The 2001 census confirmed this pattern, noting that 13 per cent of men did nothing and men evaded equal shares of care of children and aging parents.

Increasingly the real economic value of housework and child rearing is recognized, though it remains unpaid. In 1996, Statistics Canada estimated that the 1992 value of unpaid domestic labour, based on the cost to hire someone to do the work (replacement cost), was $235 billion, about one-third of Canada's Gross Domestic Product and the equivalent of about 14 million full-time jobs.[3] Further, as families have become increasingly dependent on two earners, the costs of services to replace a wife have astonished many men. Whether it's the escalating costs of daycare, or the investment in the "new necessities" like freezers, microwave ovens and dishwashers,[4] or the 30 cents of each food budget dollar that families of full-time working women spend on eating out,[5] it is impossible for Canadians not to recognize the economic value of domestic labour. Indeed, "pay for housework," a proposal that enjoyed some brief prominence in the feminist movement over a decade ago, only to be largely rejected because it did not solve the alienation, isolation, and psychological oppression of housework, now is being picked up by the anti-feminist lobby. Chantal Devine, the wife of Saskatchewan's ex-premier, proposed that perhaps women might have to be paid to stay home with the children in order to defeat "the anti-family agenda led by radical feminists."[6] That view — paying women to stay home as traditional wives and mothers — has been pushed repeatedly by the conservative traditional family lobby and prominent neoconservative politicians.

According to the Economic Council of Canada, the contribution of husbands to average family income between 1973 and 1986 *dropped* by 5 per cent, while the contribution of other family members, largely working wives and mothers, *rose* by 46 per cent, mainly because there has been no real growth in earnings since the mid-1970s. By 1990 wives contributed 29 per cent of family income overall, up from 26 per cent in 1967. Husbands contributed 56 per cent, down from 63 per cent in 1967. The balance was composed primarily of transfer payments and, less significantly, investment income. By 1994, almost one in four working wives was earning more than her husband, in one half of the cases contributing more than 75 per cent of family income.[7] How has this massive change affected the sharing of housework and child care between working husbands and working wives?

A fair distribution over time of domestic and child care work is still exceptional. Studies in the late 1970s and early 1980s generally found that husbands resisted sharing domestic work, and studies in the mid-1980s suggested there had been only a marginal improvement.[8] In 1985, a Toronto Family Services Association survey found that when both spouses work full-time outside the home, men contribute less than half the time to housework that women do, and one-third of the time to child care. When women moved from part-time to full-time work, their husbands contributed an average of nine minutes more a day to housework, while actually contributing one minute less per day to child care. Men also enjoyed much more "passive leisure time" — reading or watching TV — than women. In 1988, a Dalhousie University survey found that working married women did three-and-one-half hours of housework each day compared to one-and-one-half hours for their husbands.[9]

In 1989, Hochschild and Machung reported on their eight-year study of dual-earner families and the sharing of domestic work in the U.S.[10] They found that about 20 per cent of men shared "the second shift" equally, about 70 per cent did more than one-third of the domestic work but less than one-half, and there was a 10 per cent group of hard-core holdouts who did less than one-third. Further, Hochschild and Machung found that even in those marriages that came closest to equal sharing, the women got the less satisfying tasks while the men got the more interesting ones. In other words, men with working wives are just doing a bit more of the same kind of domestic chores they did for non-working wives. In Canada, Statistics Canada's 1990 General Social Survey (GSS) found patterns similar to the Hochschild and Machung research. Examining only *full-time* working wives and husbands in dual-earner families, the GSS found that in 52 per cent of such families the wives did all of the domestic work; in 28 per cent of cases the wife did most; and in only 10 per cent of cases was there an equal sharing (in another 10 per cent, the husband was solely or largely responsible).[11]

The stress of the double burden for women, and the resentment provoked among them by the unwillingness of men to share the second shift, have increased dramatically as the dual-earner family has become a permanent fact of life for a majority of husband/wife families. Furthermore, the situation becomes worse with the arrival of children. While the working wife of a childless couple might accept a husband's failure to share domestic work fairly, when children arrive the problems redouble because children require "compulsory and full-time" care.[12]

A study of the transition from childlessness to parenthood among dual-earner couples reports that women experience much more pressure than men and that sometimes the stress is "extreme." Yet, interestingly, new parents in single-earner families experience a steeper fall in "life satisfaction" than new parents in dual-earner families.[13] A study of 680 husbands and wives by Ross and Mirowsky found that the impact of a wife working on the psychological well-being of a family depends on four factors: the presence of children; the type of child care used; the presence of difficulties relating to child care; and a husband's participation in child care.[14] The results represent yet another setback for advocates of the traditional family. For wives with jobs outside the home, levels of well-being were not affected by the presence of children, but by whether there were difficulties relating to arranging child care and by whether the husbands shared child care responsibilities. Wives whose husbands did not participate in child care experienced higher levels of depression and lower levels of psychological well-being than those whose husbands helped. Indeed, working mothers and wives who had problems arranging child care and who had the *sole* responsibility for child care manifested "extremely high depression levels." Yet, in general, it was found that wives who did not work also experienced high depression levels when children were present.

As a result of this primary responsibility for child care and domestic labour, women at work suffer great stress. A U.S. study of 30,000 employees at 30 corporations found that 40 per cent of working women with babies and toddlers claim that worries about child care make them less productive at work, 50 per cent turned down transfers and 30 per cent turned down promotions because of child care difficulties, and more than 50 per cent felt stress both at work and at home because of the conflicts between work and family obligations.[15] A Conference Board of Canada survey found that most firms estimated that at least 25 per cent of employee absenteeism resulted from work/family conflicts,[16] and a larger 1988 study found that two in three employees experienced difficulty reconciling work and family obligations, and 80 per cent of these said they experienced stress and anxiety because of such conflicts.[17] A report prepared for the Canadian Advisory Council on the Status of Women asserted that the stress resulting from balancing domestic and job obligations is also a hazard to women's physical health, since stress is implicated in as much as 80 per cent of all illnesses. A University of Michigan study found that, on average, working women sleep 25 minutes less a day than working men because of their primary responsibility for domestic work.[18] Despite promises from employers throughout the 1980s to respond to the double burden, and new laws protecting women's rights on the job, research in the 1990s revealed that the stresses borne by working women who are also mothers and wives have not lessened. In some ways they've worsened as real family income falls despite two working spouses and as corporate and government cuts create an atmosphere of tension and insecurity. Working wives with children have twice the absenteeism of equivalent men, due to family and work conflicts. Working wives with children suffer twice the "severe time-crunch stress" as equivalent men. And, ironically, working men find firms allegedly more responsive to family/job problems to be more congenial than working women do, suggesting the changes are cosmetic rather than substantial.[19] So far there is no evidence that such increased levels of stress have begun to close the age of death gap between men and women, as many traditionalists warned; long-term paid employment does not appear to increase women's average risk of mortality, even among those struggling under the double burden.[20] At least not yet.

In *The Second Shift*, Hochschild and Machung note that working women have developed three basic stratagems for dealing with the double burden. Some try to excel at both job and home, pursuing the superwoman or "supermom" course. Some cut back their commitment to work, thereby relinquishing some of their career aspirations. And some cut corners at home, scaling down the high expectations they previously had about what they could do as a wife and mother. And many have surrendered and discontinued putting pressure on men in an effort to ease domestic tension. Overall, Hochschild and Machung found that there is a novel secret to marital happiness in this era of the changing family. And it has nothing to do with candlelight and wine. Women are now increasingly claiming that the most important component of marital bliss is rooted in a husband's willingness to share domestic and child care work fairly. Not very romantic. It may be hard for men to realize that the secure way to a woman's heart is through the mop pail, the laundry room, and the kitchen sink. But there it is.

While Hochschild and Machung's work suggests that many working women swallow their resentment in the interests of marital harmony, there are contrary indications that it is coming more and more to the surface. The U.S. National Center for Health Statistics reports that about 62 per cent of divorces in the U.S. are initiated by women, 33 per cent are initiated by men, and the rest are mutually initiated.[21] The figures are similar in Canada. But the U.S. report also tells us that when children are present, 66 per cent of divorces are initiated by women, while when no children are present, only 57 per cent are. These figures suggest, at least in part, that the double burden becomes truly onerous for women with the arrival of children.

Perhaps, in order to get a full sense of their feelings of injustice and resentment, we should let some women experiencing the double burden speak for themselves.[22] One cook and the mother of two says:

> A mother that works and raises a family has to be pretty strong, very strong. I really feel sorry for the mother with the little kids — have to bundle them up in the morning and take them to the daycare centre and pick them up again at night. I wouldn't go through that again that way. It's too hard.

Another comments on the problems of reconciling traditional sex role socialization with the new family reality:

> It's still very different for men and women. You can divide up all the tasks in the world, but the feeling of responsibility of every working mother I know is vastly different [from that of] her working husband. I mean, I don't know any man who would call home to see what's doing with the babysitter. You know, the men walk out the door and that's the end. But for the mothers, there's a sense of responsibility and there are different levels of guilt.

Or take the case of a woman lawyer who said she was reaching her "breaking point" in her marriage. Involved in a difficult case, she had called her husband at work and asked him to pick up the children at the daycare "just this once." "He absolutely refused, said it was impossible. He had an important meeting, and I had to do it."

Finally, a working mother of two explains why divorce and the absence of a husband brought a measure of relief:

> Remove the male and it's easier to organize. It is true. When I was a single parent I found that there is yourself. And it's easy to deal with yourself by yourself. You know that you have to do these things. No one else is going to be there to do them. You make your decisions whether they're right, wrong, whatever ... It's much easier. You can come home and throw on a hot dog.

The double burden borne by women is a central dimension of the family crisis provoked by our rapid move to new family forms. As the Canadian husband/wife family has come to rely on two earners, women have been forced to assume two jobs. The resulting stress and resentment have in no small part contributed to the rising rate of marriage failure. Men's general failure to accept a fair sharing of domestic and child care tasks has presented many women with a hard choice: either accept the double burden in order to sustain the family or opt for divorce and a period of single parenthood. More and more women are making the second choice.

As we examine the three central areas of women's continuing oppression — economic, emotional, and physical/sexual — the reality of the double burden, and the fundamental sexist assumptions and structures it is based upon, permeate all the other costs women are bearing as a result of the transformation of the family.

8 / Women's Economic Oppression

The General Pattern of Economic Oppression

Women do not get paid as much as men for the work they do. In 1900, full-time working women earned about 60 per cent of what full-time working men earned.[1] Such comparative income data on the sexes only began to be regularly collected by Statistics Canada in 1967, when it was found that full-time working women earned just over 58 per cent of the pay earned by full-time working men.[2] In 1977, the figure was an unimpressive 62 per cent. By 1985 the figure had climbed slowly to just under 65 per cent. In two years it inched up to 66 per cent, and by 1991 up to just under 70 per cent. During the 1990s, the pay gap has see-sawed, up to 72 per cent in 1992 and 1993, back down to 70 per cent in 1994, and back up to 72 per cent in 1998.[3] Thus the 40 years characterized by a Royal Commission on the Status of Women, an inundation of studies and inquiries, a blizzard of laws forbidding sexual discrimination, and countless specific programs to improve the economic position of women resulted in only a very modest upward shift. Indeed, this slight improvement had little to do with such symbolic acts and more to do with women's improved labour market qualifications as they flocked to universities in the last two decades in record numbers, now taking up over 53 per cent of undergraduate and 40 per cent of graduate places, compared to just over 25 per cent and 15 per cent, respectively, in 1961.[4] And in the 1970s, 1980s, and 1990s more and more women have entered university specialties that were formerly the near-exclusive preserve of men. Women are taking 57 per cent of places in agriculture and the biological sciences, 28 per cent of places in mathematics and physical sciences, and 18 per cent of places in engineering and the applied sciences.

Another factor helping to close the gender pay gap has to do with declines in both the real incomes and labour force participation rates of men. The average pay for a man working full-time rose by 11 per cent between 1971 and 1996, while the average for a woman working full-time rose 35 per cent over the same period. However, since 1977 average incomes for men have declined by over 8 per cent, while those for women have continued a modest incremental growth. This decline in average male earning is partly due to the loss of many high-paying, high-skill jobs formerly dominated by men. This has resulted from managerial restructuring, downsizing, and deindustrialization due to the impact of free trade, and it is partly a result of declines in labour force participation rates by men under 25 and over 55.[5]

The picture that emerges is one of chronic and change-resistant economic injustice.[6] Full-time working women aged 45 to 54 earn 70 per cent of their male colleagues' salaries, while those aged 15 to 24 earn 81 per cent. Women with grade nine education or less earn 70 per cent of equivalent men's salaries, while those with some university training earn 74 per cent. Married women earn 68 per cent of what married men earn, while single, never-married women earn 92 per cent of single never-married men's salaries. Women in male-dominated professions earn 71 per cent of what men in those professions earn. A survey of 201 occupations based on 1980/81 data found that in the top 10 occupations by annual earnings, women ranged from a low of 46 per cent of men's earnings to a high of 66 per cent, while in the bottom 10 occupations by annual earnings, women ranged from a low of 47 per cent of men's earnings to a high of 84 per cent. Perhaps an illustration from Statistics Canada's 2000 report, *Women in Canada*, makes the point most dramatically regarding the systematic pay inequities women face. In 1997, a woman with a university degree earned just $7,294 *more* than a man with some high school education. Meanwhile, a man with less than grade nine earned $2,371 *more* than a woman with some post-secondary education. Comparing those with university degrees, a man with a degree earned $15,269 *more* than a woman with such a degree, while a man with less than a grade nine education earned $9,328 *more* than an equivalent woman.

Typically the pay gap between the sexes is explained in terms of the ghettoization or segregation of women in the labour force. In the early 1900s, two in three working women were employed in the following occupational categories: (1) professional (mainly nursing and teaching); (2) clerical; (3) commercial and financial; and (4) service. In 1980, four in five Canadian women in the labour force were employed in those broad categories.[7] Armstrong and Armstrong refined this by identifying the 10 leading female occupations in Canada in 1981 where women made up over 72 per cent of the occupation and which accounted for about 40 per cent of all working women.[8]

In 1991, the leading female occupations changed. "Telephone operator" virtually disappeared and was replaced by "managerial and administrative" and "social sciences related," reflecting the new pink-collar opportunities for women. Women moved into lower and middle manager/administration positions and professions related to the social sciences (mainly social workers), due to both a dramatic growth in these occupations and women's marginal gains in occupational status. However, with the exception of these two new categories, and nursing and teaching, together comprising 32 per cent of all employed women, the other six categories of jobs are largely unskilled and largely non-union. As a result, the pay is low, and it is not surprising that global female earnings lag well behind those of men. As long as women as a group remain in such jobs, they will not succeed in closing the overall pay gap. Further, the breakthrough into pink-collar jobs has not resulted in pay rates remotely equal to those of men. Indeed, the segregation of women in the labour force appears to be worsening, since the jobs available are increasingly concentrated in the clerical and sales sector, as well as in the lower-paid managerial categories.[9] In 1982, the 10 leading female occupations employed 89 per cent of all working women. By 1994, the figure increased to 91 per cent, while clerical jobs' top spot was dramatically confirmed as the number of working women in clerical work rose from 1.5 million in 1982 to 1.6 million in 1994, despite the so-called "office revolution." Returning to the four broad occupational categories that employed two in three women in 1900, and four in five women in

1980, we find that these categories (nursing and teaching, clerical, sales, and service) still employ four in five working women in 1994 (4.8 million of 6 million working women), despite the gains in the new "pink collar" categories (see Table 3).

Table 3: The ten leading female job ghettoes in 1982 and 1994				
	Females as a % of Occupation		% of all females Working	
	1982	*1994*	*1982*	*1994*
Nursing and related	85	86	9	9
Clerical	79	80	34	27
Teaching	59	63	6	7
Social sciences	43	57	2	3
Service	54	56	18	17
Artistic/Literary/Recreational	39	46	1	2
Sales	40	46	10	10
Manager/Administrative	29	43	6	13
Doctors/Dentists	18	32	0.3	0.5
Primary goods producing	20	21	3	2
			89	**91**

Sources: Statistics Canada, *Work in Canada: A Statistical Report*, 3rd ed., Ottawa: Minister of Industry, 1995, p. 76.

The occupational segregation argument by no means explains the pay gap completely. In fact, men in the leading female occupations still earn significantly more than women, ranging from a low of women earning just 59 per cent of men's wages in sales occupations to a high of 93 per cent of men's wages in nursing.[10] So, in fact, women face a double segregation: not only do they tend to be concentrated in low-paying occupational categories, but they also tend to be at the lower paying end of those categories.

But this still cannot fully account for the enormous wage gap between the sexes. Thus, another argument is added: owing to their socialization, women tend to have less training and experience than men. This contributes to the wage gap since they do not move upward in a chosen career path, either because of lower motivation or of interruptions in their labour force participation. As Phillips and Phillips point out, as with the occupational segregation argument, there is some small truth in this.

> Studies both in Canada and elsewhere that try to standardize for training and work experience suggest that about half the difference in earnings at the level of the broad occupational categories is accounted for by the above two factors. The *Ontario Green Paper*'s [a 1985 government study of pay equity] estimate is somewhat lower, a quarter or less of the difference in full-time earnings.[11]

In other words, if women had the same training and work experience as men, women's earnings would rise from around 60 per cent to 70 or 80 per cent, depending on the estimate accepted. Such model building cannot control or account for the effects of sexist attitudes and discrimination. Such discrimination is so widespread that an Economic Council of Canada study expressed a shocking conclusion:

> In short, full-time native born paid employees who are women earn less than men because they do not benefit from their income relevant characteristics (education, training and experience) in the same manner as men.[12]

The fact is that in the 1990s, only women with a university education and working full-time earned more in wages than the average full-time male worker in the labour force, and then only slightly more, less than $100 more.[13]

Nowhere is this made more starkly clear than when we leave the low-paid segregated occupations of "women's work" and examine what happens to the women who join men in the more highly paid and privileged occupations. A study of 800 executives in the U.S., reported in the *Harvard Business Review*, carried out a survey of women executives and their experiences over two decades. A 1985–1990 study in Canada of 676 Crown corporations confirmed the pattern: women are essentially locked out of the boardrooms of the nation.[14] Although the number of female executives has increased dramatically, the studies still found that women had to be exceptional to succeed and that even then they failed to win dollar recognition equivalent to men — 48 per cent of male executives, compared to just 10 per cent of female executives, were earning six figures a year or more.

Professional Advancement

In Canada, women have made remarkable progress in breaking into male-dominated professional occupations.[15] (A professional occupation is defined by Statistics Canada as one where 45 per cent or more of the incumbents in 1981 had at least a bachelor's degree. A male-dominated profession is one where 65 per cent or more of the incumbents in 1971 were male). In a Statistics Canada survey of 46 professional occupations, including 34 male-dominated professions, between 1981 and 1986, women accounted for 69 per cent of the growth in all professions and over 52 per cent of the growth in the male-dominated professions. Between 1971 and 1986, women's participation in the male-dominated professions grew from 11 per cent to 23 per cent. Indeed, female growth in some of the male-dominated professions had been so marked that a number of them no longer fit Statistics Canada's definition of a male-dominated profession. But women in these male-dominated professions in 1986 earned only 71 per cent of their male colleagues, while women in other professions earned 83 per cent of their male colleagues. One could argue that some of this difference has to do with the fact that the recent female arrivals are younger and less experienced and therefore, as a group, will tend to earn less than men. But the fact remains that when women and men aged 25 to 34 were compared the earnings gap did not disappear — women earned 81 per cent of their male colleagues. Evidently, a professional woman of that age loses 19 cents of every salary dollar for no other apparent reason than she is a woman.

This trend of women breaking into formerly male-dominated occupations continued into the 1990s. A 1995 study by University of

Alberta sociologist Karen Hughes found that women had success-fully crashed the gates of 22 non-traditional occupations, including insurance sales, dispensing opticians, optometry, financial man-agement, osteopathy, chiropractic, and farmers and farm managers. Nevertheless, women in these occupations, on average, only earn 80 per cent of their male colleagues' wages.[16]

In the legal profession the situation is similar. Between 1966–67 and 1982–83, female full-time enrolment in Canada's law schools went up from 281 (just over 5 per cent of law school places) to 4,153 (just over 40 per cent of places) — an increase of 1,378 per cent![17] But in 1980, female lawyers earned just 58 per cent of what male lawyers earned, and by 1985 that limped up to 60 per cent. By the early 1990s, women held one in five positions as judges or magistrates and almost three in 10 lawyers were women. Yet female judges earned only 73 per cent of their male counterparts' salaries, and the earnings of women lawyers had slipped to 58 per cent of that of their male colleagues. This was partly because women lawyers were more likely to be salaried or to work part-time than their male peers. And job segregation is also at work, since women lawyers in Canada tend to be in lower-paid legal jobs and smaller practices, including family law, legal aid, and govern-ment jobs, while men dominate the high-profile, much more highly paid legal specialties.[18]

Women have also made great gains in medicine. By 1987, women made up 43 per cent of all medical students in Canada, including close to 60 per cent in Quebec, and comprised over one in five of all practising physicians.[19] Over 40 per cent of medical school graduates in 1987 were women. And an examination of medical students training for specialties in 1987 indicated that women outnumbered men in general practice (53 per cent), and have come close to matching them in pediatrics, obstetrics, and gynecology (about 47 per cent). But job segregation afflicts women in medicine as well, since they have failed to break significantly into the glamorous specialties like cardiovascular surgery (8 per cent) and neurosurgery (9 per cent). And the pay gap remains; women physicians earn about 60 per cent of their male counter-parts. By the early 1990s, women physicians and surgeons had improved their position only marginally, now comprising almost one in four practising physicians while earning 66 per cent of their male colleagues' salaries. Furthermore, ironically, women's emerging pre-eminence in certain medical areas is occurring just when a process of relative proletarianization is taking hold. Incomes for non-specialist physicians and family specialists are falling relative to other incomes in general and particularly relative to the incomes of the male-dominated medical specialties. Governments are also moving to put caps on billings, to control access to billing numbers, and to continue to underfund medicare. By the time women come to dominate the lower ends of the medical profession in Canada, as they must in the new millennium if present trends continue, they may find themselves no better off than their sisters in Russia, where women dominate the profession but cannot expect to earn much more than a technician.

One final example. Women have also made great strides as teachers at Canada's universities.[20] In 1960 there were fewer than 750 female university teachers in all of Canada. In 1985 there were almost 6,000 — an increase of 713 per cent. Though the number of women university teachers has grown more rapidly than that of men, the gap has not greatly narrowed. In 1960, 11 per cent of full-time faculty were women; in 1985 the percentage was 17; in 1990, 22 per cent. Job segregation also characterizes women's participation in university teaching, both by discipline and rank. Women faculty tend to be concentrated in the areas of education, social sciences, humanities, and health sciences. And female university teachers tend to be concentrated in the lower academic ranks and tend to advance much more slowly than men. Therefore, overall, women teachers at Canadian universities are paid less than men — in 1985, 81 per cent of the salary paid to men, falling to 75 per cent in 1990, reflecting a growth in the use of cheaper, part-time professors, many of whom are women. Furthermore, women in the same academic rank and with the same qualifications as men earn significantly less than their male colleagues.

All this is not to diminish the significance of women's tremendous advances in acquiring post-secondary education and in breaking increasingly into the professions. But many women have experienced dismay and even anger at the continuing barriers. A Statistics Canada study comparing almost 30,000 men and women university graduates found that men generally obtained significantly higher-paying jobs and that in many areas of work men earn more than women for the same job and with comparable qualifications and experience. Another Statistics Canada study of the employment outcomes for degree holders in the humanities and sciences confirmed the problem.[21] As expected, a university degree improved women's employment prospects and salary levels, but not as much as for men. Not only do women graduates in the humanities and sciences have lower levels of employment than men, but they earn less. Women aged 25 to 34 with degrees in the humanities earned 87 per cent of their male colleagues, while in the sciences they earned 84 per cent. And things do not seem to improve with age — women aged 45 to 54 with humanities degrees earned 81 per cent, and with degrees in the sciences 68 per cent of their equivalent male co-workers. Though the sex wage gap remains for female university graduates, it is not as large as the average gap faced by all working women as a group. All full-time working women from age 25 to 34 earned 76 per cent of what all full-time working men of that age earned, while from age 45 to 54 the gap widens considerably. Such women earned only 67 per cent of men of the same age.

Another aspect of the sexual segregation of women in the labour force is that such segregation also tends to limit women's opportunities for advancement at any level. A study of university graduates found that many women stay in traditional female jobs even when they get an education in a typically male area — for example, a male graduate of a business school tends to get on the career track to a management job, while a female graduate often gets side-tracked into the career dead-end of a clerk.[22]

This lack of opportunity has persisted, as confirmed by a series of mandatory affirmative action reports filed during the 1980s. Among Canada's 120 diplomatic missions, only 10 were headed by women.[23] Among 4,538 managers in the federal public service, only 481 were women. Among 22,702 scientific and professional personnel in the federal public service, only 5,563 were women.

Among Canada's 366 full colonels, there were five women, and among our 87 brigadier generals you could only find one lonely woman. Among the higher reaches of Quebec's public service there were 2,319 men and 179 women — and this excluded the public service stratosphere of deputy ministers, associate deputy ministers, and directors of government commissions and agencies.[24] Among the army of women who worked in six Canadian banks — the Canadian Imperial Bank of Commerce, the Toronto-Dominion, the Royal Bank, the Bank of Nova Scotia, the Bank of Montreal and the National Bank of Canada — who outnumbered men by a ratio of 70 to one, there were almost no women in upper management.[25]

Thus, even access to the formerly male-dominated professions does not narrow the pay gap to anywhere near equity because doors to advancement within such professions remain closed once women have overcome the hefty entry barriers. The former head of the Canadian Bar Association's Committee on Women's Issues noted that a central reason why women lawyers tend to concentrate in the lower-paid areas is that they reach a sort of "glass ceiling," beyond which it is very difficult to advance,[26] a barrier their male colleagues don't see.

Women in Canadian universities also hit a glass ceiling within the system. This inequitable situation has been documented and redocumented. The frustrations resulting from lack of gains led two scholars to conclude that blatant sexism is the only possible explanation of women's lack of opportunities to gain *access* to university faculty jobs and the lack of opportunities for *advancement* for those few women who have gained access.[27] In 1986, the University of Western Ontario won a prize for its voluntary affirmative action plan to advance women. Three years later, Western actually had to admit that the percentage of female professors was in fact *lower* than it had been in the 1930s and 1940s.[28] As Michele Landsberg noted, "All parties to the debate seem to agree that this grotesque imbalance is the result of widespread, covert and entrenched discrimination against women in university hiring."[29]

As a result of Ottawa's 1986 Employment Equity Act a clearer picture of the global situation emerged. The legislation requires that federally regulated businesses file reports regarding the situation of women, and in 1988, 371 such reports were filed. *Globe and Mail* analysts reviewed reports filed by 27 organizations employing around 400,000 people.[30] The reports revealed that women continued to occupy the "lower work rungs" and received lower salaries compared to men. Women tended to be concentrated in jobs paying less than $25,000 annually, while men tended to be concentrated in jobs paying more than $35,000 a year. Air Canada reported they had 18,800 full-time male employees and that 1,373 of these earned more than $70,000 per year. Meanwhile, Air Canada had 6,300 full-time female employees, only four of whom earned more than $70,000. According to Canada Post, most male and female employees earned between $25,000 and $30,000. But the corporation also had 5,400 women earning less than $20,000 and 7,600 men earning between $30,000 and $70,000. The survey concluded that "in almost every enterprise, employers favour men when hiring or promoting middle managers, skilled tradesmen, and semi-skilled and manual workers." Women benefitted in only one category of hiring and promotion: clerical.

This helps explain the results of a Statistics Canada study on the changing wage distribution of jobs.[31] The study uncovered a worrisome trend that began in the 1970s and accelerated dramatically between the 1981, 1986, and 1991 census years. It seems that the lowest-paying jobs in the Canadian economy are the fastest-growing category of jobs, and most of these are taken up by younger workers. As a result, the wages enjoyed by younger workers are declining in relative and real terms, while the wages of middle-aged and older workers are climbing. However, if men and women as groups are compared, the wages of women workers as a group fell while those of men rose. Women, therefore, experience an additional disadvantage to add to job ghettoization and barriers to opportunity. As relatively recent arrivals in the labour force, many women have hit the job market at a time when low-waged jobs are more and more the only ones available and at a time of declining real wages for young workers.

Given the situation of women in terms of pay and opportunity, it is not surprising that there is an increasing "feminization of poverty" in Canada. The fact is "women face a greater risk of poverty than men in almost every category" and "make up a larger percentage of the poor ... in most categories."[32] The ratios of female to male poverty rates in the different categories show a consistent pattern of women's greater risk: all persons, 1.24; persons in families, 1.18; all family heads, 4.30; aged family heads, 1.9; non-aged family heads, 4.62; unattached individuals, 1.32. The only poverty categories in which men face ever so slightly higher poverty rates than women are "children" and "aged persons in families." And in these categories the rates are about equal, 0.99 and 0.93 respectively. In 1998, there were over two million women in Canada below the poverty line, compared to 1.5 million men, a ratio of women to men of 1.30.

Economic Oppression and the Crisis of the Family

This general economic oppression of women is intimately linked with the crisis of the family and the unjust burdens that it imposes on women. The "revolution in women's labour market participation" from the 1960s to the 1990s most importantly included a massive movement of "married women between the ages of twenty-four and fifty-five" into paid work.[33] Starting in the early 1980s and continuing into the 1990s, this movement most dramatically included married women with young children. Clearly this revolution is the result of a complex web of causation, and no doubt the growing instability of marriage has contributed to women's determination to decrease their economic dependence. Yet a major push has to do with the economic needs of the family. In 1989, Statistics Canada reported that the traditional two-parent, one-earner family experienced a slight *decline* in real family income between 1980 and 1988. Meanwhile, average family income had experienced "little real growth in the 1980s" and will remain "flat for the foreseeable future." The only families that experienced growth in real terms during the 1980s were those with two earners. In fact, in November 1989 the Economic Council of Canada reported that rises in real family income during the last decade and a half have been the primary result of married women entering the labour force. It has become clear that families need two earners just to mark time.

In the 1990s, for the first time in 50 years, average family income as a whole began to fall in real terms. The drop was most precipitous among traditional, one-earner families, who earned an average of 21 per cent less than dual-earner families. The hardest hit were traditional-earner families headed by men under 55, with the gap increasing as age decreased. Further, in the 1990s traditional-earner families suffer *three-and-one-half times* the poverty rate of dual-earner families. Indeed, the wives' incomes in dual-earner families is what maintains this risk of poverty differential — in 1994 the national Council of Welfare reported that the poverty rate among Canadian families would more than double in the absence of the incomes of working wives and mothers. The fact is that many women are driven into wage work in order to safeguard the family from the poverty into which it would fall, in spite of enjoying the support of a full-time, wage-earning father and husband.[34]

Women pushed into the labour force by family income pressures are clearly at a disadvantage. They will take any job available, and most will end up in traditional female job ghettoes. Part-time jobs tend to be lower paid and carry few benefits. In 1993, over 70 per cent of Canada's 2.1 million part-time workers were women, and over one in three of these worked part-time because that was the only job they could find.[35] But the unwilling acceptance of part-time work is but part of a larger problem that plagues the careers of many women in the labour force. Studies in occupational mobility have confirmed the importance of the "occupation of entry" for future occupational attainment.[36] Take the earlier case of a young man and a young woman, both graduates of a business school. The young man succeeds in obtaining a place in a management trainee intake program — he is on the career track toward promotions and higher pay. The young woman, on the other hand, because of family income pressures, takes the first job she can get — as a clerk in an accounting firm. Their work futures will be heavily influenced by these occupations of entry.

Taking any job available is only one of many labour market sac-rifices women routinely make. Much of the economic inequity women experience occurs long before they enter the labour mar-ket. Socialized to see themselves realizing a central aspect of their identities as wives and mothers, women are often not encouraged to take their role in the world of work seriously. Therefore, they tend not to be as well prepared as men when they launch their careers. That is why, in a study over the decade of 1976 to 1985, it was found that men obtained twice the rate of trade certificates as women; that women, though earning more undergraduate degrees than men, were far less likely to pursue graduate work; that, despite female predominance as university undergraduates, women still only occupy a tiny percentage of places in the more employment-oriented university courses like mathematics, sci-ences, and engineering; and that women were far more likely than men to pursue university education on a part-time basis. These pat-terns persisted into the 1990s, despite significant advances by women into traditionally male areas. In 1993, 63 per cent of all women at university were still concentrated in fine arts, humani-ties, social sciences, and education. Sixty-seven per cent of women attending community colleges were enrolled in nursing and relat-ed health courses, counselling and social services, secretarial and commerce, and fine arts, while only about 10 per cent were enrolled in applied sciences, mathematics, and technology cours-es. Further, by 1992 twice the number of women were enrolled in trade apprenticeship programs compared to 1988, but they still only accounted for less than 2 per cent of total enrolments.[37]

If women choose to marry and to have children, they make major labour market sacrifices. They drop out of school. They attend part-time. They leave their jobs to have kids. Then they look for jobs compatible with raising kids. They enter, exit, and re-enter and then enter, exit, and re-enter the labour force again to suit the ebb and flow of family demands. They search for part-time work to reconcile the need for income, the desire to work, and the demands of children and husbands. They look for work that fits the daycare they can find, when it becomes impossible to find daycare to suit the work they want to do. Even highly motivated and well-educated women, having embarked on the first steps of a rewarding career, find such career compromises inescapable.

Women who work, and then opt to have children, or women who have children and then realize that they must find some paid work, learn very quickly that often only the inferior jobs can be easily reconciled with being wives and mothers. For the majority of women these are jobs in the traditional female ghettoes. For female teachers, it involves the "choice" not to pursue further education for a high school job or an administrative post — or perhaps to do "just a few years" of "subbing." For female nurses, it involves the "choice" to work only two or three days a week. For the female doctor, it involves giving up post-graduate training, "at least for now" and perhaps practising part-time. For the female lawyer, it involves a part-time job at a legal aid clinic. For the aspiring female university teacher, it involves putting off the Ph.D. and "teaching the odd course" until the kids are in school. The variations on the theme are endless.

The modern family's success therefore rests importantly on the abandoned aspirations of many women: foregone training, postponed education, rejected promotions, transfers dismissed out of hand, jobs unapplied for. This point is made considerably more drily by the Canadian Mobility Study:

> Additional sex differences in the occupational attainment process among married men and women occur with child-bearing and child-rearing. Number of children depresses the occupational attainment of women under age 45 but it has no influence on the attainment of married men.[38]

And while it is true that many of these working mothers, perhaps most, make significant career sacrifices willingly, the fact remains they have no real choice. Unlike men, women cannot easily "have it all." Studies in the 1990s suggest that the situation of working women may in fact be deteriorating, despite claims of responsiveness from public and private employers. Career sacrifices — quitting jobs, working part-time, and dropping out of the labour force — have clear, negative impacts on one in four working women aged 25 to 54. Over 50 per cent of 25 to 34-year-old women in the labour force who quit jobs, or delayed re-entry into active paid work, did so in response to family obligations. Overall, working women with children face double the load of balancing job and home obligations when compared to equivalent working men, including twice the severe time stress. Indeed, working men are actually benefitting more from flex-time arrangements than working women, since working women often respond to time stress and job/home balancing problems by moving to part-time work. Women often find full-time work with flex-time more stressful than continuing with regular full-time hours.[39]

Indeed, the one group of women in Canada who have come closest to closing the sex pay gap are "single, never married" women, who in 1997 averaged 92 per cent of the pay gained by single, never-married men.[40] The only group of women to surpass equivalent men in income is single, never married women aged 45 to 54 who in 1997 earned 5 per cent more on average. And the women who have succeeded in breaking into the male-dominated professions are more likely, compared to women working in other areas, *not* to be married, and to have *fewer* children, or *none* at all. They are also most likely to have *never* married. As Katherine Marshall says, in her study of women's success in male-dominated professions, "it is still far easier for men to maintain both a professional career and a family. For many women, unlike men, the decision to pursue such a career may mean limiting marital and parental options."[41] A study of women lawyers who did advance to reach near equality with their male colleagues found that such women did so at "great personal sacrifice." The fact is that "most successful male lawyers are married and have children, most successful female lawyers are not."[42]

More than a decade ago a U.S. executive search company surveyed 485 women executives in the 1,500 largest U.S. corporations. The study found that the highest-paid women executives tend to work longer hours and to be divorced when compared to less well-paid women executives. Over one in three was divorced. Fewer than half had children, and those under 40 were less likely to have children than those over 40.[43] Almost a decade later, Edith Gilson's study of 250 U.S. women executives, appropriately entitled *Unnecessary Choices: The Hidden Life of the Executive Woman*, found that things had not improved, indeed they appear to have deteriorated in some ways.[44] Success for women in the U.S. executive suite can be emotionally expensive for some women: loneliness, unhappiness, unsuccessful marriages, childlessness. And even success brings lower pay than men, fewer promotions, less recognition, and pressure to deny and suppress their femaleness as they learn to model themselves on successful men in order to get ahead.

In the 1990s, more women began to break into the top executive suite. Though they still represented only 2 per cent of senior executives in large U.S. corporations, they were promptly dubbed the "breakthrough generation" of women who had launched their corporate careers in the 1970s and who had benefitted from affirmative action pressure. Others called them "window-dressing," "tokenism," or "guideline fillers." Nevertheless, such women took over major positions in large corporate empires like AT&T, Autodesk, Kraft Foods, and General Motors. The fact that each breakthrough was accompanied by major headlines reminded everyone how exceptional such cases were. These women had to be tougher and more aggressive than the men they outperformed. Carol Bartz, CEO of Autodesk, the fourth-largest personal computer software manufacturer in the U.S., was diagnosed with breast cancer two days after her appointment. She had an emergency lumpectomy and stayed at the job for a month before a radical mastectomy, returning to work four weeks after surgery. She said that, "having a female illness could be fodder for anyone inclined to question whether a woman should be doing this job, and I wanted to avoid that at all costs." Gail McGovern, head of AT&T's $26-billion consumer business, learned about baseball, deliberately became a devoted fan to fit in with her male peers, and consciously sought out jobs in male-dominated corporate sectors like technology, sales, and marketing in her climb to the top. A 1996 study by Dun and Bradstreet found that almost one in three Canadian businesses have a woman in command and the greatest increase occurred in the early 1990s. Women-led firms tend to be concentrated in the retail sector and to be smaller than average, but they are breaking into traditional "male" sectors like agriculture, mining, finance, and real estate. Two *Wall Street Journal* writers sum up these glass ceiling crashers:

> [They] still live in what is largely a man's world, where the rules are the same as they ever were: work hard, make the numbers, be a team player. But to stand out, women have had to do more. They have tackled assignments others have shunned as losers and they've even taken brief career detours to get tough jobs done for bosses who almost always are male.[45]

Often, such women have succeeded by taking jobs their corporate male colleagues avoid, as in the case of Irene Rosenfeld, president of Kraft Canada. Rosenfeld volunteered to take over the food giant's failing beverage division and succeeded in turning around the faltering Kool-Aid brand. She then took on the desserts and snacks division, and again succeeded, rescuing Jell-O from imminent oblivion.

And, of course, at work such successful women, despite their sacrifices, still face forms of discrimination that inhibit their advancement. As a result of differences in behaviour and personality, women are often judged differently from men.[46] Professor Ron Burke reported that compared to men, women executives tend to be friendlier, more willing to help associates and subordinates, better listeners, and more prone to try to persuade others to their point of view rather than using confrontation. Hence such women may speak up less at conferences and meetings and therefore might be viewed as "timid" or "reticent" and hence less valuable. Nina Colwill found similar sex differences in behaviour in corporate boardrooms: women allow themselves to be interrupted more often than men, are more polite in their business interactions, and tend to make "softer" requests and suggestions. In other words, the behaviour that earns maximum rewards in the executive suite still tends to be that expected of stereotypical males.

Despite the fact that women outperform men in 28 of 31 management categories, particularly on the keys to corporate success

— high productivity and generating new ideas — and continue to outperform men in the corporate suite on intuitive and nurturing skills, they continue to be held back and, as one study found in the 1990s, appear to have begun to have trouble handling frustration. Further, even women who have made it into management and have decided either to postpone children or to ensure children do not disrupt their careers face prejudicial attitudes. Dr. Alice Nakamura found that whether or not a woman quit upon bearing a child was predicted more successfully by the woman's past work record than by the fact of having a child. A woman who worked 48 weeks in the previous year and bore a child was almost as likely to continue to work after the child's birth as a woman who bore no child.

Career advisors to corporate and professional women warn job seekers to beware of the Big Chill that can set in if a woman is overly frank about family commitments and priorities during job interviews. One warns women to be prepared for family questions as probes about job commitment — one expert suggests that, if a woman is asked an innocent-appearing question about what kind of child care she has, she should say, "I assume your concern is, 'Am I a reliable employee?' and I can assure you that I absolutely am. It means a lot to me to perform my duties and I take every measure to make sure I can get to work."[47] It appears, then, that even those women who are determined not to allow children to disrupt their careers suffer from the assumption on the part of their employers that children will interfere with their continuing commitment to the job.

New Patterns

As a result, some astute women are seeking success first and postponing having children until their careers are well-established. This strategy is not without its costs, costs that men do not have to bear. One cost is the act of deferring children until a later age, thus postponing the emotional fulfillment ten or twenty years. Another is the increased risks of bearing children at a later age.

This trend also includes senior women executives leaving work to have a baby and to spend a few years at home. Corporations that have committed themselves to the advancement of women up the ladder are now concerned about how flexible they should be with talented and successful women asking for time off to have a baby. More and more are responding with extended leaves, flex-time, temporary contract work, and extended part-time work. Yet such attitudes are rare. And the number of women willing to, or able to, postpone children until they reach managerial success are few. There is just not that much room at the top. As Judge Rosalie Abella found in her Royal Commission on Equal Employment Opportunities, prejudice and discrimination against working women of all classes are so widespread and tolerated that only harsh interventionist measures will succeed in achieving equity in the world of work for women.[48]

One of the choices women can make to avoid trying to balance work and family is simple. They can stay single and childless. More and more women are doing just that — in 1986 Statistics Canada estimated that 14 per cent of Canadian women would never marry, up from about 10 per cent in 1971, and by 1991 one in five women had never married, almost double the 1981 figure.[49] But the choice most women make involves work, spouse, and children. A woman making that choice faces clear consequences. Her career takes second place to that of her husband and to the needs of her children. She will always earn much less than her male colleagues, even those with the same qualifications and experience doing the same work. She will routinely lose out on promotions, partly as a result of her family obligations and partly as a result of discrimination. Her husband will give her little help with child care and housework. She will find little support and sympathy, and almost no career concessions, from her employer and her colleagues when she decides to have children. Family crises and problems that disrupt, or *appear* to disrupt, her work commitment and job performance will most definitely be held against her. Indeed, the fact that such disruptions *might* occur will be held against her almost as much as actual disruptions. She will work 12- to 16-hour days once the kids arrive and until they grow up and leave home. She will work almost as hard on weekends and holidays as on regular workdays. The other option is to remain single and childless, at least until she has fulfilled her career aspirations. She will have to work harder than her male colleagues, and routinely outperform them, in order to receive the same treatment. Or nearly the same, since she will still receive less pay on the average. Promotions will be harder to come by than for men, but easier than for her married sisters, especially those with children. She can come and go as she pleases at home, weekends and holidays will be hers, and her psychological space after work will not be cluttered with the insistent demands of husband and children.

Life's choices are rarely posed with such clarity. Indeed, we have often made life choices without realizing it until much later. But faced with such a set of choices, I have no doubt which option most men would chose without a moment's hesitation. The fact that the overwhelming majority of women choose the messy and difficult choice involving work, husband, and children is a confirmation of their abiding commitment to making the family work.

And at no time is that commitment more clearly revealed — nor is the reality of women's economic oppression more unmistakably confirmed — then when the family breaks down. The economic consequences of family breakdown for women — and for their children, as we've seen — are catastrophic. Families headed by working women not only lose the man's income, but now rely on the woman's income, which is much less from a job with fewer prospects. Further, single-parent mothers have a greater difficulty maintaining their commitment to the labour force. In 1999, only 55 per cent of female single parents with preschool children, and 61 per cent of those with kids at home, were in the labour force. (This compared with 68 per cent and 74 per cent, respectively, for married women with children of those ages.[50]) It is not surprising, therefore, that female single parents and their children are among the major beneficiaries of social programs like welfare, unemployment insurance, and family allowance.

Furthermore, despite improvements in laws affecting the sharing of family assets after marriage failure, women still do not experience economic justice upon family breakdown. Judges now more frequently insist that a divorced woman, even those who remained at home, should eventually become self-sufficient. Thus, ongoing support awards, as distinct from the one-time split in all family assets, are tending to be smaller in amount and shorter in duration. As one Montreal family lawyer put it,

> Divorce judgements used to reflect the fact that the husband definitely had to look after her. Now women are being told to fend for themselves. You change the rules in the middle of the game and it creates very grave handicaps.[51]

Further, such awards are rarely realistic. The same lawyer alleged that support orders — including child support payments — are often less than half the cost of raising a child and often go no higher than 20 per cent of the husband's net income. As a Manitoba study argued, courts are increasingly operating on the mistaken assumption that Canadian men and women have managed to achieve something approaching economic and social equality, "but the reality is that Canadian women ... have fewer resources, lower status and less flexibility."[52]

But even court-awarded maintenance and child support payments, however inadequate, often do not find their way into the hands of divorced single-parent mothers. In 1985, a Canadian Advisory Council on the Status of Women study reported that 50 to 85 per cent of divorced husbands and fathers default on such payments,[53] and the situation has not improved much.[54] Only about 26 per cent of Ontario's 62,000 court-ordered support payments in 1989 were complied with — up from 15 per cent in 1987. These results were achieved through the Ontario Attorney-General's department spending about $14 million a year on enforcement. The success rate in Alberta is about 33 per cent, and in Quebec it is about 50 per cent. These modest success rates have been achieved as a result of Ottawa's, and most provinces', recent "get tough" policies with delinquent ex-husbands and fathers. Contrary to popular belief, such court-ordered payments are largely for the support of children. For example, 97 per cent of Ontario's cases are orders for men to pay; of these, 73 per cent are orders for the support of children, 16 per cent are for an ex-spouse and children, and only 11 per cent are orders for the support of the ex-spouse alone. In response, in the 1990s, provincial governments began to get even tougher. By 1996 only 23 per cent of court-ordered child support payments were in full compliance and the arrears had climbed to $1 billion in Ontario (97 per cent of defaulters are men). Both Manitoba and Ontario have begun to crack down on defaulters through suspending drivers' licenses, notifying credit bureaus, accessing income tax records, and hiring aggressive collection agents. Manitoba claims such measures have realized a dramatically increased success rate.[55]

Clearly the major cause of the trend toward the feminization of poverty has to do with the economic consequences of marriage breakdown. In Quebec an estimated 10,000 women and their children have been forced to go on welfare as a result of defaulted maintenance payments. Between 1987 and 1989, over 16,000 Ontario ex-spouses, overwhelmingly women, and their children received welfare because of support payment defaults. In Ontario about 70 per cent of families on social assistance are headed by single mothers. In two out of three of these families, the mothers were previously married. A 1997 Statistics Canada Report, *Family Income After Separation*, found that between 1987 and 1993, separated and divorced mothers experienced income reductions of 23 per cent in the year following the breakup, while the fathers were 10 per cent better off.[56] Throughout the 1980s and 1990s, the percentage of female single-parent families below the official poverty line was shocking: 1980, 58 per cent; 1988, 57 per cent; 1990, 61 per cent; 1993, 60 per cent; 1998, 54 per cent. The rate goes up dramatically for single-parent families headed by young women. For example, the rate is 85 per cent for those families headed by women under 25. It also goes up for single parent families headed by women with young children — single-parent mothers with two children under the age of seven endure a poverty rate of 87 per cent.[57]

Women's economic oppression cannot be separated from their roles as wives and mothers. In the traditional family the economic sacrifices women were expected to make were clear. They were expected to devote themselves to domestic careers. Thus, they became economically dependent and vulnerable. That domestic legacy affected the fate of women as they moved into the labour force and sought to reconcile domestic obligations and paid work. Whether it was in the form of "women's work," or of lower pay, or of the assumption that women's commitment to the paid labour force was temporary, women were (and are) expected to make economic sacrifices because their primary tasks remained domestic. When women's commitment to the labour force became clearly permanent and irreversible, and families increasingly needed two earners to survive and flourish, that domestic legacy continued to demand economic sacrifices of women. Most of the economic crises of the changing family are imposed primarily on the shoulders of women and their children.

9 / Women's Emotional Oppression

The emotional oppression of women is not simply a consequence of the difficulties imposed by the double burden and economic injustice. Indeed, the double burden and the new forms of economic oppression are themselves merely the more recent historical expressions of women's general oppression. Women have always been economically, emotionally, and physically oppressed in the interests of the family. Certainly that oppression is taking novel forms as the family changes and as women's resistance increases, but in many ways it's the same old oppression.

The emotional sacrifices women have made, and continue to make, for the family have been thoroughly documented. As the traditional guardians of hearth and heart, women were assigned the "expressive functions" in the family, according to functionalist Talcott Parsons, while men were assigned the "instrumental functions."[1] For men, women are expected to provide emotional support and reaffirmation. For children, women are expected to provide "warmth, security, and unconditional love." Different authors have selected different words, but the reality is the same: women are viewed as the primary emotional guardians and sustainers of husbands and children. And in order to do so, women have been expected to give emotional priority to the needs of husbands and children. Indeed, women's personal aspirations, their access to an enjoyment of privacy, their emotional needs, and even their health are expected to be forever offered up on the family altar.[2] For example, one classic study in the U.S. found that women in "adequate" or "normal" families were "overwhelmed with responsibility," "obese," "psychosomatically ill," and "sexually dissatisfied," while the men were "functioning well" and felt no sexual dissatisfaction.[3] As Luepnitz argues:

Thus, according to the authors, an adequate family consists of a husband and children who are functioning adequately and a wife who is not ... There is no greater devaluation of female leadership ... nor a more profound training in sex roles than in a family in which a mother's needs are sacrificed for the good of the whole.[4]

In the orthodox psychological literature, characteristics traditionally associated with the male — assertiveness, independence, autonomy — are usually posited as those which come closest to characterizing an emotionally mature and mentally healthy adult, while the traditional female characteristics — dependence, submissiveness, responsiveness, subordination — are typically associated with an emotionally immature and less than psychologically healthy adult.[5] A report for the Canadian Mental Health Association argues that since women in the family are "devalued" and "oppressed," they have "poor self-esteem" and "lowered aspirations."[6] As the role of housewife is viewed as less important in the "real" world, women who occupy that role receive less attention and concern and less recognition of their desires and problems.[7] Indeed, there is a new pathogenic category increasingly recognized in psychiatry: "the belittled wife."[8]

The belittling process goes beyond merely a devaluation of women and their role in the family. Women are also frequently blamed for the emotional problems of others. In the clinical literature, mothers are routinely blamed for 72 different categories of psychopathology.[9] They are blamed for their own problems as well as the problems of other family members: they "provoke" their husbands' physical abuse, they contribute to their husbands' alcoholism, or they neglect their psychologically maladjusted children. Even for psychological disturbances among young women in which fathers play a significant role — depression, anorexia, agoraphobia — the mothers are often still blamed.[10] As a result, women often accept the blame and consider themselves inadequate. The tendency to engage in "mother blaming and father coddling" is so widespread that one therapist concluded that the family in "modern culture is irrefutably father-absent ... and patriarchal."[11]

Not satisfied with merely blaming women for the emotional and psychological problems of children and men, neo-conservatives and the traditional-family lobby recently began blaming women, especially working women who are wives and mothers, and feminism in general, for a long list of problems. They have been blamed for the rise in the divorce rate and the resulting growth in single-parent families; the decline of the family; the social decay of community life; the rising rates of crime and violence; child hunger, poverty, neglect, and abuse; and the rising rate of suicide and emotional disorders among our adolescents. Regrettably, there is sufficient public confusion, uncertainty, and anxiety that such shallow woman-blaming analyses strike a responsive chord among some — for example, 53 per cent of Canadians still believe that when a wife and mother works for wages, it has a harmful effect on the family.[12]

Marriage and Mental Illness

The overwhelming preponderance of evidence tells us not only that women benefit less from marriage than men, but also that marriage appears to increase the risk for women of falling victim to forms of psychopathology.[13] For women, marriage brings with it an increased risk of social and psychiatric problems, often of marked severity. Married women who remain at home, and therefore dependent on men, experience a greater risk, compared to single women, of anxiety, phobias, and depression. In fact, married women experience a greater risk of depression than single women, and married women with three or more children have a higher risk of depression. Between 60 and 80 per cent of mothers experience emotional problems after the birth of a child, and one in five such mothers experiences serious depression for many months after birth. For unemployed wives, the arrival of children increased levels of depression; but for employed wives, depression was not affected by children, but by the ease or difficulty of child care arrangements and whether husbands helped out.

Overall, rates of mental illness among women are higher than those among men. Married women experience higher rates of anxiety than single women and men in general. Girls, for example, suffer three times the rate of clinical depression of boys, largely as a result, one suspects, of their preparation for future roles where they will be expected to define themselves and their priorities as based on sustaining others in relationships. In fact, the higher rates of anxiety and depression among women suggest that these psychopathologies are quite sex specific: anxiety and depression result frequently when one feels worthless and useless as a result of a fear of failure or failures in fulfilling responsibilities and obligations to others. Anorexia nervosa and bulimia nervosa, which are clearly women's psychopathologies, have mushroomed in recent years, and clinical descriptions of young women most at risk sound very much like a characterization of the psychological and emotional problems and contradictions women typically face.

> Girls and women who are particularly vulnerable appear to be those who have a premorbid sense of helplessness and powerlessness about their lives ... their sense of self-efficacy is impaired ... most of these women identify problems with appropriate identification of internal feeling states, perfectionistic attitudes, trouble with expression of direct and appropriate anger, difficulty with assertiveness and decision-making, and trouble with appropriate separation and autonomy from the family of origin.[14]

A recent "Health of Youth Survey," which studied 100,000 middle adolescents aged 11, 13, and 15 in 14 countries, found that Canadian girls, compared to boys the same age, are much more uncertain and negative about body image, body weight, and self-esteem; suffer significantly more headaches; use more prescription mood modifying drugs; and suffer triple the stress rate.[15]

Of course, a global comparison of psychopathological rates between men and women is deceptive. Married women are more at risk of mental illness than married men. But unmarried men have a greater risk than unmarried women. Hence the conclusion is rather stark: marriage is psychologically bad for women and good for men; singleness is psychologically good for women but bad for men.

As a consequence of the increased risk of psychopathological disturbance women face, other facts make sense. Women and girls receive anywhere from 66 to 72 per cent of tranquilizer prescriptions.[16] Indeed, they are increasingly the treatment of choice among many doctors for middle-class housewives. One study at the University of Ottawa found that women aged 45 to 65 receive most new prescriptions for tranquilizers, suffer more frequently from emotional crises and seek psychiatric help more often. Another clinical study at Queen's University found that women were 30 per cent more likely to be prescribed tranquilizers than men for the following categories of presenting problems: tension headaches, anxiety, alcohol abuse, marital and sexual problems.

A common explanation of the mental health differences between men and women is that women are more willing than men to seek help for their problems. Some feminists have also alleged that male physicians and psychiatrists tend to see women as emotionally weak and therefore too readily diagnose psychological problems. Others argue that women in fact appear to suffer more than men. Vancouver psychiatrist Susan Penfold believes that indeed many male psychiatrists have a sexist bias and embrace traditional views of women. They tend to see unhappy women as needing help to cope with their family life situation, but rarely suggest that their family situation could be part of the problem and could be changed. Also, she concedes that male psychiatrists might be quicker to label women's problems as emotional rather than situational. But the evidence also shows that women do suffer more. Furthermore, as Montreal psychiatrist Suzanne Lamarre argues, women suffer more anxiety because of a "sense of powerlessness." Women are simply not allowed to refuse demands placed upon them by husbands, children, or employers. In the context of low control in a situation containing high and ever-escalating demands, the resulting stress makes women more vulnerable.

Other Data

Other data tell us, however, that traditional marriage and dependency is also very much implicated in women's greater vulnerability. As women become less dependent economically and psychologically, their risk of psychopathology decreases dramatically. Married women who work outside the home are not only less vulnerable, but positively psychologically healthier than women who do not. As women become less dependent, they attain a greater sense of self-determination and mastery. Furthermore, since work extends the self into the larger community and establishes a wider network of both support and social confirmation as a person independent of husband and children, women have stronger identities and more coping resources. Despite the great stress for working wives and mothers of juggling the double burden, they are psychologically healthier than those locked up in traditional roles in traditional families.

Let us leave for the moment the area of greater psychopathological risk and focus on the "normal" situation. Besides the emotional sacrifices all women are expected to make for husbands and children, what are some of the other specific emotional frustrations that women in general bear? Two U.S. studies, one at the University of Michigan and the other at the University of Washington, provide some insight. Neglect, condescension, unfaithfulness, physical or verbal abuse, sexual aggressiveness, and inconsideration were all listed as male characteristics that make women unhappy. By far the biggest concern had to do with the way men dealt with their own and their partners' emotions. Women complain that men are too emotionally constricted, too unwilling to work through emotional matters. Men typically seek action solutions — "You're unhappy, well what can we do about it?" — whereas women are frequently looking for an open discussion of the situation. Furthermore, men and women appear to have opposing views on the relationship between sexual intercourse and emotional intimacy. For women, physical lovemaking is part of the expression of love and intimacy. For men, women complain, sex is too often the necessary prerequisite for a time of emotional intimacy. Women also want to hear actual expressions of love and respect, which men too often take for granted. Other studies have documented the different bases of jealousy among men and women — a woman's jealousy is provoked more by an emotional attachment than by adultery, while it tends to be the opposite for men.[17]

That men and women largely live in two emotional solitudes — responsive, emotionally sensitive women and unresponsive, emotionally controlled men — is all part of the traditional package of sexually stereotyped behaviour. Some progress has been made, and many men today are much more emotionally open and responsive than their fathers and grandfathers were, but it is slow. A Gallup poll confirmed that men are more likely than women to see their spouses as romantic.[18] Women are more likely than men to see themselves as romantic. Men are more likely to forget birthdays and anniversaries and less likely to give gifts at times other than special occasions. Women are almost three times as likely as men to feel they do not receive enough attention from their mates. Women are less likely than men to see sex as important in their relationships and more likely to feel that the excitement has gone out of the relationship. Over twice as many women as men would not marry the same person again (11 in 100).

Single women may be statistically psychologically healthier than married women, but they are not necessarily more emotionally satisfied. Women marry, usually, for love, a desire to have children, and to construct a meaningful and fulfilling family life. But if the emotional consequences of marriage are difficult for women, those of marriage breakdown and divorce are even more so. For many women, divorce is not only an economic but also an emotional catastrophe.

Certainly divorce is not nearly as psychologically devastating for men and women as it is for children. But neither is it painless.[19] Rates of mental illness among divorced or separated adults are up to 20 times higher than among the married. Divorce and separation have been causally implicated in depression, suicide, homicide, alcoholism and increasing risks of various serious physical illnesses. Studies have found that both estranged partners, one year after separation, "feel anxious, depressed, rejected and alternate between anger and despair." Women suffer from these reactions more deeply and for a longer time. Divorced couples are afflicted by very ambivalent feelings about each other, but "the anger and resentment are sustained far longer in women than in men." The only significant psychological advantage women experience after divorce is that they tend to have a stronger network of support and that ultimately they tend to become more happy than men "with their post-divorce lives and suffer lower rates of mental illness than divorced men as a result."[20]

Single mothers and poor women experience the greatest risk of mental illness. And when a woman is both poor and a single parent, as is usually the case, the risks are that much greater. One study of 83 female single-parent families found that the psychological trauma of divorce, combined with the resulting economic hardship, seriously disrupted the women's ability to cope, dramatically lowered their self-esteem, and undermined their sources of social support.[21] Other studies report that the dire economic problems associated with female single-parent families seriously impair the mothers' relationships with the children. Further, such women often have problems just coping with routine domestic work and lead highly constricted social lives.

Upon remarriage — which happens to three of four divorced women — women's emotional problems do not end.[22] Balancing the new family is difficult, and women see such emotional relationships complicated by orchestrating their new husbands' relationships with his children from the previous marriage, her children from the previous marriage, and the joint children of the new marriage. The memory of the previous failures is inescapable. The children are suspicious, resentful, and resistant; both partners are uneasy and uncertain. Family boundaries are unclear because of the continuing obligations, both tangible and emotional. Economic problems are complex and full of conflict. Through all this the woman feels enormous stress to keep it all together. So do men. But men are more prone to "let things work themselves out." By their socialization and emotional training women are expected, and expect themselves, to work diligently to ensure success. And failure — which occurs very often in remarriage families — still tends to be blamed on the woman.

What is most striking about the emotional oppression of women in the context of the crisis of the family and the emergence of new family forms is that it has not lessened. Indeed, in some ways it has worsened. Whether it's earning that needed second income, or taking on the double burden, or trying to cajole a recalcitrant and perhaps bruised male to new insights and new behaviours, or repairing as far as possible a fractured family as a single parent, or walking an emotional tightrope as a remarriage wife and mother, women today bear an infinitely more complex emotional burden than their mothers and grandmothers. It is true that the emotional burdens of the traditional family always weighed heavily on women. Today that burden is composed of contradictory expectations, aspirations, and dreams. Before, a woman, a domestic and emotional slave in the home, knew what she had to do. Today that clarity and certainty are gone: she is to be her own person yet also the person of others; she is to slug it out on the job market yet also maintain a home and raise children; she is to be free yet encircled with marital and maternal obligations; she is to be equal and autonomous yet also be there whenever she is needed.

There is, however, one crucial difference. Today a woman has a choice, at least much more so than formerly. An unhappy marriage need no longer be endured endlessly. Lost dreams, surrendered hopes, and forever postponed happiness need no longer be embraced as endless "reality." But often, as women try to exercise this newly won choice, they face the final line of defence of a threatened patriarchy — physical and sexual oppression. Options and choices can only be exercised fully in the absence of a fear of consequences. Today many women fear the consequences of freely exercising their freedom to make choices. Many also suffer the consequences they feared. And often the consequences are fatal.

10 / The Physical and Sexual Oppression of Women

Violence against Women

The phenomenon of violence against women has dominated our front pages for three decades now. Apparently rising rates of wife abuse, of sexual assault, and of sexual harassment have provoked both widespread debate and deepening concern. Is it just that violence against women has come out of the family closet? Is it that women victims of non-family violence are laying more public complaints? Is it, in the context of the rise of feminism and women's assertiveness, that male patriarchy, threatened, defied, and frustrated, is lashing out more often? We will never know for certain. As John Boswell notes in his fine study of child abandonment in the premodern period, "Conjugal relations, reproduction, and the interior life of the family are, in fact, among the most reclusive and private aspects of human existence, jealously guarded from public view in most cultures, and less likely than almost any other interpersonal activity to leave written records."[1] And it is probably even more true that the darker aspects of "the interior life of the family" were among the least likely to find their way into the public record. Similarly, the true extent of non-family physical and sexual violence against women did not find its way into the public record because of the response of the community: disbelief; woman blaming (she asked for it); and if the case were proved, often rejection ("damaged goods"). Today women are more willing to come forward to lay complaints. Public agencies of order are more likely to take the charges seriously. And the attitudes of the community have changed considerably.

However, the underreporting of violent events against women persists. A report prepared for the Solicitor General found that 750,000 Canadian couples experienced one or more episodes of conjugal violence a year and that "domestic dispute" calls were the largest category of requests to police for help. Yet only 10 per cent of such events were recorded, and there were only two prosecutions for every 10,000 incidents. Forty to 70 per cent of all violent crimes in North America occur between people who are married or living as married, and only a fraction are reported.[2] A Secretary of State study by Linda MacLeod estimated that one in four women in Canada can anticipate being sexually assaulted at some time in her life, half before the age of 17,[3] and U.S. estimates are similar. An Alberta study found that one in nine women in a marriage or common-law liaison is subjected to abuse,[4] and the national estimate is that one in 10 married or common-law women can expect to be abused.[5] The 1981 Canadian Urban Victimization Survey, carried out by Statistics Canada, found that four in every 1,000 Canadian women, aged 16 years and over, were subjected to physical and/or sexual assault by a spouse or a former spouse, and only 44 per cent of these events were reported to the police.[6]

The 1993 Violence Against Women national survey found that 29 per cent of women who had ever been married or lived common-law — over 2.6 million Canadian women — had experienced physical and/or sexual assault by their husband. Twenty-two per cent of these, over 570,000 women, had never told anyone prior to disclosing it in confidence to the researcher. (This included 15 per cent of currently married or common-law women who reported suffering violence at the hands of their current spouses.) Only 26 per cent or 676,000 women had informed police. The same survey found that 4 per cent of Canadian women 18 years of age and over, about 42,000 women, had been physically and/or sexually assaulted by a stranger in the 12 months prior to the survey, and only 37 per cent of the physical assaults and 9 per cent of the sexual assaults were reported to police.[7] In 1980 rape was the fastest growing crime of violence in Canada. Eight years later, the Women's Legal Education and Action Fund claimed that sexual

violence against women had reached the status of a "national crisis,"[8] and in 1991 Gallup found that fully 22 per cent of Canadian
adults claimed personal awareness of the physical abuse of wives
by husbands.[9] Clearly, if all such events were acted upon through
our formal agencies of justice, Canada's criminal justice system
would be inundated by a tidal wave of cases having to do with
family and non-family violence against women. But this has not
happened. As the Metro Toronto Action Commission on Violence
against Women and Children declaimed:

> We see sexual violence tolerated by our institutions, celebrated by
> our media, excused by our criminal justice system and ignored by
> many in our governments.[10]

The fact is that violence against women is still not taken seriously by many. If found guilty of beating his spouse a man rarely
faces jail or a fine, usually receiving a suspended sentence or an
absolute or conditional discharge. Among the 56 per cent of women
reporting abuse in the 1981 Urban Victimization Survey, and who
did not report the event to police, most did not do so either because
they believed the police would do nothing or because they feared
future retribution. In 1993, 74 per cent of victims of wife assault did
not report the incident to police — half of these believed the incident to be too minor to report, the remainder were about evenly
divided among a variety of reasons: desire for privacy and to avoid
embarrassment; didn't want or need help; didn't believe the police
could do anything; fear of retribution; and anxiety about involvement with police and courts. Most reasons reflected a mistrust of
the system's ability to respond effectively and to provide future protection. This was realistic, since court orders restraining assaulting
husbands from contact with their victims, even in the most extreme
and violent cases, are "routinely violated without penalty."[11] As for
sexual assault, federal statistics suggest that the police are more
prone to refuse to take seriously a complaint of sexual assault than
any other kind of allegation of criminal wrongdoing.[12]

Reforms and changing government policies exerting pressure
for mandatory charges in cases of violence against women have

slowly improved the situation, especially regarding wife assault. In the early 1980s only 10 to 20 per cent of reported wife batterers were charged in Ontario. By 1987, 47 per cent were charged. In Metro Toronto the figure reached 61 per cent. Nationally in 1993, of the 26 per cent of cases of wife assault reported to police, only slightly more than one in four resulted in a charge being laid — and most of these (80 per cent) led to a court appearance for the offending husband. But punishment is still lenient, most cases resulted in probation and in those cases involving a jail sentence, the typical sentence was one day. Nevertheless, police/court intervention effectively stopped the violence in 45 per cent of cases.

Similarly, there have been efforts to improve the effectiveness of the system in dealing with cases of sexual assault. In 1983, Canada's old rape laws were replaced by new sexual assault laws, designed to make prosecutions easier by being more lenient regarding rules of evidence and by being less harsh on the victim. Victims less often find their sexual histories on trial, nor need the prosecution fulfill the formerly excessively strict evidentiary rules regarding corroboration. These reforms were strengthened by a clear "no means no" law in 1992, which clarified the rules regarding sexual consent. This did not, as many expected, lead to a massive movement of victims coming forward and appears to have resulted primarily in shorter sentences for offenders. There have been more convictions, but these have typically been for the less serious forms of sexual assault.[13]

One of the major problems is that many judges harbour traditional attitudes. Some seem to believe that rape by a man known to the woman is a less serious matter than rape by a stranger. A Dauphin, Manitoba, man received a six-month jail sentence and probation for a year when convicted of the extremely violent rape of his wife. An Ontario Supreme Court judge in one case remarked that a raped erotic dancer "was in a profession that promoted lust." A Sault Ste. Marie, Ontario, man convicted of a sexual assault, involving beating and raping a woman behind an arena, received a 90-day sentence to be served on weekends, despite the prosecution's request for a penitentiary term.[14] The judge felt that the man came from a good family, and had learned his lesson. As for the woman, a divorced single parent who had been followed by her rapist from her twenty-seventh birthday party in a hotel, the judge remarked that though the assault had been traumatic, it was of short duration. Then there was the Quebec Superior Court judge, who, annoyed that a woman who murdered her husband was only found guilty of second-degree murder, and that the jury had recommended parole eligibility after 10 years, commented that when women "decide to degrade themselves, they sink to depths to which even the vilest man could not sink" and imposed the maximum sentence of 14 years while berating the jury. Another Quebec judge sentenced a man for sodomizing his nine-year-old stepdaughter over a period of two-and-a-half years to 23 months in jail because the man had "spared the virginity" of the victim. The Quebec Court of Appeal reduced the sentence of a man convicted of sexually assaulting his teenage sister-in-law over a four-year period to 90 days to be served on weekends because he was "an asset to society." One Quebec judge commented that he would "not lose any sleep" if a woman victim of abuse was killed by her abusing common-law husband. A Cape Breton judge on one occasion commented during the sentencing of a man convicted of sexually assaulting three girls — two 15-year-olds and a 12-year-old — that "if these were 35-year-old women that the accused had done this to I might smile and throw this out of court." On another occasion the same judge sentenced a man to two years probation for forcing entry into his estranged wife's home, saying "I don't know ... whether it's your own fault or you happen to have a very sensitive mate who was easily rattled." Two weeks later the man was charged with murdering his former girlfriend.[15]

Women frequently do not fare much better in cases involving family violence. The Alberta Crime Compensation Board found that a 24-year-old woman was 25 per cent responsible for the beating she received from her former boyfriend because she went to his house to collect a debt despite her knowledge that he tended to be violent.[16] And in the family violence trial that probably received the most media attention in Canada's history, Kirby Inwood received 30 days in jail after his conviction for assaulting both his Russian wife, Tatyana Sidorova, and their one-year-old baby.[17] The judge felt that Inwood should not be made the scapegoat for Canada's family violence problems. Such selective illustrations suggest that the old pattern of woman-blaming and man-coddling continues even when dealing with events of serious violence.

Troublesome attitudes about violence against women remain deeply held. A survey of 245 women and 194 men at Washington State University found that 5 per cent of the women and 19 per cent of the men did not believe that forced sexual intercourse on a date is definitely rape or that the man's behaviour in such a situation is "definitely unacceptable."[18] It is not therefore surprising that a survey of women students at Cornell University found that almost one in five "had intercourse against their will ... through coercion, threats, force or violence." A survey of 1,700 Rhode Island students in grades six to nine seemed to suggest the situation may even be worsening. One in four boys, and one in six girls, said it was "acceptable for a man to force a woman to have sexual relations if he has spent money on her."[19] The researcher commented, "Basically, the kids were very much into blaming the victim of sexual assault." Among the survey's findings: one-half of the students believed that "a woman who walks alone at night and dresses seductively is asking to be raped; ... 65 per cent of the boys and 57 per cent of the girls in grades seven through nine said it is acceptable for a man to force a woman to have sexual intercourse if they have been dating for more than six months; 87 per cent of the boys and 79 per cent of the girls said rape is acceptable if a couple is married." Two Quebec City studies of adolescents found that 54 per cent of girls in one, and 33 per cent of girls in the other, had experienced sexual violence.[20] The prevalence of such behaviours and attitudes helps us understand why a Queen's University student council's anti-rape campaign around the slogan "No Means No" was responded to by some men at the university with slogans like, "No Means More Beer," "No Means Harder," "No Means Kick Her in the Teeth," and "No Means She's a Dyke."

Sexual Harassment

A related, but considerably less serious, manifestation of the physical and sexual oppression of women is sexual harassment, particularly in the workplace and other public places. A 1983 survey by the Canadian Human Rights Commission reported that 1.2 million women faced forms of sexual harassment at their places of work. Ten years later Statistics Canada found that 6 per cent of working women — almost 400,000 women — had experienced sexual harassment at work in the previous 12 months.[21] A 1991 Gallup poll found that more than three in 10 adult Canadians are personally aware of instances of sexual harassment that either happened to them or to someone they knew.

Sexual harassment does not just include unwanted sexual attention and overtures, though that is its most common form. It also includes "any unwelcome [sexual] action, whether verbal or physical, that humiliates, insults or degrades."[22] In 1993, the study by Statistics Canada's Holly Johnson found that sexual harassment included inappropriate remarks about bodies and sex life (77 per cent); a man leaning close over them unnecessarily (73 per cent); a man repeatedly asking for a date (50 per cent); and threats of negative job consequences including possible dismissal if sexual favours were not granted (18 per cent). It happens to women in the lowest service jobs and in the highest-paid professions. It can be expressed crudely or in highly subtle ways. But it all adds up, in the words of the Canadian Bar Association's Committee on Women's Issues, to the same thing: "some men apparently continue to have problems separating the image of women as romantic possibilities from the reality of women as professionals." It can involve betting on how a female co-worker will react to having her breast pinched.[23] Or leaving doors off toilet stalls. Or sexist jokes. Or touching, bum patting, and sexual molestation.

A most extreme form occurred in the New York jail system where some female corrections officers were not only subjected to the typical forms of sexual harassment by their supervisors — dirty phone calls and offers of promotion for sexual favours — but were told, when they became pregnant, to get abortions or resign their jobs.

Again, like the more extreme forms of women's oppression, sexual harassment in the workplace is coming more into public view as a result of changes in human rights laws and important precedent-making arbitration and human rights commission decisions, which have encouraged women to come forward with complaints. And both union and management frequently have moved to establish policies and procedures to protect victims who complain and to ensure such complaints are taken seriously and acted upon fairly.

Sexual harassment in other public places continues, affected only by public disapproval. Sexual harassment can be worse for women on the streets and in the shopping malls. Sexual ogling and comments by passers-by, suggestive body language, and facial gestures are all constant backdrops for women when they are out in public. Only rarely can a woman take meaningful action. As one woman journalist put it,

> Women know what it's like to have to walk past a crowd of teen-agers after dark and try to ignore their jeers and threats.
>
> Women know what it's like to have total strangers comment on their physical appearance or stare at their breasts before bother-ing to meet their eyes — if they bother at all.
>
> Women know what it's like to face this day after day ... the small, daily indignities that degrade us — and degrade all men who perpetuate them.[24]

It is important to reflect upon the typical role of violence and harassment in the history of human affairs. They are used to con-trol the behaviour of others through fear, retribution, and example. Violence punishes those who break or resist the established rules of power and privilege and alerts them to the consequences of contin-ued resistance. Public violence against members of an oppressed group has a demonstration effect, warning through graphic exam-ple what can be expected. We find this easy to understand, if not accept, when dealing with violence between racial, economic, national, or religious groups, or with the application of legitimate violence by the state. Both critics and defenders of such violence understand why it occurs.

When feminist and other social theorists make similar arguments about the nature of violence against women, many are uneasy. They regard it as outrageous that male violence against women is a systematic effort of a patriarchal society to defend male privilege and to keep women contained and controlled. Where are the meetings where men as a power group make such policy decisions? Where are the documents to validate such claims? Of course, there are none. And most men are deeply offended by violence against women and are hurt by suggestions that violence against women is a male campaign to suppress them. Perhaps we would all like to believe that these violent acts are perpetrated by deranged individuals. Yet experts tell us again and again that rape, and other sexual assaults, are more acts of violence and domination than sexual acts. The same is true for family violence. We determinedly seek individual pathological explanations, all of which are certainly pertinent, while overlooking the larger structural issues, the persistent patterns that refuse to go away.

One lawyer has argued that sexual harassment in the workplace is part of the social oppression of women. As one of the ways in which women are kept in their subordinate place, the lawyer drew an analogy to racial harassment.[25] Most white people deplore it when white supremacists attack black or native people. But the attacks occur and take their toll, not only among the particular victims, but among all blacks and natives as they experience fear and hesitation in living and working at ease in the world.

Clear Evidence

Certainly there is clear evidence that violence against women has engendered fear among many, perhaps most, women. A Victimization Survey of 61,000 residents 16 years of age and older in seven major Canadian cities, carried out for the Solicitor General's office, found that Canadian men are almost twice as likely as women to face violent crimes, yet women are much more fearful of violence.[26] This fear results from the nature of the violent crimes women face — sexual assault and personal theft. In *The City for Women: No*

Safe Place, Linda MacLeod reports that 56 per cent of women do not feel safe and secure when walking alone after sunset in their own neighbourhoods. Gallup routinely and annually asks women if they are afraid to walk at night in their neighbourhoods, and close to half answer 'yes' each year (from a low of 42 per cent in 1997 to a high of 56 per cent in 1991).[27] Women experience fears serious enough to lead to self-imposed restrictions on their own and their children's lives. Women who experience repeated battering by their husbands often claim that it was the fear of their husbands and the potential public shame that kept them silent victims in abusive relationships. Rape victims are often fearful, depressed, and unable to work as effectively; they feel vulnerability, humiliation, and a profound loss of control. Even some wife batterers concede the purpose of violence against women: "We've [men] been raised in a society that teaches us we're expected to have power and authority and be served by women. When those expectations are either denied or frustrated, we will use violence to regain control."[28] Therefore it is safe to conclude that one of the consequences of violence against women is that women are more likely to be fearful, controlled, and restrained in their behaviour.

The whole debate about violence against women — its sources and its consequences — was horribly crystallized on 6 December 1989 by the bloody and tragic events at L'École Polytechnique de Montréal.[29] Shortly after 5:00 p.m. Marc Lépine, 25, armed with a .223 calibre semi-automatic rifle and two 30-clip magazines of ammunition, entered the engineering school affiliated with the Université de Montréal. Twenty minutes later he had roamed three floors of the building, killing 14 women, most with shots to the head, wounding 13 other men and women, until he ended his massacre by committing suicide near the bodies of his final four victims on the third floor. Lépine's actions were cold and calculated — at the first classroom he entered he separated men from women, ordered the men out of the room, and began methodically shooting the women. Witnesses heard him say, "You are all a bunch of feminists. I hate feminists" ("Vous êtes toutes une bande de féministes. J'haïs les féministes."). When asked what he was doing he replied, "I am fighting feminists" ("Je lutte contre les féministes"). Police found a three-page letter on Lépine's body that characterized his act as a political gesture ("un geste politique") against feminists, whom he accused of ruining his life. The letter also contained a list of the names of 19 prominent and successful women in Quebec society.

In the aftermath, considerable effort was made to avoid the sexual politics of the tragedy. Violette Trépanier, Quebec's minister responsible for the status of women, characterized it as "a completely isolated act" ("un geste complètement isolé"); Claude Ryan, minister of education, called it "a tragic event everyone was powerless to prevent" ("un fait tragique contre lequel on ne peut plus rien"). Others suggested it was the act of a deranged individual. Still others insisted it was merely another reflection of the growing general problem of violence in our society. The late Barbara Frum of CBC's *The Journal* almost pleaded with commentators that the event could not possibly best be seen as a deliberate act of political violence against non-traditional women and a violent gesture against feminism.

Many such reactions were understandable, and some were even accurate. It was, thankfully, an isolated event. By any reasonable standard, Lépine was deranged, at least temporarily. And yes, violence is escalating in our society. But Lépine did not just shoot people at random, nor did he just shoot women at random. He deliberately chose to shoot women engineering students. It was an act of deliberate mass murder of non-traditional women for the sole reason that they were non-traditional and symbolized feminism, which Lépine felt was his scourge and nemesis.

Although sketchy, some of the details of Lépine's life are disturbingly suggestive: an emotionally scarred product of a broken home where family violence led to family breakdown; a failure in his relationships with women; a difficulty in forming close friendships with men; a familiarity with firearms and a recognized expertise as a marksman; a chronic failure in most things he tried; unrealistic aspirations. We will probably never know the full details of his psychosocial chemistry, but we do know that before his suicide he was determined to make "un geste politique … contre les féministes."

Those who still believe that this was just the isolated act of a madman should reflect on the subsequent comments of Tyler Benson, a prominent anti-choice and anti-feminist activist in Regina.

> Violence against women is dramatically increasing in direct proportion to the success of the feminist movement in destroying the traditional family unit and values generated within that unit. If we are to eliminate such violence, we have to acknowledge the frustration, anger and hate generated by the things feminists do ...
>
> Feminists are advocating a lawless society ... the safety of women depends on how successful we are at destroying the feminist movement ...
>
> The Quebec incident was just the beginning of the backlash against feminism. Very few, I am sure, will resort to such violent methods, but there will, from time to time, be someone unable to express the agony and hate they experience in any other way.
>
> Many innocent people will get hurt in the process, but there is a war going on.[30]

There it is. Feminists are destroying the family and engendering "frustration, anger and hate." They advocate lawlessness. They must be destroyed. "There is a war going on." Extreme misogynists who perhaps secretly applaud Lépine's rage against feminists, if not his actions, can find further inspiration in the public utterances of people like Tyler Benson.

Violence and the Changing Family

This work cannot deal extensively and completely with the wider problem of violence against women in contemporary society. But we must turn our attention to family violence as it affects women and how part of the price women are paying for changing family forms is the increased risk of being abused, beaten, and murdered within the family. We do know that the tendency to seek violent solutions to problems is typically first confronted and learned in violent families. Most concede that wife beating was a fairly common event in the past, but I suspect that the factors that shape the risk of women being beaten have changed considerably. Perhaps women who were beaten in the past were put at greater risk when they defied patriarchal authority, when their husbands came home angry and stressed and perhaps drunk, or when they didn't serve their husbands with the alacrity expected. Such themes recur in old movies, novels, and plays. However, we now know more about the extent of family violence against women and the factors that put certain women more at risk and that make certain men more prone to use violence against their spouses.[31]

First, the extent. Both of Linda MacLeod's studies on wife battering (1980 and 1987) estimate that about one in 10 women in Canada who is married, or lives as married, is battered each year. Based on a survey of various studies, she claims this is a very conservative estimate.[32] A 1986 Alberta study put the figure at one in nine, and the 1982 Canadian Urban Victimization Survey (CUVS), carried out by Statistics Canada and the Solicitor General's office, found that four in every 1,000 women aged 16 and over suffered physical or sexual assault by a spouse or former spouse.[33] The discrepancy is probably the result of MacLeod's wide definition of wife battering as involving physical and sexual, as well as psychological and verbal, abuse. The CUVS study included only actual assaults and excluded all those assaults carried out by male friends or partners the victim did not describe as a spouse or ex-spouse. On the other hand, a 1986 survey of Canadian men aged 18 and over, carried out to assure anonymity, found that 12 in 100 men admitted to using physical violence against their spouses or girlfriends.

Overall, 12% of men reported that they had pushed, grabbed, or shoved their mates at least once during the previous year, and in two-thirds of these cases, the incidents had occurred more than once. Another 9% reported they had thrown an object at a mate.

Rates of more serious types of violence were lower: 6% reported kicking, biting, or hitting with a fist, 5% reported slapping, and 5% said they had hit with an object or had attempted to do so. Fewer than 3% reported beating their mates, while less than 1% claimed to have either threatened to use or actually used a knife or gun.[34]

Lest the small percentages deceive the reader, it should be noted that in 1986 there were over 9.1 million men in Canada aged 18 years and older. This means that almost 1.1 million men used forms of physical violence against their romantic partners in 1986, including 80 to 90,000 who threatened to use, or actually used, a knife or gun. This suggests that MacLeod's one million battered wives figure may be an underestimate since she includes psychological abuse. The male violence survey included only physical abuse. The survey also found that 18 per cent of married men — or over 1.1 million men — engaged in at least one in a list of eight violent acts. Further, 10 per cent of married men — or about 630,000 — committed at least one of the five most serious violent acts which carry "a high risk of serious injury."

The more complete 1993 Violence Against Women (VAW) survey provides data that indicate that the frequency of wife assault is escalating despite all our efforts. Responding to critics of previous surveys regarding the wide definition of wife abuse, the VAW survey on wife assault used strict Criminal Code definitions of assault and sexual assault. Fully 29 per cent of "ever married" (including common law) women 18 years and older have been assaulted by their spouses (over 3 million women), including 15 per cent who have been assaulted by their present partner (1.6 million women), and 3 per cent who were assaulted by their present spouse in the 12 months prior to the survey (315,000 women). If emotional/psychological abuse were included, the numbers increase substantially to over one in three married or ever married women who has suffered physical/sexual and/or emotional abuse at the hands of their spouses. The assaults included: threats to strike with an object (19 per cent); thrown objects (11 per cent); pushing, grabbing, and shoving (25 per cent); slapping (15 per cent); kicking, biting, or hitting with a fist (11 per cent); hitting with an object (6 per cent); beatings (9 per cent); chokings (7 per cent); threats to use or the use of a knife or gun (5 per cent); and sexual assault (8 per cent). In 40 per cent of cases, medical help was required, and in 50 per cent of cases the woman had to take time off regular activities in order to recover. In two-thirds of cases the assault happened more than once, and in many cases, especially in relationships that had ended, the assaults continued and frequently worsened.[35]

Suffice it to say, then, that wife battering is very widespread. When Canada had 71 transition homes for battered women in 1979, they were almost always full and had to turn women away. In 1993, when Canada had 371 such shelters, again they were virtually always full, and it is estimated that one woman was turned away for every one that gained entry. The 86,000 women who gained entry to such homes in 1992–93 represented only 13 per cent of the total who left home because of domestic violence.[36] There is no reason not to believe that the need will more than fill any foreseeable expansion of emergency shelter and support programs.

The nature of wife battering runs the whole gamut of violent, degrading, and abusive actions and words. Beatings with fists, feet, and weapons; bitings; scaldings and burnings; rape and sexual degradation of unspeakable kinds are all part of the pattern. Psychological abuse, belittling, and terrorization that frightens, controls, and degrades are also common. Indeed, frequently episodes of physical and sexual abuse and psychological terrorism alternate, increasing the victim's fear and uncertainty. An important point is that wife battering and abuse is ongoing, repetitive, and persistent. MacLeod attempts an encompassing definition:

> Wife battering is the loss of dignity, control, and safety as well as the feeling of powerlessness and entrapment experienced by women who are the direct victims of *ongoing or repeated* physical, psychological, economic, sexual and/or verbal violence or who are subjected to *persistent* threats or the witnessing of such violence against their children, other relatives, friends, pets and/or cherished possessions, by their boyfriends, husbands, live-in lovers, ex-husbands or ex-lovers.[37]

Its long-term psychological effects can destroy a woman's self-esteem, fostering feelings of self-hatred, leading to an increasing withdrawal from contacts outside the home, and often resulting in the overuse of drugs and alcohol. The batterer seeks to control through an insidious process involving the systematic dismantling of the victim's autonomous personality.

The short-term physical effects can be serious as well: bruises; cuts; concussions; burns; wounds; and broken bones. In the CUVS study cited above, 75 per cent of incidents of wife abuse were acts of physical violence: one in three caused injury serious enough to require medical attention. In 1993, four in ten cases of wife assault led to medical intervention, and in almost half of the cases the women feared for their lives. Wife battering can also lead to death. About 40 per cent of homicides in Canada involve victims and suspects in a domestic relationship; and in over half of the cases there was a known history of domestic violence. The most common type of domestic murder is that of men killing their legal or common-law wives. McMaster University researchers Margo Wilson and Martin Daly studied spousal homicides in Canada from 1974 to 1992 and found that over three times as many husbands kill wives as wives kill husbands (1435 versus 451), and that 76 per cent of spousal homicide victims are women. A woman is nine times more likely to be killed by her husband than by a stranger. Often, the husband kills the wife and the children of the union at the same time — familicide occurred in 65 cases between 1974 and 1992 involving 172 victims. In 94 per cent of the cases of familicide the husband/father was their murderer.[38]

Wife battering can also lead to another kind of murder, the murder by the victim of her assailant — her spouse. Just as in the case of physical assaults against husbands, women who murder their husbands typically do so in desperation after years of sustained, life-threatening battering. Wilson and Daly report that 1991 and 1992 police data reveal that the victim was the first to use, or to threaten to use, violence in 52 per cent of the husband-victim, and only 6 per cent of the wife-victim murders.[39] Two widely publicized cases of the murder of the husband helped spotlight the horrors of wife battering, increased public awareness, and set important legal precedents that for the first time help to protect victims of battering from first-degree murder convictions.

On 9 March 1977 in Dansville, Michigan, Francine Hughes, 30, poured gasoline around the bed containing her sleeping husband, Mickey Hughes, set it on fire, loaded her three children into the car and drove to the Ingram County Sheriff Department.[40] She was charged with first-degree murder and felony murder. Had the death occurred just a few years earlier, Francine Hughes would probably have been routinely convicted of murder. On the day of Mickey Hughes' death, he had repeatedly beaten Francine with his fists, terrorized the children, spilled food and garbage all over the floor and forced her to clean it up, smeared food on her face and back and in her hair, torn up her business college school books and forced her to burn them, threatened to smash up her car so she couldn't go to school anymore, ordered her to fix him a meal, and finally forced her to have sexual intercourse with him before falling into a semi-drunken sleep.

At the trial, the jurors and the public were subjected to the sordid details of her 12 years of brutalization at the hands of Mickey Hughes, and her repeated but always unsuccessful efforts to get help from the authorities, police and prosecutors, even on the day of the death. At the conclusion of the trial, the prosecution claimed that Francine Hughes had deliberately murdered her husband with premeditation. The defence argued that she had suffered a bout of temporary insanity as a result of the years of abuse and further that she acted in self-defence "against an evil force that was threatening her life." After five hours of deliberation, the jury returned a verdict of "not guilty — by reason of temporary insanity."[41]

The Canadian case was similar. In Queen's County, Nova Scotia, late on 11 March, or in the early morning hours of 12 March 1982, Jane Stafford, 33, killed her common-law husband Billy Stafford with the discharge of a 12-gauge shotgun.[42] After a day of drinking, Billy Stafford had passed out in his pick-up truck, but only after subjecting Jane to another day in six years of abuse, culminating in threats to kill a good friend of hers and her son by a previous marriage. Jane Stafford was charged with first-degree murder.

After hearing the testimony, and the defence arguments for a manslaughter verdict as well as the prosecution's contention that the murder was planned, deliberate, and without provocation, the jury reached a verdict of "not guilty." The prosecution, the defence lawyer, the whole courtroom was stunned — no one had expected a not guilty verdict. Many were elated, but others were disturbed that it was a mandate for beaten women to take justice into their own hands. (Just weeks after Jane Stafford's acquittal, a woman in New Brunswick shot and killed her battering husband. The jury took just over an hour to find her not guilty.) The Crown successfully appealed, and a new trial was ordered. This time the Crown prosecutor accepted the formerly rejected offer of a guilty plea to a manslaughter charge. After sentencing arguments, the judge sentenced Jane Stafford to six months in jail and two years' probation.

Experts claim that these two cases are not all that unusual as serious battering cases go. We know about these cases because of two widely reported, sensational trials that reached unexpected verdicts, verdicts that caused the judicial system and the whole community to take stock.

Because these cases received enormous attention, they, and others like them, contributed to improvements in attitudes and policies affecting cases of battering. But they did more. Together with the fine work of people working in the area, they told us something about the complexity of the phenomenon. Both men engaged in cruel and unspeakable brutalities against their wives and children. They were among the most sadistic of wife and child abusers. Yet their wives loved them, at least at first, and did everything they could to salvage the marriage and the family — including risking their very lives for an extended period of years. Why? What motivates such women? What provokes abuse? What increases the risk of abuse, and of spousal homicide? What motivates the abuser? What kind of men abuse? Why? Are there discernible risk factors?

As with child abuse, there is a widespread reluctance to seek explanations of wife battering in theories of economic stress or social class. However, the evidence from transition homes is clear: battered women tend to come from poor, economically stressed families, and the men who batter them tend to be poorly paid and only irregularly employed. MacLeod's study of battered women in Canadian transition homes in 1985 is revealing.[43] They tended to be poor and young, with an average of two young children. Three in four lived in serious poverty. Only one in five worked outside the home, and those who did tended to be in low-paying jobs. If they left their husbands, a bad economic situation would have become catastrophic. Seven in 10 had not finished high school. They often stayed with their batterers because they felt sorry for them, believing that without the relationship the battering men would have nothing left and that the men were somehow psychologically sick. Only 38 per cent of the batterers worked regularly — the others were chronically un- or underemployed. Of those who worked regularly, almost six in 10 worked in unskilled, labouring sorts of jobs. Over six in 10 had not finished high school.

Back in 1980, faced with similar patterns, MacLeod was adamant: "wife battering is just as common in middle- and upper-class homes."[44] But in 1987, having presented even stronger data on class and poverty factors, she was more tentative in her suggestions that battering occurs equally among all class and poverty groups. Her data are derived from battered women who sought the help of transition homes. Other than impressions on the part of transition home workers that many of the anonymous calls for advice come from middle- and upper-class women, there just aren't hard data to tell us clearly the extent of battering in less economically distressed families.

There are, however, other studies based on samples drawn from the population at large that provide us with some data on the risk factors associated with wife battering. The 1986 University of Alberta study was able to establish some clear risk factors.[45] It found that one in nine married or common-law wives suffered from abuse at the hands of their husbands. Also suggesting that wife battering is more extensive than is believed, the study found that 46 per cent of those surveyed knew of cases of physical or psychological abuse. (This compares to the Gallup figure of 22 per cent for physical abuse.) The highest rate by age, about one in five, occurred among younger women aged 18 to 34 years. Recently separated wives suffered rates of physical violence of about 55 per cent, while recently divorced wives suffered rates of almost 44 per cent. Lower-income households reported almost twice the rate (13.8 per cent) reported by upper-income households (7.5 per cent). The 1981 Canadian Urban Victimization Survey, which surveyed 61,000 people in seven cities and identified 11,000 incidents of physical and/or sexual assaults of wives, reported a similar set of risk factors.[46] The data reveal that separated women suffer a rate of abuse of almost *28 times* that of married women, while divorced women suffer at a rate *9 times* that of married women. As well, women in low-income families suffer a rate of abuse of over *3 times* that suffered by women in higher-income families. Women in moderate-income families experience only slightly lower rates than those in lower-income families. The male domestic violence survey in 1986 suggests similar risk factors.[47] Divorced or separated men were over one-and-one-half times as likely to use physical violence against their wives as married men. The rate of wife abuse among poorer men was *twice* that among better-off men. Younger men are more likely to use violence against their wives than older men — over one in two males admitting domestic violence was 29 years old or younger. Finally, among men aged 18 to 44, those with less education (incomplete high school) showed much higher rates of wife abuse than those with a graduate or professional degree. Interestingly, among men aged 45 years or older the highest rate was found among those with an unfinished university degree.

The 1993 Violence Against Women survey on wife assault also found clear risk factors — women in newer marriages are at most risk; young wives face four times the risk of older wives; women in low-income households are at twice the risk; women living with unemployed men are more at risk; women who become pregnant are at greater risk, as are those with disabilities; women who have ended a relationship, or are contemplating ending a relationship are at more risk — and frequency and severity of the violence often escalates in such circumstances. The male domestic violence survey also found evidence of a clear relationship between economic stress and wife abuse. The respondents were presented with a list of events that they might have experienced in the previous five years. These included: "unemployment for more than one month; personal bankruptcy; a drop in wage or salary; taking an additional job to make ends meet; child support or alimony payments that he did not have before; a move to less expensive accommodations; taking in a boarder to help make ends meet; one or more demotions; loss of income due to a return to school; some other important career setback; some other significant negative change in economic circumstances." The rate of wife abuse was lowest (eight in 100) among men who claimed to have experienced none, or only one, of the events (the overall rate was 12 in 100). Among men afflicted by two or three of the events, the rate of abuse rose to 18 in 100; for those facing four or five of the events, to 19 in 100; and for those facing six or seven of the events, to 33 in 100 — over four times the lowest rate.

Similar risk factors can be found in patterns of spousal homicide. The study by McMaster University psychologists Martin Daly and Margo Wilson suggested that family homicide emerges in the context of a sexual struggle in which the male attempts to dominate his wife, and the woman tries to minimize or resist that control.[48] The psychologists noted some significant risk factors. Women are most at risk of murder by their husbands when they attempt to end the relationship. They also found that very young wives face a higher risk of murder by their husbands — teenage wives suffer triple the risk of murder of older wives. Statistics Canada figures also confirm some of these patterns.[49] A survey of 1995 homicides notes that separated and divorced people are overrepresented, both as victims and suspects. In 1995 such people made up 6 per cent of the population, but 17 per cent of the victims, and 12 per cent of the suspects, of homicide. Over 60 per cent of all female victims of homicide in 1995 were killed by a husband or lover in a domestic relationship (this contrasts with just over 24 per cent of all male victims). In 1995, six in 10 spousal homicides involved a history of continuing domestic violence known to police. Although there aren't clear class and income indicators, Professor Chimbo's earlier study of 34 spouse murderers suggested they tended to come from "the lower socio-economic stratum."[50]

Murder/Suicide

Three family homicide cases exhibit many of these risk elements. On Saturday, 23 December 1989 in Drayton Valley, Alberta, Trevor Samuel, a 33-year-old school caretaker, stabbed to death his wife Cindy, 23, and their two daughters, Brittany, four and Erica, six, before taking his own life.[51] The couple had been married for five years, during which Trevor battered Cindy regularly. A good friend of Cindy's reported that Trevor had a "maniacal obsession with controlling his wife" and had threatened her, "I'll kill you and the kids if you ever leave me." The friend believes Cindy had finally decided definitely to end the relationship the night before her death and her husband "couldn't handle that."

On Monday, 18 September 1989 in Bridgewater, Nova Scotia, Darrell Lowe, 23, shot and killed his estranged common-law wife, Gail Naugler, 34, on the school bus she drove, and then fatally shot himself.[52] Just the week before the murder/suicide, Lowe had been charged with threatening to shoot Naugler and her children, but was released after a promise to stay away from them and not to possess firearms, and was scheduled to appear in court to answer the charge on 27 September 1989. Apparently the relationship had been stormy and Naugler had left Lowe just a month before her death.

On Sunday, 13 April 1997 in Orangeville, Ontario, Ludvik Kirec, 37, shot and killed his estranged wife Helen, 36, and their four children, Ludvik, 15, Christopher, 14, Suzy, 12, and Nancy, 11, before setting the house on fire and turning the shotgun on himself. The couple were one week short of their seventeenth anniversary. Ludvik's formerly successful general contracting business in Toronto had failed in 1990, and in 1991 the family moved to Orangeville where they lived in social isolation from the local community. But for odd jobs, Ludvik remained unemployed and the family became dependent on Helen's work as a waitress, first at a local restaurant and then at a Tim Horton's. About six weeks before the murders/suicide, Helen was promoted to manager and took the four children with her to the local shelter for abused women. On 12 April she agreed to a sleepover for the kids at the father's. The next day she went, despite fears expressed to the staff at the shelter, to talk with the husband at his request. What then happened between them will never be known, but the forensic evidence suggests Ludvik deliberately and relentlessly pursued each family member into different rooms and killed each with a shotgun blast to the chest.[53] Many of the typical risk elements were clearly present in all three cases, and in each the actual murder/suicide appears to have been provoked by the decision taken by the woman to leave the relationship.

What, then, can we conclude about violence against women within the family? Those families with lower incomes are at substantially greater risk. Men in lower-income groups, and/or experiencing greater levels of economic stress, are more likely to engage in wife abuse. Men with less education are more likely to engage in abuse than men with more education. Finally, rates of family violence against women tend to be much higher among those women about to end a relationship or who have recently ended it. Regarding this last factor, of course, we don't know if the move to separation and divorce is a cause or a consequence of violence. But we do know that when abused women do begin to show signs of assertiveness, when they begin to make moves toward independence, or when they threaten to leave, the violence escalates tremendously in intensity and frequency, and sometimes escalates to murder.

Clearly these larger social and economic epidemiological patterns of risk have to be related to particular psychosocial profiles of men who batter. The data from MacLeod's study suggest that the battering husbands of women who sought refuge in transition homes were, on the whole, a rather pathetic group — even their victims believed that their lives would be nothing without their wives and kids, whom they abused. High estimated rates of alcohol and drug abuse, high rates of criminal conviction, low rates of regular work — all suggest that these are largely men with seriously flawed personalities, a poor and underdeveloped capacity to cope with their lives, and a tendency to live multi-problem lives. Further, their proneness to use violence is symptomatic of their general inability to cope effectively with life and even its routine difficulties. Perhaps their sense of failure in the context of traditional patriarchal expectations to succeed makes them more likely to target their wives and children for abuse.

Doug Scott has tried to demonstrate the diversity of men who batter, based on a study of battered women who sought refuge at Regina's Transition House.[54] While recognizing that there was a great deal of overlap among the categories, he found nine themes that seemed to capture different "types" of battering and the "social forces" at work.

> Certainly patriarchy is prominent among the forces which promote male violence in the home. However, the association between patriarchy and battering appears more complicated than is commonly assumed. Only three of the factors could be construed as representing the type of "secure," "rational," or "instrumental" violence characteristic of feminist portrayals of battering. Several of the factors suggested that, although the relationships may have contained elements of patriarchal organization, the violence itself was more directly associated with other aspects of the men's situations, including: depression and alcohol dependency, severe loneliness, or insecurity and paranoia. Moreover, even violence which appeared to express "secure patriarchal dominance" was not all of one type. In this analysis, such violence took the form of "disinterested cruelty," "machismo," and "calculated domination."[55]

Scott also found an association between class and battering. Among middle class batterers, stress "related to incongruities between ... the men's 'status expectations' ... and their actual 'status experiences'" appeared to be a factor. Among blue-collar workers, battering seemed more associated with "a form of 'retaliation' ... for what they perceive to be attacks on their self-worth or 'maleness.'" Overall, Scott's work suggests that although the patriarchal context and the effort by men to control women are central features of violence against women within the family, only certain kinds of deeply flawed men feel it necessary to use violence to confirm their significance in the world.[56]

How has the crisis of the family and the emergence of changing family forms contributed to the risk of violence? Many of the risk factors are clearly related to the family's crisis. The traditional one-earner, male "breadwinner" family is in serious economic trouble. Such men find it difficult to "deliver the goods," and they face increasingly stiff competition from growing numbers of women in the labour force. This can only increase the kinds of stresses that the male domestic violence survey found were related to wife assault. Women are increasingly assertive, making control and domination by traditional patriarchal men more difficult. Women are seeking separation and divorce more often, and there's a clear relationship between the risk of wife assault and efforts by women to end relationships. And women have more choices today.

Whether or not violence against women within the family is more extensive today than in the past is finally really irrelevant. Since in the past it was part of the hidden "interior life of the family," it was not a contentious public issue. Today, the context in which violence against women within the family occurs has clearly changed. The public spotlight on violence against women gives the phenomenon, politically speaking, the same impact it would have had, had it suddenly increased.

The economic, domestic, emotional, and physical burdens women bear for the sake of the family are enormous. For the sake of sustaining the family, women make great sacrifices, renounce many hopes and aspirations, and often confront continuing abuse. And, when the family breaks down, women bear the lion's share of that burden as well. But women's fate — and that of children — has always been largely tied to the family. And it was, in retrospect, inevitable that the growing liberation of women would finally have to be resolved in a significant structural transformation of the family. So far, we've tried to document the costs and consequences of those structural changes for children and women. But men pay a price as well. Certainly the changes are less costly and the burdens less onerous than they are for children and women, but neither are they entirely without pain and difficulty. While we might not wish to weep copious amounts of tears as we contemplate the plight of the deposed patriarch, we must nevertheless try to understand his plight. There is a special sad poignancy about an emperor who has not only lost his throne, but whose former subjects, pity having replaced fear and respect, look upon him, not without affection, as a historical curiosity.

PART IV

Victims of the Crisis: Men

"Arguments that masculinity should change often come to grief, not on counter-arguments against reform, but on the belief that men cannot *change, so it is futile or even dangerous to try. Mass culture generally assumes there is a fixed, true masculinity beneath the ebb and flow of daily life. We hear of 'real men,' 'natural man,' the 'deep masculine.' This idea is now shared across an impressive spectrum including the mythopoetic men's movement, Jungian psychoanalysts, Christian fundamentalists, sociobiologists and the essentialist school of feminism."*

R.W. Connell, *Masculinities*
(Berkeley: University of California,) 1995, p. 45.

Introduction: Elusive Masculinity and Patriarchy

Men remain the clear beneficiaries of patriarchal social structures. Such structures bestow great powers and privileges on them: social, political, economic, and psychological. The control of economic resources, of instruments of political power, and of women and children, allowed men, even the lowliest of men, degrees of autonomy, self-determination, and self-indulgence that went far beyond even the wildest imaginings of women. During the last two centuries, a slow dismantling of structures of patriarchal privilege has resulted in the growing emancipation of women. Women's gains were not given freely by men, and as each enhanced women's power over themselves, it diminished men's control over them. At each step women met general male resistance, followed by a slow erosion of male unity as they were confronted with their own hypocrisy and contradictions, hurried by rapid social and economic changes that made women's liberation not only feasible but structurally necessary.

It may be true, as Simone de Beauvoir argued in 1949, that "the males find in women more complicity than the oppressor usually finds in the oppressed."[1] But it is equally true that few oppressed groups have had the lobbying privilege of sharing the bed and home of the oppressor; of being his obsessional object of love, even when such love was paternalistic; and of raising his children in a union that gave to the oppressor a significant portion of his sense of meaning and purpose in life. The continuing fact of woman's oppression and the slowness that has characterized her transcendence of that oppression cannot be easily separated from a degree of complicity on the part of the oppressed or from the complex links of affection that intimately bound oppressed and oppressor together. The complicity of women and the final willingness of men to begin to yield or, at least, to use de Beauvoir's words, "to resign themselves to the new status of woman"[2] are deeply related. And men paid, and continue to pay, a price for their patriarchal privileges. They paid, and pay, a price to keep them. And they pay a price when they lose some of their privileges, whether they render them up willingly, or with resistance and ill-grace.

Men have deeply ambivalent feelings about women.[3] They love them but want to be free of them. They depend upon them but want to assert their autonomy. They need their approval but cannot ask for it. They want them there when needed, but resist the turnabout. According to Chodorow, Dinnerstein, Horrocks, and Easlea, this ambivalence results from mother-dominated and father-absent child care. Mother becomes all-important and apparently omnipotent in the experience of male infants and children. The absence of the father from the child's immediate experience deprives boys of the opportunity to establish a meaningful identification with a male figure in their formative years.[4] This leads to an early sense of sexual insecurity and uncertainty. Since Mother appears all-powerful, the male child develops great expectations that can never be completely fulfilled. There is never enough love. The world is never perfect enough. Feelings of insecurity and anxiety can never be completely laid to rest. Thus the male child, in addition to a strong love attachment, also feels resentment and anger toward Mother.

As the boy grows and develops a need for autonomy, he commences with a rejection of the authority of Mother. The first most crucial steps in his self-determination, then, are taken *against* women. This is exacerbated because the main male role model in his experience — the father — is rarely implicated in the immediate domestic scene. This encourages the boy's view that to be a man is to be absent from, or "free" of, the woman; to be a man is to be aloof from the domestic scene. All this begins and feeds a psychological need to be dominant over and superior to women. Thus the first tentative steps to masculinity are taken against women, and most importantly against the most significant and powerful adult in the boy's experience, Mother. But since masculinity is initially developed in such an ambivalent context, it remains forever elusive, and it must be forever confirmed to others and to oneself. Furthermore, since the first relationship of a boy with a woman is fraught with ambivalence, all future relationships with women are complicated by such feelings.

The content of traditional masculinity in men is full of this ambivalence about women, the need to be dominant and superior yet dependent, and the need to constantly reaffirm their "maleness" to themselves and to others. To be masculine is to be individualistic, competitive, and tough. A man must control his emotions and not express them too freely. He struggles and competes to succeed, but each triumph merely sets the stage for the next struggle. A man grants affection and intimacy only rarely, and in carefully controlled circumstances. Masculinity means to fear intimacy, indeed to strive for power and control. Masculinity means to seek superiority, public superiority, and to continue to confirm it. Real men judge each other's jobs in terms of pay, power, and control over others.

Men do, of course, seek out women, wanting relationships in which they can become dependent without admitting it. The confident macho male of 20 becomes the dependent husband of 40. The sexually satisfied married man still peers furtively at his neighbour's penis at the urinal, comparing size. Men want to escape the charade and the competitive game — usually through love and commitment with a woman — but can never finally do so with complete ease. Because, finally, traditional masculinity is elusive precisely because it is a myth, a myth that collapses almost completely in the absence of supporting patriarchal structures.

And I am not just talking about the traditional masculinity of our fathers and grandfathers. I am talking about much of the content of masculinity now. Many men still feel a need to define themselves against "the other" — women. One family therapist argues that masculinity is still seen by many men as a sort of "ritualistic combat" with other men and that "a man's greatest fear is to be thought to be like a woman."[5] A study of 150 male college students found that male fears resulting from the stress of masculinity cluster in five areas: "physical inadequacy; emotional inexpressiveness; subordination to women; intellectual inferiority; and performance failures in work and sex."[6] Another study investigated the extent to which the traditional masculine role — involving "restricted emotionality, preoccupation with success, and the inhibition of expressions of affection" — increased the vulnerability of men, compared to women, to the negative effects of difficult life situations. The researchers found elevated levels of distress in men as a consequence of the traditional masculine role.[7] A study of "divorce prone" and "marriage phobic" men found that both groups exhibited a "wariness" of women and felt an irresistible need to dominate and control their relationships with women. Marriage phobic men expressed this by withholding commitment, while divorce prone men made tentative commitments that were quickly withdrawn.[8] A California psychologist interviewed 227 fathers of recently born or about-to-be-born children and uncovered a number of "secret fears" that privately haunted the men.[9] The biggest fear — affecting about 60 per cent of the men — was one of the most ancient, "uncertain parentage." In a seven-year study of 1,632 couples by a U.S. psychologist, it was found that good job news — like a promotion or raise in pay — tended to increase a man's desire for sex, while bad job news — like being demoted or fired — tended to diminish a man's sexual appetite. (By contrast, women tended to respond to good job news with a small celebration with friends.)[10] A study relating a child's sex with the content of father-child interactions with one-year-olds found that men tend to enforce, often quite rigidly, traditional sex behavioural stereotypes much more than women.[11] Contemporary studies like these indicate that many men are still ensnared in the traditional masculine role and remain afflicted by uncertainties, doubts, and anxieties that accompany sustaining that role. Evidently a large part of occupying the traditional masculine role is a fear of failing to live up to the expectations embodied in it.

The problems posed for men by the traditional, old-fashioned masculine role have in fact increased markedly. Certainly, as Millett asserted, "patriarchy's chief institution is the family."[12] And as long as the traditional patriarchal family remained strong and secure, the "dilemmas of masculinity" were more or less tolerable. The evident benefits far outweighed the less tangible costs. There was a synchronization between masculine and feminine roles. But there were still costs — or renunciations — exacted from the man: the suppression of his tender side, a loss of freedom, a feeling of oppression by the economic burdens and responsibilities imposed by the family, the fear of failure, and the awful consequences of actual failure. So while women pointed to their oppression *in* the family, men pointed to how the obligations of the family oppressed them and complained of their oppression *by* the family. Gains for women, like the vote and full legal citizenship, did not fundamentally change the reality of the position of women in the patriarchal family. According to de Beauvoir, "in their exchanges, woman appeals to the theoretical equality she has been guaranteed, and the man to the concrete inequality that exists. The result is that in every association an endless debate goes on concerning the ambiguous meaning of the words give and take: she complains of giving her all, he protests that she takes his all."[13]

The "dilemmas of masculinity" for men accelerated as women began to achieve a measure of economic independence, particularly since the 1960s. As long as women remained economically dependent on men, the patriarchal family remained secure and women remained locked up inside of it, even if increasingly restively. As Millett noted, "In general, the position of women in patriarchy is a continuous function of their economic dependence."[14] Twenty years earlier, de Beauvoir had made the same central point:

> It is through gainful employment that woman has traversed most of the distance that separated her from the male; and nothing else can guarantee her liberty in practice. Once she ceases to be a parasite, the system based on her dependence crumbles; between her and the universe there is no longer any need for a masculine mediator ... [She has found] a means of economic and social autonomy.[15]

Today the changing status of women, and the new emerging family forms, are confronting men with not just the wisdom and justice of changing their commitment to the old traditional masculine role, but with the necessity of doing so. Thirty years ago the women's movement appealed to men to renounce their sexist ways. Today the changing structure of the economy and the family are forcing men to do so whether they want to or not.

11 / Men and Economic Stress

The economic stress faced by the traditional male carrying the sole burden of supporting the family was central to the price men paid for the privileges bestowed upon them by a patriarchal society. A key component of the traditional masculine mystique, the role of economic provider, was fundamental to a man's identity. The stresses and anxieties generated by these obligations were carried without complaint. A real man got out there on behalf of those who depended on him and competed relentlessly throughout his working life to bring home the bacon, to put bread on the table, and to keep a roof over the family's heads. Even if the man were poor and less than successful, even if the bread were day-old, the bacon a tiny portion, and the roof covered a modest slum, he could still stride manfully into the kitchen confident that, within the limitations imposed on him by his station and circumstances, he had done his duty as a husband and father. Such men were portrayed in novels and movies, and the behaviours and expectations involved in living up to this masculine ideal were drummed into little boys from birth onwards. The image of the ideal male was simple and clear. He was a man of few words, a man of action. He felt deeply but rarely showed it. He would face challenges to his manhood, and threats to his family, courageously. His life was spent on the endless treadmill, the rat race. Even if he succeeded, he kept on competing and striving. There was always someone with a bigger salary, a better job, a bigger house; there was always more to be got for the family.

Few men really measured up to this stereotype. There can be only so many successes in a hierarchical society, and every success means the failures of many others. Even those who succeeded felt little comfort and security because competition is not just getting there, but an endless process of staying there. And there were cultural images of failure, like Willy Loman in Arthur Miller's *The Death of a Salesman*. But most men confronted their failure to measure up less catastrophically than Willy. Achievement goals were scaled down. Acceptable rationalizations were proffered. Bruised and wounded egos were carried gingerly back to the privacy of the family for mending and reconstruction, with the essential ministrations of the wife and children. In many ways, each family embarked on a secret psychological conspiracy to convince the man that he was a success in his own way, that he was the most important man in the world, or at least in their world. And, of course, he was the head of the house. His lack of power and control outside the family was somewhat compensated for by his power and control within the family.

But this was not always enough, and the stresses were never completely expunged. The burden of being the sole provider was overlaid with playing out a role that denied and suppressed a whole dimension of a man's life — the emotional, tender side. The toll on a man was sometimes physical; in other cases it was exacted from the family, when a bitter man came home drunk and frustrated and hopeless. Most often the toll was a surrender to a chronic sense of insecurity, of failure, of dissatisfaction, of disillusionment. Since the essence of the traditional masculine role was impossible to achieve, men were rarely able to be completely content, even if they succeeded materially. But there were payoffs. Those men who did achieve the outward trappings of manly success, however modest, could hide their inner anxieties as they enjoyed the deference of those who depended upon them. Even for those who failed, a submissive wife and loving and obedient children could go a long way to compensate for perceived or real failures.

Traditional men today, faced with the changing status of women and the new emerging family forms, confront enormous, even insuperable, problems in sustaining their role as sole economic provider and head of the family. Harsh economic reality has confirmed the end of the myth to all but the most willfully blind of traditional men. A traditional husband is having more difficulty sustaining the economic viability of the family on his income

alone. Such families face well over triple the risk of poverty compared with two-earner families (14 per cent versus 4 per cent in
1986, 1990, and 1995; and 13 versus 3 per cent in 1998)[1] and have
experienced virtually no growth in real income since 1973. In fact,
traditional-earner families experienced a slight fall in real income
between 1980 and 1988, and again in the early 1990s.[2] Indeed,
being a traditional-earner family, relying solely on the husband's
paycheque, has become one of the major poverty risk factors
today. At the other end of the scale, traditional-earner families are
increasingly less likely to make it to the top of the income pyramid
— over 80 per cent of all families in the top fifth of income distribution are dual-earner families.

Moreover, traditional men face increasing job competition from
women, and the drive for economic justice for women involving
affirmative action and pay equity programs can only make their
own career and salary potentials more uncertain. Moreover, they
see their colleagues in two-earner families able to provide extras
and in general to exude a more manifest sense of economic security. All the things that were supposed to go to the traditional
successful male's family are increasingly beyond his grasp, yet
within the grasp of dual-earner families in which men have, at least
partly, abandoned the traditional role. Today, a man appears to be
economically punished for clinging to the old ways.

For a young man, sustaining a family based on the traditional-
earner model is even more impossible. As a result of declining
real family incomes and declines in real wages for younger workers, families headed by young couples have an enhanced risk of
poverty, and those dependent on just the husband's income are
among the most vulnerable. As of the 1991 census, less than one
in five families where the husband was under the age of 40 was
a traditional-earner family, while almost one in three husbands of
traditional-earner families were aged 55 or over. Further, traditional-earner families have been declining rapidly as a share of
all families — 24 per cent in the 1980s, 15 per cent in the 1990s,
and projected at 13 per cent by 2016. If these trends continue, the
traditional family, economically dependent solely on the husband's income, will virtually disappear in this century.

The economic circumstances of the traditional male in the context of the growing rate of family breakdown are equally bleak. Families headed by single-parent men, though much better off than those headed by single-parent women, face almost twice the poverty rate of two-parent families.[3] Divorced men on whom the wife and children were solely dependent face child support and alimony payments considerably higher than those faced by divorced men from dual-earner families. Upon remarriage, if such a traditional man wants to continue to be the sole earner and must meet support payments from a previous marriage, the situation becomes even more difficult. In the past, most such men were able to abandon their former obligations more or less completely with relative impunity. This is more difficult today as governments embark on tougher enforcement and collection measures. A divorced and remarried man, determined to continue to be the sole provider, even one who earns a high income, cannot hope to fulfill his economic obligations without major stress and sacrifice.

A combination of women's insistence on change and economic reality is thus forcing even traditional men to accept the new reality of the dual-earner family. Yet a reluctant move to the dual-job family poses serious adjustment problems. Studies have found that marriage to an "overeducated" wife is often stressful for men; that non-traditional occupations of wives are associated with either divorce or pressure on the woman to move to a lower-ranking job; that a wife's income is negatively associated with difficulties in marital adjustment (the higher the income, the lower the quality of adjustment); that "problem" marriages tend to be those where there are serious discrepancies between the couple's sex role attitudes; that the highest marital satisfaction occurs in egalitarian or man-dominated marriages, the lowest in woman-dominated marriages; and that among the poorest marriages in terms of quality are those that bring together a traditional male and an even moderately liberated woman.[4] Certain economic trends will inevitably increase these marital tensions. As men aged 55–64 leave, or are forced out of, the labour market, Statistics Canada reports that they face dramatically increased poverty levels (27 per cent). One of the fastest growing husband/wife family forms is the "wife-only work-ing," which grew from four per cent of husband/wife families in the 1980s to five per cent in the 1990s, and is projected to go up to six or seven per cent by 2016. Further, a combination of declines in men's real wages, declines in labour force participation rates for younger and older men, and wage gains for women, has led to women out-earning men in one of four dual-earner families, over twice the rate of the late 1960s.[5]

Such findings merely reflect the painful process of adjustment that is going on as traditional men adapt to the new family and female realities. In individual cases the adjustment may be suc-cessful or unsuccessful, but it is occurring as men make the transition and as women learn the best means of helping them to do so. Perhaps the whole process is most analogous to a funeral rite: anger and resentment at the loss, followed by mourning for what has been irretrievably lost as a prelude to accepting the loss and getting on with life. Each of us in his or her own way is thus involved, willingly or unwillingly, in the ceremonial burial of the traditional patriarchal family.

12 / Men and Emotional Stress

The problems of emotional adjustment differ for different men, but they all face the same stressful context. Komarovsky's landmark study of U.S. male college seniors discovered "a basic contradiction" between "sex equality of opportunity outside the home" and "traditional sex-role segregation within the family," as she characterized the new "dilemmas of masculinity" faced by young men in the era of the new feminism. Many experienced severe strains in their relationships with women and felt dubious about their personal adequacy. Many complained of the "shallow and aloof paternal relationship" that had characterized the homes in which they were raised.[1] Raised to see women primarily in sexual terms either as potential objects of sexual consumption or as wives and mothers, men increasingly complain about the uncertainties they face about how to approach and relate to women. Therefore male children suffer from a serious cultural lag between the sexist values many are taught and the feminist reality they must face. Such a lag inevitably produces stress. Samuel Luker put it this way:

> The basic challenge facing contemporary men is to develop role models that are consistent with reality ...
>
> The traditional male played the game. He paid the penalty — he died younger, he was out there alone, sort of leading the charge and getting the arrows through his hat — but it was a man's world. If he played the game right, he got the respect of his wife and the love of his children and that was worth it all.
>
> Now, he does all the right moves and he still doesn't get the guarantee that his wife and family think he's No. 1. And it is not just in the working world that men are finding their childhood images of a real man are not up to real life.

Women that I see in my practice want the man to be strong and
a provider and all the things that a traditional male did automati-
cally, but now it's not enough, you've got to be strong, you've got
to be tender and you've got to be open about your feelings.

The new woman is demanding a lot more of the same old man.[2]

Herbert Freudenberger, the New York psychologist who came
up with the term "burnout," concurs, but he goes further by suggesting that "men are in a much more significant state of transition
now than women. They are often uncertain, ambivalent about
themselves and sometimes quite confused about the meaning of
masculinity and what it means to act and 'be a man.'" The reverse
of the fact that women "have more clearly defined ... goals and
desires" is that "men have lost their sense of purpose" in life.[3]
Freudenberger reported that most of the psychologically distressed
men in his practice were between the ages of 25 and 50. Often
these men were very successful in their professions and businesses, but felt depressed, uncertain about the future, and trapped in
orthodox family relationships. They had difficulty adjusting to the
new woman. They complained of having limited intimate relationships and of feeling lonely. They sometimes became narcissistic
and compulsive, abused alcohol and/or drugs, or dropped out of
their traditional supporting roles and became dependent on a
woman. While suggesting that both women and men must change
and adapt to cope with the new situation, Freudenberger alleges
that "the biggest change needs to be made by the men."

Self-evidently, a man who has accepted the need to redress the
economic injustices faced by women will find it easier to accept
programs of affirmative action or pay equity which may have a negative impact on his own career prospects and future earning
potential. But he will still have to cope with the new competition of
women and the consequences of his lost privileges including, for
many, resentment, anger, and frustration. So too, a man who agrees
that his wife should work outside the home, and that he ought to do
a bit more to help out around the house, will find it less traumatic
to cope with the problems presented by a working wife. And clearly when there is more congruence between the sex role expectations

of the man and the woman in the relationship, the coping process will be less stressful and marriage quality will be higher.[4] But if the man retains traditional attitudes, resents competition from women, resists his wife's desire to work, or expects to maintain the family's style of life on just his income, the stresses of coping can be quite horrendous. The results can include not only the possibility of failure at work, but the loss of wife and family. There is a clear positive correlation between the divorce rate and the labour force participation rate of wives, indicating that a wife's full-time work is implicated in the failure of some relationships.[5] California psychotherapist Herb Goldberg, a leading critic of feminism, was much more blunt about the failures of traditional men in the new context. He claimed to have seen evidence of a "role-reversal" in which formerly submissive women have left or threatened to leave their macho husbands, despite the fact that such men were "good providers, hard workers and dedicated family men" on the grounds that the relationship was emotionally unsatisfying.[6]

Men and Marriage

Men have had a different stake in marriage and the family than women have had. Just because the traditional masculine role has been instrumentally oriented to the competitive struggle in the marketplace does not mean marriage and the family were of peripheral significance to men. Men have been at least as emotionally and psychologically dependent on marriage and the family as women, if not more so. The nature of the traditional masculine role makes intimacy difficult, particularly with men with whom they compete at work. When men leave their families of birth they seldom maintain as close an emotional relationship as women do with their families. Again, part of the traditional masculine role is to become independent; as a result, they tend to become emotionally isolated, anchored by few close emotional ties that transcend their worldly, instrumental obligations. This has been typically presented as an outward manifestation of male strength and autonomy and as evidence of men's emotional coldness, aloofness, and irresponsibility. But it can be equally seen as a manifestation of men's emotional vulnerability.

Marriage and the family, in fact, became central to the emotional life of a traditional male. It was in a relationship with a woman that a traditional male found emotional fulfillment and meaning. He needed her love, understanding, and unqualified support. For it was there, in a relationship based on sexual intimacy and bonds of affectional obligation, that he could let down his guard, open up a bit, and be himself. And when children came, the family became the place where a man sought a more complex and rich emotional life.

Marriage and the family therefore became places of emotional permanence and security for traditional men, pivotal anchors in an otherwise insecure and hostile world. In the mind of the traditional man, his wife and children were the reasons for his daily struggle and were the struggle's ultimate justification. Women were simply expected to give the men what they needed emotionally. A woman's economic dependence, and careful socialization, ensured she would do so. She was not to question what he did or what he felt obliged to do. But while it is evident that women were therefore subordinated and oppressed in the family, men certainly needed and depended on marriage and the family for their emotional meaning.

That is why, as we saw in Chapter 9, marriage has typically delivered more psychological benefits to men than to women, benefits delivered largely at the expense of women.[7] Marriage is psychologically good for men but bad for women; singleness is psychologically bad for men but good for women. This stark pattern should tell us more than anything else just how central marriage and the family have been to the traditional masculine identity. Without marriage — and all the material and psychological benefits it brings — men are more vulnerable, more at risk of psychiatric and emotional disorders. Married men live happier and longer lives than unmarried men.[8] And married men live happier, if not longer, lives than married women.

Consequently, the loss of marriage and the family through separation or divorce is a profound shock for many men. As we've seen, divorced adults generally exhibit higher rates of psychiatric disturbance, but divorced men experience higher rates of mental illness than divorced women. Indeed, just focussing on marital status, divorced men have the highest rates of mental illness of all marital groups. Separated and/or divorced men, when compared to similar married men, suffered significantly elevated feelings of "distress" and "loneliness" and a higher rate of more recent physical illness.[9] Divorced men face a higher risk of suicide, of admission to psychiatric hospitals, of being victims of violence, and of vulnerability to major and minor physical illness.[10] Even extremely self-centred, macho men experience severe distress upon divorce.

> [O]ne group of divorced men seem to feel very little. These men come from marriages that involved little sense of commitment. They are the "easy come, easy go" men with narcissistic character disorders; men who are capable of only shallow relationships and low levels of intimacy. *The loss of context of their lives* seems more important to them than the loss of any specific attachment. They may be very angry or depressed about their own immediate disruption, but they quickly move on to new relationships and leave their children behind with remarkable lack of bereavement. These are the true "disappearing" fathers. In stark contrast psychodynamically are the group of men who experience *a severe narcissistic injury, a sense of intense betrayal and damage.* These are frequently the men for whom the wife's leaving was *a total surprise, who were not aware that the divorce was on its way.*[11]

Clearly, some men are deeply disturbed by divorce in all spheres of their psychological life. There is a loss of self-esteem, of purpose, of emotional meaning. For others, the disturbance is real, but for more clearly selfish reasons: bruised egos, public humiliation, a "loss of context in their lives" rather than the loss of the particular wife and children. Caught up in the preoccupation with self, the divorce leaves them bereft of the justification that was so central to their public "presentation of self."[12] Given the tenuous and insecure nature of traditional masculinity, the blow can be psychologically devastating, and for those who deeply loved their wives and children, the blow can be doubly devastating: not only is the private and public masculine ego in tatters for all to see, but they grieve for the love lost.

There is a clear relationship between divorce and suicide. Travato's analysis of the historical relationship between divorce and suicide in Canada between 1950 and 1982 demonstrated a clear positive correlation. As the divorce rate went up, the suicide rate went up.[13] This was true for both sexes, but successful suicide is and has always been much more common among men than women, and divorce is also directly correlated to the risk of suicide among children, particularly adolescent boys. Indeed, divorce, as a general phenomenon, is directly related to suicide rates in all groups affected by divorce: men, women, and children. From the early 1960s to the 1990s, the suicide rate doubled for both men and women. But since the late 1970s, the rate for women has fallen, while that for men has continued to grow. The most dramatic growth in male suicide between the 1960s and the 1990s occurred among the 15 to 19 year age group, up over four times, and the 20 to 24 year age group, up almost three times. Overall, the rate for men aged 25 to 44 doubled. Up until the early 1960s, suicide was most common among older men over 60, but by the mid-1990s suicide rates for men aged 20 to 44 either equalled or exceeded those of older men. And this rapid rise in suicide rates among men, especially younger men, uncannily and almost perfectly tracks the accelerating divorce rate.[14]

The possible reasons for consistently high rates of suicide among men over 60 are easily understandable: terminal illness or physical infirmity; bereavement; the shock of retirement. But for young men, even those on what should be the optimistic threshold of their adult lives, the high rate of suicide is perplexing and bewildering. And the increase has been so astonishing that an explanation must be sought.

Striking Difference

In studying suicide rates in nineteenth-century Europe, Durkheim found patterns similar to the ones noted above.[15] Examining the relationship between suicide and divorce, he noted that the highest rates of suicide occurred among divorced men and women. But the rate was much higher among the men. Indeed, Durkheim found that the risk of suicide goes up for men and down for women as divorce becomes easier to obtain, which led him to talk about the "immunity of married persons" to suicide and the general "preservative effect of marriage and children." But the striking differences in suicide rates between the sexes led him to point to the "salutary discipline" of the family and children for men and to suggest that the consequences of "conjugal anomy" — divorce or separation — included less "calmness and tranquility" and "more uneasiness" for men than for women. He concluded, therefore, that men benefit from marriage more than women:

> Thus we reach a conclusion quite different from the current idea of marriage and its role. It is supposed to have been originated for the wife, to protect her weakness against masculine caprice. Monogamy, especially, is often represented as a sacrifice made by a man of his polygamous instincts, to raise and improve woman's condition in marriage. Actually, whatever historical causes may have made him accept this restriction, he benefits more by it.[16]

Durkheim was trying to demonstrate that even such an apparently personal act as suicide resulted from larger social causes. Suicide, he argued, occurred more frequently when great social structural changes threatened the serenity of people's daily lives. Rising rates of suicide were therefore reflective of the weakening ties of social integration. As people's social structural maps are disrupted, personal indices of social disintegration, like suicide or divorce, will go up. Durkheim also demonstrated not only the protective factors for men and women associated with marriage and children, but also the considerable advantages enjoyed by men over women regarding the gender-related share of the social psychological benefits of marriage and family life. Such benefits continue today, as revealed by the differing rates of risk of psychopathology by marital category, as well as by overwhelming evidence that marriage steers both men and women, but especially men, away from high-risk behaviour, particularly smoking, drinking, and "recreational" drug use.[17]

Modern men, particularly men committed to the traditional masculine role, are facing major distress. As a result, many men find their expectations out of step with social reality. In an effort to explain the spiralling rate of suicide among men, especially younger men, psychiatrist and suicide expert Diane Syer-Solursh said,

> The strong, silent macho role society expects of young men is a major reason why they are seven times more likely to kill themselves than are younger women ... Boys are supposed to learn how to cope alone, to be a man and not to cry. Asking for help has become extremely difficult ... Young men are reluctant to reveal their troubles, and those who could help them — friends, parents, teachers and doctors — are equally unaccustomed to offering assistance. There are taboos for boys; culturally we allow young women to express much more distress.[18]

Traditional men today face many difficulties in obtaining and retaining Durkheim's "preservative effect of marriage and children." Women are less admiring of traditional masculine behaviour, and men are therefore often forced to change their ways. While this can be a positive step, the stress of balancing the inner self with the new outer self can be significant. Further, within the intimacy of marriage the effort to change is difficult to sustain, particularly when families face troubled times. Some men carry on as men have always done, perhaps agreeing to tolerate a more assertive woman than they would really like. But the stress of that compromise, particularly the economic stress if the wife doesn't work, can be great, and such a compartmentalization can quickly disintegrate. A traditional man may even try to carry on when it becomes clear that he is in an impossible situation and snap, as in the case of Lawrence DeLisle of Wyandotte, Michigan. DeLisle, 30, drove his station wagon containing himself, his wife, and four children aged eight months to eight years, into the Detroit River. During interrogation, he allegedly said that "as the car hurtled toward the river" he was "thinking of no longer having to pay bills." In a statement proclaiming his innocence after he was found guilty of four counts of first-degree murder and one count of attempted murder, DeLisle said, "A father's job is to protect his children, and I failed ... That is my guilt, not murder."[19]

Far too many men are going through an unprecedented period of chronic stress, and fragmentation of their identities, as their socioeconomic realities and personal circumstances shift radically in response to deep structural changes, both in the nature of their intimate relationships with women, and in the essential character of the new emerging family. As the structures of patriarchal privilege are dismantled, certain categories of men are at greater risk of serious stress. Men over 50 are being driven from the labour force due to economic restructuring and downsizing. The disappearance of traditional male-dominated occupations makes them possessors of now unmarketable skills that once gave them pride, social recognition, good incomes, and lifetime economic security. Young men find themselves competing on an increasingly level playing field with young women who, suddenly full of an exuberant sense of liberation and independence, are beginning to outperform them at school and on the job. Further, young men face the disappearance of traditional male jobs, and face chronic unemployment or the acceptance of low-wage work in the service sector, historically seen as "women's work." Successful men in relatively secure jobs and careers, still well-paid and sheltered from, or survivors of, the worst effects of economic restructuring, face daunting challenges from increasingly competent and well-educated women on the road to advancement and promotion. One consequence, particularly for poorly educated men of the lower classes, is a future without work characterized by a growing economic dependence on women. As W.J. Wilson has pointed out in *When Work Disappears*, this has already happened in the inner cities of North America, and contributed to the rising rates of crime, violence, and social desperation. If present trends continue, it could be a portrait of a more general future for society as a whole. The future of the family, and harmonious gender relations, in an economy where a growing army of young and older men cannot find work and can therefore play no meaningful productive economic role in society is deeply disturbing and represents one of the biggest challenges faced by our social structure.[20]

Most men are adjusting more or less successfully. Many are not, and face separation, divorce, and remarriage, perhaps more than once, as they strive to adapt. Many experience depression, anxiety, lowered self-esteem, and uncertainty. Many also experience anger and resentment, which are often internalized and manifest themselves in psychiatric illness, alcoholism, or suicide. Sometimes this anger and resentment are expressed against women and children, whether through abuse directed at his wife and children in the home, or through sexual harassment and expressions of misogynist sentiments at work. It may be the anger and resentment of the traditional male who cannot accept or deal with assertiveness and independence on the part of his wife, or from women in general. It may be the anger and resentment of the traditional male who cannot accept the fact that his wife has finally rejected him and seeks a divorce.

The Lépine Syndrome

There is no doubt that a goodly portion of contemporary male violence against women and children can be attributed to the strains and stresses faced by men as they try to cope with the impacts upon them of the general crisis of the family. Perhaps it is true that much of such violence in the past was routinely the result of male frustration and failure to live up successfully to the masculine ideal. But today, added to that historical legacy, is the failure of modern marriage and the family, and the larger social structure, to mesh with many men's traditional notions. And although we will never know for certain, many express the uneasy feeling that such violence has been increasing in recent years. As we have seen, data from studies of domestic violence in the 1980s and 1990s strongly indicate a dramatic *increase* of such violence to near-epidemic proportions. Indeed, we may be on the threshold of the emergence of a "Lépine syndrome" in much of male violence against women. In fact, it may well have already emerged, as the events in Montreal ominously suggest. This is male violence arising from a man's sense of failure and frustration, both in intimate relationships with women and in occupational attainment and economic achievement, directed increasingly and more or less consciously at women who are seen as the causes of his failures. Whether it is the wife who is blamed for the failure of the marriage because she didn't accept or understand the husband, or had been too assertive and independent, or whether it is women in general in the job market who are depriving him of the success that is his due, such women are targeted as scapegoats and become the repository for all his anger, resentment and bitterness. Many men already suffer from a sort of "Lépine syndrome" without the explicit violence, expressing it in anti-feminist attitudes and petty hostile acts.

Perhaps I have painted an unnecessarily dark picture by focussing on the more extreme ways in which men are victims of the crisis of the family (and in which they, in turn, often victimize others). Typically, men's reactions are rarely the extremes — outwardly directed violence against women or inwardly directed violence against themselves. Yet sometimes the reactions are worrisome, and oftentimes they are ominous. I can't help but remember a television interview with an obviously very prosperous male rancher after a fundraising rally held by Colin Thatcher's Moose Jaw defence committee. At the time, Thatcher had finally been charged with the murder of his former wife, JoAnn Wilson, after a marriage breakup marked by bitter disputes over matrimonial property and child custody. The rancher said that there would be more and more men driven by economic desperation to murder their estranged wives if the legal principle of the equal division of matrimonial property remained unchanged. The impression was that the man believed Thatcher was possibly guilty, but that Thatcher's actions were at least understandable if not completely justified.[21]

Perhaps less ominous, but nevertheless worrisome, were Winston Cole's anti-feminist efforts at Dalhousie Law School in the early 1980s.[22] Cole, a law student, established a group called Men and the Law as a reaction against the law school's Women and the Law group, organized to promote women's concerns regarding sexism in the law and its administration. Comprised of 24 men and only one woman, who served as the group's secretary, the group was, Cole admitted, a "half-serious backlash against the feminism espoused by Women and the Law." Men were confused, he lamented, because they didn't "know whether the female students they sit beside want to be treated as academic colleagues or women."

Even more worrisome is the growing use of the law by men to control women.[23] Efforts by boyfriends to use the courts to prevent women from obtaining abortions are among the most highly publicized, and so far unsuccessful, of such efforts. More and more fathers' rights groups, largely composed of divorced and angry men, are being established. Although involving a very small number of men, they are obtaining some supportive responses from conservative politicians and the courts. The groups, like Toronto's In Search of Justice and Kitchener's Fathers for Justice, are explicitly anti-women and anti-women's equality. They are against any special treatment for women; therefore they oppose affirmative action and pay equity programs, the right of women to have reproductive choice, and the disbursement of government money to activist women's groups. They favour the father's right to have a veto on a woman's abortion decision and better legal protections for men accused of sexual assault. One fathers' rights activist said, "Women's groups say rape is rape. Rape is not rape … we know the difference between a 90-year-old Sunday school teacher and the woman who's screwed every guy in Toronto. In Search of Truth provides aid to men accused of sexual assault by providing peer support and understanding." But the focus of such groups is "family issues — arrangement for custody, access, child support, parental benefits and alimony." Most importantly, they favour compulsory joint custody and forced mediation upon divorce. In an effort to gain wider support, the groups have begun muffling their more stridently anti-women positions, and many have joined the more moderate coalition, the Canadian Council for Family Rights, which calls for more equal treatment for men and women in the case of divorce, especially divorce involving children. As one father's rights activist said, "It's easier to sell equality than rights for men."

A series of court decisions restricting the mobility of female custodial parents suggest that fathers' rights groups are beginning to influence the courts. These were cases where women who had custody of the children after a marriage breakdown wanted to relocate to another city. In each case, the father was able to use the courts to prevent the woman's move on the grounds that it would restrict his access to the children and thus have a harmful effect on the children. In an analysis of the issue, *The Globe and Mail*'s Dorothy Lipovenko asked:

> If the shoe were on the other foot, would the courts compel a father who had custody to regulate his romantic interests or career ambitions around the needs of his children? Or, would a court tell a man who had access but not custody that he could not move because the children would be deprived of regular visits?

A law professor believes that indeed "the tables have been turned: the onus is no longer on the non-custodial parent to prove that changing living arrangements would harm a child's best interests; rather, it's the custodial parent who must now convince a court that changing the status quo ... would benefit a child." For Margrit Eichler, what is happening is crystal clear:

> It's an issue of control. What I find interesting is that fathers, via the courts, are having more of a say about their ex-wives than they did with their wives.

Regarding the generally increasing use of the law by aggrieved men, Susan Crean agrees: "This is part of an anti-feminist backlash. It is a regaining of control, or a way of regaining manhood." So does Michele Landsberg:

> It's one of those ironies of history that women, in fighting for rights, have handed the weapons to those who want to take away all the rights of women. It's all about control. It's really a comment on how angry and frustrated men are over the areas that used to be under their control.

There have therefore been significant shifts and splits in the men's movement, which initially emerged in the 1960s and 1970s as a positive and supportive response to the new feminism.[24] At first, particularly in the 1970s, the movement was an important ally of feminism and the demands of women for justice and an end to sexism. These groups often focussed their activities at two levels, the personal and the political. At the personal level, the movement held men's educational and group therapy meetings in an effort to help men to understand and to adjust to the new feminist reality. At the political level, the movement joined in public advocacy — marches, demonstrations, rallies — supporting the political and economic demands of the women's movement. But in the 1980s, many of feminism's allies among the intellectuals and spokesmen of the men's movement began to turn against the women's movement, and some became explicitly hostile and anti-feminist. Some retreated from politics, focussing entirely on a personal, therapeutic solution. Others embrace a mythopoetic response, probably best epitomized by Robert Bly in his bestselling *Iron John*, looking for the deep inner source of masculinity by probing the past, the depths of their psyches, ancient myths, and even fairy tales in search of "the wild man" and "the warrior," while "sustaining the tension between opposites" — the masculine and the feminine. Some embrace right-wing politics and/or evangelical Christianity, enthusiastically joining the conservative crusade against feminism, often with the shrillness, vindictiveness, and hostility so characteristic of the recently deeply disillusioned and personally wounded.

During the 1980s and 1990s, this backlash among men occurred around certain persistent themes: Men are not to blame for the plight of women and should not feel personally guilty for the oppression of women. Men have suffered from the burdens of traditional masculinity and suffer now from the unjust attacks of feminists. Men have to rediscover, reassert, and celebrate their deeper masculine tendencies. Feminism maliciously exaggerates the true extent of male violence in the home (some even argue that men suffer spousal abuse and violence equally, and that women are more guilty of child abuse than men). Men are unfairly victimized by affirmative action and pay equity programs. Men suffer at the hands of a pro-feminist court system and social service state bureaucracy, routinely losing legal battles for child custody and fair child support agreements. Middle-class, white males are the scapegoats and are unfairly harassed and hounded by feminists and their political allies in government and the courts. As a result, the uneasiness, anxieties, resentments, and sense of hurt of many men have found an intellectual rationale around which to focus a political resistance to feminism and to base a denial of the reform demands of the women's movement.

The anti-feminist men's movement has many faces, but similar messages. For example, in the secular stream of the backlash there's "A Manifesto for Men" by Andrew Kimbrell, author of *The Masculine Mystique*, which boldly declares, "The movement among men is ... generated by the millions of men who, having devoted their lives to work and family, have grown weary of the continuing assault on their gender identity. They no longer find ... society's misandry and constant scapegoating of men acceptable. For many years they have endured male bashing in relative silence. However, many are now proclaiming, 'We're not going to take it anymore!'"[25] Then there's the religious stream of the anti-feminist backlash, perhaps best epitomized by the Promise Keepers movement, calling on men to rededicate their lives to God, the church, and their families, in that order, and insisting that, in the words of its founder, "a man's man is a godly man." The movement believes that men have been drawn by worldly pursuits away from their central role in the family as husbands and fathers, and though professing a belief in equality between husband and wife, some in the movement are fond of citing Ephesians 5:22, "As the Church submits to Christ, so also wives should submit to their husbands." The movement also encourages men to get together apart from women to reaffirm their pledges and to support each other.[26] As one critic put it, "the followers of Bly get into male bonding by running in groups naked through the woods, beating drums, searching for the hairy man within; the more restrained Promise Keepers, meanwhile, seek the deep masculine in male-only prayer and Bible reading circles, helping each other through the seven-step program." All the streams come together in public debate behind the secular, political movement. This is reflected best in Canada by the Canadian Alliance party, and in the U.S. by the evangelical right of the Republican party. Both are publicly dedicated to reversing programs like pay equity and affirmative action, to establishing publicly funded programs to keep women at home with the children, and to leading the charge against the "feminist conspiracy" during election campaigns.

At the same time there is a more moderate, reasonable wing of the recent men's movement with a strong case that many men have suffered unfairly in the gender skirmishes provoked during the family's crisis: men who have been unjustly denied reasonable access to their children after divorce; men who have suffered brutal economic burdens in property division and maintenance decisions; men who have been falsely labelled as sexual and physical abusers of their children by vindictive ex-wives. Though far from commonplace events, such injustices have happened frequently enough to provide ammunition to the feminist-bashers and traditionalists who want to go back to the good old days of the patriarchal, traditional family. This would appeal to the new generation of young men who have known little but the era of uncertain and confused gender relations and often personally traumatic marital wars between bitter fathers and mothers. The fact is that many men who embrace equality between the sexes in principle, who reject traditional masculinity and the patriarchal family, and who want to be more involved as parenting fathers, find serious obstacles, and little sympathy or support, after separation and divorce. Such men do not want to become "the disappearing father" of the past, but in fact want joint custody and ongoing parental involvement with the children.[27] Some even try to win primary custody, attempting to make a case that they are the better partner to ensure the best interests of the child. Such men have organized the National Shared Parenting Association (NSPA), led by Randy Liberet, who insists that the organization is "not trying to promote the rights of fathers. We're trying to promote the rights of non-custodial parents and their children." The NSPA argues that the economic injustices women face in the labour market compel them to use custody battles to prevent economic disaster for themselves and their children. Therefore, pay equity and affirmative action need to be implemented in order to ensure harmonious shared custody and joint parenting after a marriage breakdown.[28]

The ambivalence of most men — supporting the principle of justice and equality for women while resisting the realities and costs of achieving such principles — is well reflected in recent Gallup polls.[29] Forty-nine per cent of men do not believe women are treated fairly and 61 per cent support the goals of the feminist movement. Yet 54 per cent of men believe that a working wife and mother has "a harmful effect on family life" and 78 per cent oppose programs of employment equity for women. To be fair, this ambivalence is shared by Canadian women — 51 per cent of whom agree that a working wife and mother is harmful for family life, and 69 per cent of whom oppose employment equity programs for women. Further, one in three women actually believe women are in fact treated fairly, and only 58 per cent support the goals of the feminist movement. This ambivalence among both men and women reflects the fact we are going through a major transition in both gender relations and the shape of the family, a transition that is both structural and ideological, uniting men and women on all sides in the larger debates. That is why some of the most virulent critics of feminism are traditional women, and some of the most articulate advocates of the feminist movement are men.

On the more positive side, there are thousands of men in various groups across Canada trying to adjust to the new reality in ways more supportive of women and the changing family. The biggest network of such groups was set up by Ken Fisher's New Men, Partners in Change. And there are many informal and local groups from coast to coast. The specific concerns of the groups vary, but they are all trying to get troubled men together to help each other change. They discuss questions like the restrictiveness of sexual stereotyping, the oppression of the masculine ideal, the price of masculinity, the nature and practice of sexism, the need to support affirmative action and pay equity programs for women, and the sources and consequences of sexual and physical male violence against women. Some of them engage in lobbying efforts on behalf of reforms of benefit to women. A few of the groups are composed of abusive men trying to change their behaviour.

The problems of adjustment men face clearly vary with the kind of family situation in which they participate. Men in traditional marriages face elevated levels of economic stress and a growing contradiction between their old-fashioned family life and the new reality of the increasing economic liberation of women. If their wives are traditional women, then the home front will not pose enormous difficulties, but outside the home in the marketplace, where they face competition from less traditional women, they will face elevated stress. Remarriage families and male-headed single parent families also pose unique coping problems for men. And the new norm in husband/wife families, the dual-income or dual-career family, requires tremendous readjustments on the part of men.

In fact, the dual-income, dual-career family is the most significant variation among the new emerging family forms, and the men involved in this family are making the most successful adjustment. Such a family is a decisive break with the traditional patriarchal family because it represents an attempted structural reconciliation of marriage and the family with women's growing economic independence. While all men must somehow adjust to growing female participation in the labour force, it is in the dual-income, dual-career family where that adjustment must occur most intimately. A traditional male can avoid or rationalize the new economic reality, and given the continuing advantages enjoyed by men in the world of work, he can even to some extent insulate himself from increasing female economic competition. But such insulation is more difficult to carry off if such a man's wife works outside the home. Even if the woman earns significantly less than her husband, and therefore her income can be seen as merely secondary or supplementary; even if she agrees to put the husband's career first; even if she continues to carry the full child care and housekeeping load, the new domestic reality forces even the most traditional of men to make adjustments and concessions.

The new future of marriage and the family is being charted in the dual-income, dual-career family. For it is there, if anywhere, that Komarovsky's call for "a more harmonious society, which would release the creative potential of the female half of its citizens and provide a less constricted range of choices for males"[30] will be initially constructed and tested. It is there, if anywhere, that, following de Beauvoir, "men and women [will be able to] unequivocally affirm their brotherhood."[31] It is there, if anywhere, that Ehrenreich's hope for "some renewal of loyalty and trust between adult men and women"[32] will occur. And it is there, if anywhere, that Millett's

> [S]econd wave of the sexual revolution might at last accomplish
> its aim of freeing half the race from its immemorial subordination
> — and in the process bring us all a great deal closer to humanity.
> It may be that we shall even be able to retire sex from the harsh
> realities of politics, but not until we have created a world we can
> bear out of the desert we inhabit.[33]

Historically, women's oppression was inseparable from their economic dependence within the patriarchal family. It follows that women can never achieve liberation until the patriarchal family is dismantled and replaced by a family form that deliberately seeks to reconcile women's economic independence with fairly shared marital and parental obligations.

13 / The Double Burden: Men's Version

Although the double burden is primarily a female affliction, the problems associated with balancing job and family obligations are also confronted by men in two-earner families. Eichler has argued that "sexist [social] science fails to understand men" by tending "to downplay or ignore a potential conflict between work and home for men."[1] Surveying the paucity of research concerning the impact of the double burden on men, Eichler noted that in all work-related decisions — hours of work, overtime decisions, shift decisions, commuting distances, accepting a promotion or a transfer — many men seriously consider family impacts. Indeed, the available evidence is that work/family conflicts are felt by men almost as strongly as by women. Existing studies suggest "that men are aware of family/work conflicts within their own roles and that there are situations in which they are obviously willing to give precedence to the family role." Further, according to Eichler, available evidence indicates that men tend to *believe* in the principle of the equal sharing of domestic labour, but fail actually to live up to that belief. There is also a disagreement between the sexes regarding the perception of such sharing: men often perceive they are doing a larger share than the women perceive the men to be doing. Further, "There is a remarkable inelasticity in men's contribution to household tasks." Regardless of the amount of work, the marital context, or the age of the spouses, men tend to do about the same small share.[2]

The reality of the double burden for men in dual-earner families was confirmed by Statistics Canada's General Social Survey of a sample of about 10,000 households.[3] Working men spend slightly under two hours a day on domestic work and child care, while working women spend just over three hours. Further, "83 per cent of employed women participated in activities such as housecleaning and meal preparation, compared with just 51 per cent of men." On the other hand, men worked at their jobs over an hour a day longer than working women. As a result, "the total time invested in work outside the home and family care by employed men and women are roughly equal." Of course, these averages tell us little about variation among men. A follow-up General Social Survey focussing just on responsibility for housework in dual-earner families found that only a small minority of couples shared domestic work equally — 15 per cent or less depending on the task. Full-time working women in dual-earner families are almost as likely to have sole responsibility for housework as women working part-time or as women in traditional one-earner families.[4] The eight-year study of two career families by Hochschild and Machung, cited in Chapter 7, found enormous variations among men regarding their commitment to sharing "the second shift."[5] While four in five men failed to engage in equal sharing, the other one did so. Only one in 10 men took on less than one-third of the household burden. Thus one must conclude some degree of a double burden conflict for nine out of 10 working husbands of working wives. Of course, doing the actual work is only part of the double burden. The other part is organizing and orchestrating the domestic campaign. Indeed, some marriage counsellors report that domestic chore conflicts are really of three kinds: conflicts over the sharing of the actual labour and time involved; complaints from wives about the hopeless incompetence of husbands and their need for constant supervision and encouragement; and complaints from husbands that their wives are too perfectionistic and often refuse to let them do certain tasks, preferring to do the work themselves to make sure it gets done right the first time.

It is clear that equal sharing of domestic work is very rare.[6] In those couples where the husband's job is viewed as most important, even when working women do triple the domestic work of men and willingly reduce their own commitment to their jobs, women largely express the feeling that their husbands are doing a reasonable share. Women often continue to choose work easily reconciled with their primary obligation for the family and often consciously assign domestic chores to the husband that least disrupt his sense of "maleness." Interestingly, a husband's share of domestic work tends to go up when his wife's work has high prestige and high income. Indeed, some researchers have found a clear and direct positive correlation between the size of the wife's pay packet and the amount of domestic work the husband takes on. When the wife earns much less than the husband, he does much less domestic work. As the pay gap closes, his share of domestic work increases.

A major study by Gilbert of men in dual-career families found that the men's sex-role attitudes were reflected in their participation in domestic work.[7] She identified three categories of such men. "Traditional" husbands help out, but leave the major responsibility to the working wife. "Participant" husbands take on a major share of domestic and child-care responsibilities, but still do considerably less than the women. "Role-sharing" husbands are more strongly committed to doing a fair share and strive to do so. Gilbert's study suggests that the husbands of working wives are going through a significant process of change and adjustment on the question of the double burden: even traditional husbands of working wives are acutely aware of, and concerned about, the injustices faced by women at work and at home.

Family and Job

Yet men do experience serious problems balancing work and family obligations. A U.S. study found that, while women indeed faced the greatest conflict, men were not all that far behind.[8] Twenty-five per cent of working fathers of babies and toddlers claimed that worries about child-care problems interfered with their productivity (this was true for 40 per cent of working mothers). Thirty-nine per cent claimed to have declined transfers, and 22 per cent claimed to have declined promotions as a result of child-care problems (the figures for women were 50 per cent and 30 per cent, respectively). The study reported that four in five working parents had had to cope with family problems or crises during working hours, and 50 per cent of both working mothers and working fathers claimed to have felt stress both at work and in the home as a result of conflicts between family and job obligations. Among those experiencing stress, the rate of missed work, reports of difficulty getting up in the morning, perceived failures in job performance, and indications of health problems were all elevated. One should be cautious in interpreting such results. How each sex deals with the conflict they both emotionally feel is probably quite different, and the actual consequences might be very different. The man may *feel* the stress but carry on with his job commitments nonetheless. The woman would be more likely to act on the stress, say by cancelling an appointment or leaving work early. At the same time, however, we should not dismiss such evidence, either.

There is one group of family men who cannot avoid the full impact of conflicts posed by the double burden — Canada's over 245,000 single fathers, especially the estimated 80,000 working fathers with sole custody.[9] They face the same problems as single mothers, but have two distinct advantages: higher incomes and much shorter durations of singleness. But until they remarry, they must balance job and kids and deal with loneliness and isolation, as well as sexual and emotional frustration. They experience much more uncertainty and doubt about their parenting abilities. The social awkwardness of being a male single parent is much greater than being a female single parent, if only because such families are so unusual and violate so many of our traditional sexist norms. Being a single father also challenges a man psychologically. As one social work professor put it: "The problems faced by the working single father are more than merely the logistical problems shared by all working parents. He has to change the way he feels about himself as a man."[10]

Single-parent fatherhood interferes with a working father's career, just as it does a working mother's, but the impact can be more traumatic for the man because of his own self-expectations. Two U.S. studies on working single fathers reported that about 5 per cent were fired from their jobs and another 8 per cent quit because of work/family conflicts. Other negative impacts on the job included a reduction in work-related travel, a higher frequency of absenteeism, and more lateness and early leaving. About eight in 10 of the fathers in the study found raising children either "very difficult" or "somewhat difficult." Such men have fewer emotional coping resources since they do not have the kind of female support networks that women often have. Obviously, the fact that single fathers have much shorter durations of single-parent episodes has to do with their superior economic situation compared to women and the greater ease men have in explicitly pursuing a new spouse. But it also undoubtedly has to do with their desperation resulting from coping with the double burden and the looming potential economic crisis posed by career setbacks. Such men discover very quickly that successful careers do not mix easily with the obligations of a primary parent.

Costs and Trade-offs

Clearly, men in dual-job families are not routinely expected to make career-related sacrifices for the sake of sustaining the family. Indeed, the assumption that a man's family life and career or job are quite independent of each other is still so widely held that there is very little research on the issue. The jobs men do are largely organized as if the man's family did not exist. Further, men face stronger negative reactions when they engage in "cross-sex role behaviour."[11] Women in traditional male occupations are admired, if stressed, whereas men in traditional female occupations are looked at somewhat askance. Additionally, when men begin to take on family obligations in ways that interfere with the job, they face stronger negative reactions from colleagues and employers than women face. If a man leaves meetings, declines promotions, says no to transfers, or throttles back on his time on the job, he is breaking the first rule of success — the job comes first. And it's frequently true that men face a double standard: "Employers may tolerate the tug of parental obligations in a woman, but they see it as the mark of a wimp in a man."[12] As one executive trying to balance job success with more time with his family put it: "There's a cumulative impact of saying no to your kids, but there's also a cumulative impact of walking out of meetings. It's a tough balancing act."

There are certain "costs or trade-offs" perceived by men in dual-career families.[13] Among men in such families with children, some note increased stress as a result of "physical and emotional over-load." Some regret that they had fewer children than they might have had, while others regret that they remained childless as a result of the couple's career commitments. There is decreased time for leisure activities and increased time spent on household tasks. A large group complain of decreased sexual activity, though many concede this could have as much to do with the presence of small children as with their wife's job commitment. Others note that their job mobility and career options are limited. Although many note that having a wife with a career usually enhances their prestige among their colleagues, they do experience some hostility, envy, and jealousy, especially economic envy. This is particularly true of their more traditional colleagues and employers. But these men do not appear to express resentments about these "trade-offs," typically viewing them as having been freely negotiated and freely chosen.

Interestingly, only a handful mention the loss of male power, privilege, and prestige as costs associated with a commitment to a dual-career family. This suggests that the old patriarchal axiom — men benefit from women's oppression — is beginning to be eroded, especially among men with working wives. At a general level, men clearly benefit from women's economic oppression. Less pay for women in general means more pay for men in general. Fewer opportunities for women mean more opportunities for men. A promotion granted a woman is a promotion denied a man. A pay equity program for women in a corporation or civil service bureaucracy means less of the salary pie left over to be shared out among the men. But that very real set of general structural privileges is less attractive to men in two-earner families. A lower income for the wife means a smaller contribution to the family income and hence more economic pressure on the husband. Fewer opportunities for women means a cut in his wife's advancement and future salary. A pay equity program that increases his wife's paycheque means more family income. In other words, men implicated in the concrete new family form — the two-earner or dual-job family — benefit less and less from the remnants of male privilege and, in fact, *as individuals*, begin to suffer from the structure of male privilege. Structures of unjust and undeserved privilege are shaken by appeals to justice and equity. They are even more shaken when those on whose oppression the structure of privilege rests become restive and resistant and politically mobilized. They finally collapse utterly when those who benefitted from the structure finally realize that the former benefits have become costs. That process is well-advanced in two-earner families.

By and large, the men making the most successful adjustment are therefore those involved in dual-income, dual-job families. The adjustment may be tentative, as in the case of one such man who said, "Sometimes I think, 'My father didn't do it that way, my friends don't do it that way, why should I?' But then I realize that those rules aren't in effect and it turns things from black and white to grey."[14] Or the adjustment may be full of lingering doubt, as expressed by another:

> There is no question that the rewards of sharing career, achievement, and childrearing with one's spouse are great, but the price paid can be high. It is a price, finally, that many of us never imagined we would have to pay, and therein lies much of the trouble ... We might learn to exult in the career attainment of our wives, even if we must sacrifice some of our own professional ambitions. We might find the time as well to be with our children and to be involved as a matter of course in the necessary household chores. We might even learn to give up the anger and resentment that is often engendered by the need to do all these things.[15]

But the adjustment is occurring, if sometimes reluctantly, as men come to realize that the only way they can have a satisfying and happy relationship with the changing woman is in the new family form that provides her with a degree of economic independence, while presenting him with the need to change his ways. And social science is beginning to explode some persisting myths. One study, for example, found that men in dual-earner families are not more likely to be sexually unhappy than "real men" in traditional families. In fact, the very opposite was the case. Men married to working women were far less likely to suffer from "desire disorders" and "inhibited sexual excitement difficulties" than single-earner husbands.[16]

Studies report that men in dual-income, dual-job marriages must be consciously committed to making the relationship work, in marked contrast to traditional marriage, which men tended to take for granted and in which women were required to carry most of the load of sustaining the relationship.[17] Men must be willing to be more "flexible," "co-operative," "tolerant," and "accommodating." In other words, family arrangements become constantly negotiable and require continuing renewal through compromise. When a man becomes involved in such a family arrangement, even if he begins as a traditional male, the situation will require that he begin to change, and as his behaviour changes, his views, his self-concept, and his expectations inevitably begin to change. And as the marriage and family survives, and perhaps even flourishes, the man is awakened to the benefits of the arrangement.

Even so-called "traditional" men are acutely aware of the benefits of this new husband/wife family. These men agree that there are three major clear benefits and a few minor ones. The increased family income enriches family life and provides a greater sense of economic security. The men believe that their spouses enjoy increased contentment. Furthermore, they find that the establishment of independent identities enriches the lives of both partners. Many of the men in dual-income families, especially traditional men, also note that they feel less economic pressure. Finally, the overwhelming majority of men in such families feel they receive "greater rewards from parenting."

Even more heartening for the future of the family are the effects of dual-income, dual-job families on the children raised in such families.[18] Most studies find only positive effects, especially for adolescent girls, who are "more outgoing, independent, active, highly motivated" than girls raised in traditional families. The positive effects are only slightly less for boys, probably because they are encouraged to develop positive attributes in any family situation. Children of dual-career families "are more independent, more resourceful ... more able to draw on a wide repertoire of role models ... they feel more self-directed, score higher on tests of verbal ability, and have a more affective relationship with their fathers ... than do peers raised in relatively traditional households." Such children are more flexible and less rigid in their views about sex-role behaviour. Boys raised in dual-career families, most particularly, manifest "fewer sex-related stereotypes." Interestingly and importantly, fathers in two-job families "place greater emphasis on expressivity and independence for sons *and* daughters and less emphasis on conformity to social norms" than fathers in more traditional marital arrangements. Fathers in dual-income families confirm this positive picture, mentioning the following benefits for their children of the dual-career arrangement: "exposure to a broader range of values and experiences," "greater independence and responsibility," "happier parents because of their career involvement," "quality time with parents," "the fathers being more involved with the children" and a wider range of "rolemodeling." These positive consequences suggest that when the current generation of children, a majority of whom will have been raised in dual-career families, establish families in this century, we may finally transcend the crisis of the family.

PART V

Conclusion:
Easing the Crisis

Families are the crucibles in which our personalities are formed, and, as such, are crucial to us as individuals. They are equally important for society. If families, as the major caring units, fall apart, society will ultimately fall apart ... If we want to have strong families, gender equality, and a healthy society, we need to make it possible for people to care for inevitable dependents — that is, children and adults who are unable to look after themselves — by supporting them in this task morally, economically, and socially. Unfortunately, we are faced with a political climate in which the opposite is currently being practised — we are making the task harder and sometimes impossible.

Margrit Eichler,
Family Shifts: Families,
Policies, and Gender Equality
(Toronto: Oxford University Press, 1997),
pp. 3 and 5.

Introduction: Toward a New Family Policy

Neither Ottawa nor the provinces have a comprehensive, effective family policy. And vital areas — like child neglect and abuse — that are not politically glamorous suffer from an indefensible neglect. Beset on the one side by a lobby hysterically defending the near-extinct traditional family, loudly supported by aggrieved fathers' rights and anti-choice groups, and on the other by feminists and others advocating family policies based on reality, many politicians equivocate. Others proclaim their unalterable dedication to dragging the family back into a past that exists only in their sentimental memories.

In other words, Canada does not have a family policy worthy of the name. Perhaps this is understandable, for major structural and policy changes inevitably result in pitched political battles. Incumbent politicians would insist that Canada does have a family policy. Any prime minister would point to the targeted family allowance, the maternity leave benefits under employment insurance, the child tax credit, the child tax exemption, the daycare deduction, and the billions Ottawa annually transfers to the provinces through the Canada Health and Social Transfer. He or she would point to long-overdue reforms in family law affecting divorce, birth control, and abortion, as well as to the equalization of women's legal status as a result of human rights legislation and the Canadian Charter of Rights and Freedoms. Provincial premiers would cite daycare subsidies, improvements in the laws governing the division of matrimonial property upon marriage breakdown, family income supports, human rights laws and commissions, child protection agencies, and shelters for battered women. The problem, of course, is that the basic premise of these policies, accumulated over the years, is the traditional family.

Furthermore, governments have not seen their role as intruding into family affairs, except in the most extreme circumstances. The policies were seen as "add-ons" to help the traditional family. And more recently they have often been seen as defences for that family. Even policies that responded to the new realities were implemented piece by piece, rather than as a comprehensive response to general structural change.

As Eichler points out, our existing complex array of policies is fundamentally flawed.[1] They either fail to recognize new emerging family forms altogether or discriminate against non-traditional families.

> The only case in which so-called family policies actually advantaged people on the basis of their marital status were those of breadwinner families, in which the wife is economically dependent on the husband.[2]

Besides this bias against women, which presumes and therefore reinforces their dependency, many such policies, especially those delivered through the tax system, are biased against the poor, and often the poor and women are the same.

The full extent of the failure of Canada's family policies becomes clear when we assess their lack of effect. Family poverty has not decreased significantly since the 1960s, the slight gains made in the 1970s were largely erased in the 1980s, and in the 1990s, in the context of neo-conservative cuts to social programs, family poverty has become epidemic. Income policies have largely failed to redistribute income since the 1950s — the main difference is that low-income individuals and families are now more dependent on government programs for a greater share of their meagre incomes. The programs have not prevented growing poverty among women, and indeed they have contributed to it by failing to address the economic problems of women with children after marriage failure. They have not rescued our children from poverty; child poverty rates have gone up alarmingly in the 1990s. Eichler provides a summary indictment:

The major problems with the current system of [family oriented] social policies then, are that the system as a whole is confusing and hard to understand. It does not redistribute wealth from the rich to the poor, it penalizes women for bearing and rearing children, and does not facilitate the integration of fathers into the child-rearing process.[3]

More recently, Eichler has proposed that family policy developments and debates can be best addressed around three models of the family: the patriarchal, individual responsibility, and social responsibility models.[4] As we have gradually moved to a rejection of the patriarchal model, premised on male domination and male privilege and the traditional gender division of labour, we have largely embraced the individual responsibility model, premised on gender equality and the equal responsibility of husbands and wives. In both these models, the role of the public, or of society, in individual families is minimal and carefully circumscribed. It is limited in the patriarchal case to rare assistance in cases of an absent and/or disabled parent, and in the individual responsibility case to rough guarantees of temporary assistance if necessary and only in cases of extreme need. The social responsibility model, which does not yet exist, is premised on gender equality in principle, is committed to realistic and effective programs to minimize gender inequality, and to shared parenting responsibility even in the case of divorce or separation. The public, or society, would share responsibility for the care of dependent children and "inevitably dependent adults" (through illness, aging, incapacity) with both parents.

It can be argued, however, that Canada, in common with other western industrialized societies, was moving tentatively towards the social responsibility model of the family in the post-Great Depression, World War II period during the construction and extension of the welfare state through programs in health, education and social welfare. Universal public kindergarten to grade 12 education, medicare, universal family allowance, the lowering of barriers to post-secondary education, family income support programs, guaranteed access to dignified if minimal universal standards of living through social assistance as a right of Canadian citizenship, and programs to protect children at risk are but some examples. These can be seen as the incremental construction of the social responsibility model of the family as society's basic social unit, with public agencies taking more and more responsibility for supporting and sustaining families.

Further, as we collectively responded, however tentatively and indecisively, to the demands of the women's movement for gender equality, to the dramatic rise of wives and mothers in the paid labour force, to the new realities of family breakdown through divorce or separation, and the emergence of new family forms, an ideological consensus was beginning to take shape — that the community as a whole, through government agencies and publicly funded non-governmental organizations, had an obligation to aid in the transition process. When asked, Canadians have long agreed that child poverty should be eliminated, that a publicly funded universal daycare program ought to be established, that men and women should get equal pay for work of equal value, that sexual discrimination should end, that children and women should be protected from violence, and that children at risk of abuse or neglect should be effectively rescued and protected. Indeed, there was much to be proud of in the speed and candour with which Canadians were willing to change their views on many family issues that were both deeply personal and publicly controversial.

A good part of the 1970s and early 1980s were taken up with political debates about such initiatives and moves toward their implementation. That era ended with the triumph of neo-conservativism in the Canadian political system, and the watershed was the 1984 federal election, when all parties agreed in principle to establish a universal, publicly funded national daycare program. The refusal of the Mulroney government, after the 1984 sweep and after re-election in 1988, when the program was again promised, to move on daycare on the grounds of fiscal restraint marked the end of that era of gains. Indeed, throughout the 1980s and 1990s not only was the idea of a publicly funded universal daycare program dismissed as a fantasy out of touch with fiscal reality, but a blizzard of cuts to the existing social safety net has wiped out many of the tentative gains made since the 1960s, and in some cases, since the end of World War II.

As we enter the new millennium, Canada's family policy is now clearly premised on the individual responsibility model, indeed, increasingly on the rugged individual responsibility model, as the social support system for vulnerable individuals and families has been, and continues to be, systematically dismantled. At a time when individual Canadian women, men, and children have never needed each other's support more — through a comprehensive network of social support systems — to help in the transition to new family forms, there is less and less help available. And as people are thrown back on their own limited resources, hunger and homelessness grow, and social and individual desperation become the routine daily experience of growing numbers of Canadian men, women, and their children.

Canada desperately needs a new comprehensive mix of family policies that accomplishes a number of related, indeed inseparable, objectives. We need policies that recognize the changing nature of the family and contribute to the healthy emergence of the new family forms without discriminating against those who remain committed to the traditional family. We need policies to help the victims of the crisis of the family — children, women and men — make the transition and the adjustment more easily. These self-evident policy objectives merely amount to a recognition of reality. But we also need policies that recognize that women's oppression, and the slowness of their climb to full justice, has been, and continues to be, importantly linked to their obligations to sustain the family. Further, since Canadian women bear the major burdens of the family's transition, primarily as a result of their child-bearing and -rearing responsibilities, we need policies that ensure a more equitable sharing of those responsibilities. Finally, since women's continuing economic inequality results importantly, though not completely, from the legacy of their traditional role in the family, we need policies designed to accelerate women's achievement of economic equality. In short, we need policies that recognize that the full emancipation of women can only occur when the family's transition to new, non-patriarchal forms has been completed.

Our wanton neglect of the family's crisis and urgent family policy needs is closely associated with the imposition of the neo-conservative business agenda involving the withdrawal of government from society and the economy, as we return to a classical free market model of social and economic development. This has resulted in a deepening social crisis, creating the political instability which saw the defeat of leading neo-conservative governments in the early 1990s and the growth of voter cynicism with politics in general. With the election to power of parties that had opposed neo-conservatism as the opposition, many expected a return to a civilized society in which democratic government would again become a tool to solve the community's problems, rather than a tool of social and economic discipline imposed on the people on behalf of the business lobby. This did not occur, resulting in a deep and widespread sense of betrayal. Our politicians and policy-makers remain ensnared and enraptured by the siren song of neo-conservatism, remain prisoners of the corporate lobby. As we enter the new millennium, neo-conservatism and accompanying social harshness have triumphed as the new political consensus.[5]

Negative family trends are therefore accelerating. The family's crisis is deepening and broadening. Our population is aging. Family breakdown continues to be so epidemic as to be a routine experience. More and more couples are living common law. More and more are living alone. Fewer couples are having children. Single-parent families continue to grow in number, especially those headed by women. The poverty risk factors for children continue to be closely related to the family's crisis: over 40 per cent of our 1.3 million officially poor children live in single-mother families. Single-mother families suffer five to six times the poverty risk of two-parent families. About one in five Canadian children is officially poor, the rate we left behind in the 1960s. The feminization and juvenescence of poverty continues.

As the neo-conservative wrecking crew continues to dismantle our social support system, worse is yet to come. Unwilling to pay for a civilized society, we are creating one characterized by social barbarism. As we enter the new millennium and move beyond, assuming we continue to dismantle our social security system and do little or nothing to intervene to help families at risk and in crisis, the future is stark.

We can expect a continuing acceleration in the incidence of physical and sexual abuse of women and children.

We can expect even more disastrous horror stories as a result of our refusal to provide public, universal, quality, licensed daycare for our children, even as our typical two-earner family works harder for longer hours in response to falling real incomes.

We can expect increasingly routine reports of death from hunger and health neglect among children, the elderly, and even some younger parents.

We can expect more and more runaways among our children, and the pleasure market in the flesh of children will continue to grow.

We can expect further pressure on the family as more and more young people after high school find no work, and the barriers to post-secondary education get higher and higher.

We can expect extreme stress on the family, especially female caregivers, as the so-called Wellness Model of health cuts kicks in and imposes more and more of the primary health care burden — in money and time — on the already fragile family.

We can expect, therefore, increases in abuse and neglect of the chronically ill and the elderly.

We can expect the suicide rate among men after divorce to continue its upward march, and the gap which has historically separated male and female suicide rates to continue to close.

All this, and more, we can expect as a result of the worsening crisis of the family as we enter the new millennium, unless the sleeping Canadian people awaken from the slumber induced by the official cant about deficits and debts, and governments' deceitful claims of an incapacity to govern. We must demand policies and programs to ease the crisis, to help us through, to support the new emerging family forms. To do otherwise is to abandon hope for our future as a civilized, humanitarian society.

These are not auspicious times to be talking about major new initiatives in social programs. The debates now tend to be how much to cut from social spending, and where to make those reductions, rather than about whether they should happen at all or about where social spending needs to be dramatically increased. But the same was true during the Great Depression and World War II. However, many persisted in advocating new policy departures in the interests of relieving human suffering and building a better future. Out of that debate, Canada embarked on the elaboration of the social security net that became the envy of the world and is now at serious risk. And those programs were proposed, defended, and finally supported by Canadians because they promised a better life for Canadian families. Those same arguments need repeating now.

Today the family is in serious crisis. The policy proposals that follow represent a tentative effort to come to grips with the family's crisis. They are presented as ideas that logically flow from our considerations of that crisis. They are presented as an effort to provoke debate about what we can do to alleviate the self-evident suffering of so many Canadians.

14 / Proposed Directions in Family Policy

Daycare

The debate about daycare has been particularly heated during the last 20 years. But there are certain agreements. Most people agree on the need for more spaces. Most people also agree that more public money should be targeted at daycare. In fact, 49 per cent of Canadians favour "increased tax spending to provide government subsidized daycare centres for preschool children," including 66 per cent of those aged 18 to 29 years and 58 per cent of those aged 30 to 39 years.[1] Very few now argue that daycare is harmful to children, and most agree that good-quality daycare is psychologically beneficial. There the agreement ends. Should daycare be non-profit, or should we allow commercial centres? Or a mixture? How can we regulate the safety of the centres and the quality of care the children receive? How far should we extend licensing requirements? Should there be exceptions? How should the federal government's money for daycare be spent? Where should daycare centres be established?

Certain features of the debate are clear. Governments prefer payments to parents, leaving the actual establishment of daycare spaces up to the co-operative efforts of parents, to the marketplace, or to institutional decisions at parents' places of work.

Parents and daycare advocates are more concerned about *quality* and *accessibility*. A working parent wants to know that her or his child will receive excellent care, involving enriching programs and competent staff. A working parent wants daycare that is accessible, both financially and in terms of location. Indirect funding makes quality control difficult. If parents receive a fixed subsidy or tax break, they face serious financial constraints on how much they can pay daycare workers. A for-profit daycare faces market constraints and the bottom line: quality will be as low as the market will bear. Even when governments are strongly committed to quality control through licensing and inspection, corners are cut if for no other reason than the chronic shortage of spaces. The desire of neo-conservative governments to stay out of direct involvement in daycare and parents' desire for quality and accessible daycare are just not compatible.

What is urgently needed in Canada is a *publicly funded, universally accessible*, quality-ensured daycare system. A national, shared-cost program, funded and delivered in the same way as the existing social health safety net programs, could be jointly administered by provincial agencies to set and enforce standards, to distribute funds, and to provide program support services and a local, parent-elected board at each centre to hire the staff and to supervise day-to-day operations. A network of centres established in existing schools could also provide before and after-school care for school-age children. There would also be more convenient access for the parents, since their children's care would be in the neighbourhood.

In other words, the daycare system would become the logical extension of our existing public and separate school systems. In the nineteenth century, we opted for a universally accessible, publicly funded school system for all children. Now the same arguments can be made to extend that system to all preschool children of working parents, as well as to provide care before and after school for school-age children of working parents. With good programming, such a system will produce more independent and happier kids. And it will provide immense practical and psychological comfort to their parents.

Further, the occupation of daycare worker needs to be professionalized. Daycare training programs, and more early childhood education programs, could be established and become a prerequisite for those who wish to pursue careers as daycare educators. And daycare work could become a career, much like teaching, with a decent income, a future, security, recognition, and prestige. Daycare work today is characterized by low wages, few benefits, little prestige, and no future. Even well-educated and competent people attracted to daycare work can rarely afford to stay very long, even when the work is a source of much satisfaction.

Ideally, the program might be entirely publicly funded, while making some provision for degrees of accessibility for non-working mothers in traditional families. An alternative could be to establish a transitional system funded primarily by federal and provincial money, plus a reasonable user fee based on income. The problems of freedom of choice could be initially resolved by continuing the daycare tax deduction for those who want an alternative to the public system. But that problem would quickly disappear as the public system proved itself and gained wide acceptance.

The benefits of such public daycare cannot be overstated. The anxieties of working parents, especially single parents and working mothers, would be alleviated. The problems associated with the poor supervision of many of the children of working parents would be resolved. The negative psychological consequences for children of poor-quality care would become things of the past. Most importantly, such a system would systematically grant women, as a recognized community sanctioned public right, degrees of freedom during significant portions of the day from primary parenting responsibilities. And the decision to have children would be less profound in its consequences for both parents. Assured access to quality daycare would make the decision to have a child rendered somewhat less fraught with difficulty.

Maternity, Paternity, and Parental Leave

Canada's maternity leave program, administered through the employment insurance system, has filled an obvious need. Federal and provincial labour laws currently grant women the legal right to 17 or 18 weeks of unpaid maternity leave. The employment insurance program guarantees a working woman a compensated maternity leave of 15 weeks at 55 per cent of her wage to a maximum in 2001 of $413 weekly, and similar benefits are available for an additional 35 weeks' parental leave. The woman or her partner must have worked at least 600 hours in the previous 12 months. Quebec has the best system of maternity leave.[2]

While our current system is much better than that prevailing in the U.S., Canada lags far behind most other industrialized nations, which provide 90 to 100 per cent compensation for lost wages, with a variable cap, for periods extending up to a year and more. For example, Germany provides six months at full pay, while Italy provides a more modest five months at 80 per cent of pay. Sweden is probably best — 18 months at 90 per cent of pay. Such benefits are often available to either parent. In Canada biological fathers initially were not eligible for the benefits, but adoptive fathers were. Ottawa removed that anomaly by adding 35 weeks of paid parental leave to the existing 15 weeks, and allowing the parents to decide whether the father or the mother will take the leave. Adoptive parents are restricted to the 35 weeks parental leave only.

Canada needs to go further. Why not entitle women to a full year of maternity leave at 100 per cent of their foregone pay, with a maximum based at least on the average full-time industrial wage? The waiting period could be eliminated. But lost wages are only one of the economic penalties women face. There are also negative consequences in terms of normal salary increments, merit pay, and promotions. Therefore, federal and provincial labour laws could provide a statutory prohibition of any employer's use of a pregnancy-related absence to deny a woman job advancement and salary increments. Furthermore, women returning from maternity leave, which they had taken as a legal right despite an employer's displeasure, sometimes find themselves dismissed from the job very soon after. Quebec currently forbids the dismissal of a woman returning from maternity leave during the first 20 weeks back on the job. Why not extend this protection to a year and provide it to women across Canada?

The move to a full year of maternity/parental benefits has gone some distance in resolving the controversy regarding paid paternity leave. Although Gallup reports that a majority of Canadians — 52 per cent — oppose paid paternity leave,[3] court decisions have made it clear that it is discriminatory to deny men some form of paid leave. Ottawa's response of adding 35 weeks of paid leave that can be shared, while retaining the initial 15 weeks for the mother, was an effort to respond to these court decisions. Extending the period of paid pregnancy-related parental leave to a full year, while stipulating that at least the first 15 weeks must go to the mother, enables couples more easily to negotiate how the rest of the leave might be shared.

Canada's working parents require another kind of parental leave relating to ongoing child care responsibilities. Currently when a parent misses work for a family-related reason, most feel compelled to use sick leave days or holiday time to avoid a loss of pay. What has been called "family responsibility leave" is extremely rare in Canada. Most federal civil servants, and public employees in some provinces, have been able to negotiate paid "personal leave" clauses into their contracts, ranging from two to 10 days a year. Few unions in the private sector have been as successful, and the business lobby — like the Canadian Manufacturers' Association and the Canadian Federation of Independent Business — is stridently opposed to such benefits. Again, Quebec has led the way, granting employees the statutory right to five days parental responsibility leave each year, including two with pay. Quebec also provides parents a degree of protection when job obligations might conflict with family obligations — employees with children must be given at least 12 hours notice by an employer requesting overtime. Federal and provincial labour laws could be amended granting parents up to 10 days of paid family responsibility leave each year. Further, parents should be provided with the statutory right to refuse, without penalty, unusual job demands — like overtime or work-related travel — that interfere with their family obligations.

The general objective of such policies is clear. If we want parents, particularly mothers, to work; if we want to ensure that parents, especially women, do not pay economic penalties as a result of bearing and rearing children; if we want to establish conditions that ease the decision to have children for working parents; and if we want to ease the stress faced by working parents carrying the double burden, then work ought to stop being organized in ways which assume that family obligations do not exist. We already know that family obligations are not easy to reconcile with work obligations, again,

more particularly for working women. Work, therefore, must become more reconcilable with family obligations.

Family Breakdown, Mediation, and Counselling

Though the grounds have been eased, divorce remains largely
adversarial, especially over the division of property and child custody. There has been progress on the property question with the
presumption of the joint contribution to marital property and its
more or less equal division. But child custody battles frequently
continue to be very bitter. The notion of no-fault divorce and the
realization that at some point it is best for all concerned to end a
troubled marriage have both gained wide acceptance. Given that
divorce is no longer an exceptional event, perhaps it is time to refer
questions of separation, divorce, property division, and child custody to a system of non-adversarial family courts with exclusive
jurisdiction, including an appeal mechanism that excludes the use
of the adversarial court system. Guided by the principles of natural justice and sexual equality, such a system could minimize the
suffering that is frequently inflicted by our present system.

More extensive family counselling services are urgently
required, to help not just those going through the divorce process,
but also those in troubled marriages who might avoid divorce.
More adequate preparation for marriage could ensure more realistic decisions.[4] Studies have also shown the diminishing satisfaction
with marriage among new parents and the positive effect of intervention and counselling on marital adjustment to a first child.[5] The
counselled couples felt more in control and more hopeful, whereas
those who did not receive counselling felt "overwhelmed, impo-
tent, hopeless and alienated." Such studies suggest that a wider
network of counselling and support services and a deeper commitment to family life education, including marriage and parenting
preparation, could help many adjust successfully to marriage and to
children who might otherwise fail.

The most important negative impact on children of divorce is
the loss of a parent. Studies have shown that frequently even non-
custodial fathers have more to do with their children after a divorce

than before, that continuing non-conflictful access to both parents is good for children, and that children in joint custody arrangements adjust better than those in sole custody arrangements. Joint custody also tends to reduce relitigation rates between estranged spouses, and other studies have suggested that parents in joint-custody arrangements are happier than those in sole-custody arrangements. But studies of joint custody have found that children still feel conflicting loyalties and experience stress as a result of living in two different homes. As well, joint custody creates particular adjustment difficulties for preschool children and for adolescents. Further, joint custody ought not to be forced, since it puts many women at a grave disadvantage, particularly in family breakdowns resulting from domestic violence. The question of custody, therefore, might then be determined on a case-by-case basis. If the divorce process can be made less angry and conflictful, and if both parents recognize the importance to the child of a continuing relationship with both parents, joint custody will become increasingly the arrangement of choice.[6]

Finally, the economic consequences of marriage breakdown for women and their children have to be remembered. Although the 1986 divorce reforms make clear that the principal objective of support payments to formerly dependent spouses (overwhelmingly women) is to encourage the achievement of economic independence after a reasonable period, most men continue to evade their economic obligations. Similarly, men often evade paying child support. The current willingness of most provinces to pursue men who try to renege on these obligations is to be applauded. Indeed, enforcement must become more vigorous.

Family Violence

Society has acknowledged the seriousness of family violence, but women and children who are beaten and otherwise abused need a more comprehensive network of shelters. The shortage of safe havens often drives desperate women back to their battering husbands because they do not have anyone to turn to for help and protection.

By the time a battered woman calls for help, usually only after many previous violent episodes, the situation calls for vigorous action. Police forces and crown prosecutors could establish a policy that every battering husband will be charged and that the charge will be laid independent of the wishes of the victim. If battering men knew with certainty that they would be charged and tried, they might reflect before the violent event, and certainly they would be forced publicly to confront what they had done afterwards. And if battered wives knew that the response to a plea for help would be prompt, they might be more likely to ask for help.

Courts have to become much less lenient with men who are convicted. This means that the attitudes of many judges, prosecutors, and police officers have to be changed. As long as sexist attitudes exist among the police, prosecutors, and the judiciary, violence against women will be taken less than seriously, and men will continue to believe that they can get away with battering. A policy of prompt arrest, the laying of charges, and the move to a speedy trial would send a clear message that the community finds such behaviour intolerable.

In cases of family violence against children, the problems of detection are paramount. Children can rarely call for help, and if they do they are unlikely to be taken seriously. All provinces should strengthen and more vigorously enforce existing laws that place a clear obligation on those who regularly come into contact with children to report suspected cases of abuse or neglect. Effective education and propaganda campaigns among such groups of professionals could teach them how to detect, and to deal with, suspected cases. Child protection agencies need more social workers and a clearer mandate to intervene to protect abused children. And the foster homes and other facilities where children are placed for their protection cry out for improvement and more close supervision.

The message must be clear and unmistakable. No institution — not even the family — is so sacred and private that the community will take no action to protect victims of violence.

Family Poverty and Child Hunger

Family policy alone cannot solve the problems of economic injustice. But we could eliminate child hunger easily. And we could eliminate child poverty. Hot breakfast and lunch programs in schools and community centres in targeted areas afflicted by child hunger are an obvious and vital first step. The overwhelming majority of Canadians would agree that no child in this country should suffer from hunger and would therefore support the measures necessary to feed children. More controversial, and more costly, would be a policy commitment to end child poverty. If we indeed believe that the impact of poverty on children in their formative years is unacceptable, and if we realize that the long-term emotional and economic costs of child poverty are incalculably high, then a commitment to end child poverty is not beyond our grasp.

Back in the optimistic sixties there was a lot of talk about the guaranteed annual income. The idea was simple. Abolish all programs involving government income transfers to individuals and families and substitute a comprehensive guaranteed annual income to ensure that all Canadians enjoy income levels sufficient to live a reasonable life. The idea was suffocated by the economic difficulties of the 1970s and 1980s, and the cuts of the 1990s, but every now and then the idea is reproposed by a politician or an interest group. Canadians do believe that everyone should be guaranteed a tolerable level of material existence, and they are willing to consider new ideas of how that might be best achieved as long as such "new" ideas do not camouflage a hidden agenda to dismantle some of the social security gains made over the years. But such ideas raise anxieties about means tests, criteria for cut-offs, and the threat to universality.

Canadians might therefore support the idea of a guaranteed annual income, fixed at the Statistics Canada poverty line (or at a more generous one, like the Senate's or CCSD's), *for all families with dependent children.* Such an income would not be great, and poverty, in the real rather than the official sense, would not disappear. But it would be an important step in the elimination of some of the more extreme forms of deprivation faced daily by 1.3 million Canadian children.

Well-Family Clinics

Schools are an expensive public infrastructure that exists from coast to coast, and to which all who have school-age children are daily linked. When one reflects on how to deliver many of the family programs proposed, the task seems complex and expensive. But school buildings need not just be used for educational and recreational purposes. Schools could become important neighbourhood centres where programs are established and delivered to improve family life. The daycare program could be delivered in existing schools. Schools, and perhaps targeted community centres, are probably the best places to deliver breakfast and lunch programs. And it is the teachers, more than any single group, who will be most likely first to notice evidence of possible child abuse and/or neglect.

Schools, or at least selected schools, would also be a logical place to establish a network of Well-Family Clinics, staffed by family physicians, nurses, and counsellors. Such clinics could run family life educational programs, provide sexual and birth control counselling for adolescents, help troubled families, and deliver primary health care. Schools could then become centres of support for family life in the neighbourhood. For children, schools could become places of protection and nurturance in times of trouble and conflict.

A fantasy? Perhaps. But let us not forget that our very recent ancestors went through the disruptions and horrors of the Industrial Revolution, many political revolutions, two World Wars, and a devastating depression, leaving us with one of the most advanced, prosperous, and caring countries in the world. Comparatively, building a network of family support programs, and centres to house them, to help us through the present crisis of the family seems an eminently modest proposal.

More Government Funding for NGO Advocacy and Service Groups

Many of the supports the family in transition requires cannot be directly provided by government bureaucracies. Indeed, government agencies may be the least efficient and acceptable means of delivering many programs. Therefore, more public funds could be made available to non-government organizations (NGOs) involved in family-related and women-related advocacy and service activities. Programs involving family life education, abortion and birth control counselling, and early marriage preparation are probably best left to groups like Planned Parenthood, with the active co-operation of federal, provincial, and local government agencies. Counselling groups for battering males might best be established by men's groups that include former batterers as counsellors. Troubled families might more readily seek help from family counselling services that are clearly independent of government, perhaps established by the social agencies of churches or groups of professionals organized in community-controlled practices. Shelters for battered women are probably best run by sympathetic women's groups or voluntary community organizations, whose staff would include former victims. But such efforts need government funds, organizational help, and some degree of inspection and regulation. Perhaps a line should be drawn at services for abused, neglected, and disturbed children. The record of private agencies has not been very reassuring. Child welfare and protection programs would be best run by government agencies with clear policies and regular inspection to ensure that the interests of the children in care are always paramount.

Although the service function of NGOs is clearly important, of perhaps more general importance is their advocacy function through education and propaganda efforts. Women's groups, pro-women men's groups, non-government service organizations, and the reproductive choice movement can all go much further in advocacy and in alerting the public to family and women-related problem areas than government agencies are typically willing or allowed to go. A great many of the problems of adjustment to the new realities are attitudinal. We should not therefore underestimate the effectiveness of education and propaganda not only in convincing people to accept the changes, but also in helping them to come to terms with them in their minds, hearts, and personal lives.

All these policy proposals imply a profound shift in our attitude to the family. Community supports and interventions amount to a recognition that sustaining the family is a shared social responsibility. The desire to resist the intrusion of public policy into the family is understandable. But surely there is no basic contradiction between our individual right to a private family life and our collective obligation to provide supports essential to helping the new emerging family forms survive and flourish, and to protecting vulnerable victims of violence, abuse, and neglect.

15 / Proposed Directions in Feminist Policy

Family policies developed in isolation from policies designed to deliver justice to women cannot hope to succeed. The fact is women's struggle for justice has moved forward in tandem with emerging family forms. Any policy mix to deal with the family's crisis must also come to grips with the central issues on the feminist agenda today.

Reproductive Choice

Women's reproductive choice, including the unfettered access to abortion services, is not a family issue. It is an issue of women's rights and freedoms. Indeed, it is arguably one of the most profound issues of women's rights.[1] Forced pregnancy was a central feature of the traditional patriarchal family. Until 1969, women were legally proscribed from abortion under any circumstances; indeed birth control measures were illegal if practised for birth control rather than for an acceptable "medical" reason — to prevent venereal disease or to deal with problems of menstrual regularity. After 1969, birth control was legal, but women seeking abortions had to go through the degrading process of seeking the permission of a therapeutic abortion committee at "an accredited or approved hospital" for medical reasons. Many women routinely got around the effort at control with the help of sympathetic doctors and abortion committees, but access was limited and uncertain. Anti-choice activists harassed doctors and hospitals and launched court actions to deny access to abortion.

Dr. Henry Morgentaler symbolized the crusade for women's right to reproductive choice by establishing free-standing abortion clinics and openly defying the law. In 1970, he was charged with two counts of conspiracy to perform an abortion. In 1973, a Montreal jury acquitted him. In 1974, the Quebec Court of Appeals quashed the acquittal, and Morgentaler was sentenced to 18 months in jail. He was acquitted of similar charges in 1975 and 1976, whereupon the Quebec Attorney-General ordered a stop to prosecutions against him. In 1983 Morgentaler and seven others were charged with procuring abortions in Winnipeg, and he and two others were charged in Toronto. In 1984 Morgentaler lost his challenge to the abortion law under the Charter in the Ontario Supreme Court. That same year a Toronto jury again acquitted him, but in 1985 the Ontario Court of Appeal overturned the jury's decision and ordered a new trial. In 1986 Morgentaler appealed to the Supreme Court of Canada, alleging that the abortion law violated women's rights under the Charter. In January 1988, he was completely vindicated — the Supreme Court restored the original jury acquittals in the 1984 Toronto case and ruled, five to two, that the federal abortion law was unconstitutional. In the majority decision, Chief Justice Brian Dickson and Justice Antonio Lamer said:

> Forcing a woman, by threat of criminal sanction, to carry a fetus to term unless she meets certain criteria unrelated to her own priorities and aspirations, is a profound interference with a woman's body and thus an infringement of security of the person.

But Justice Bertha Wilson went further:

> The right to liberty contained in section 7 guarantees to every individual a degree of personal autonomy over important decisions intimately affecting his or her private life. Liberty in a free and democratic society does not require the state to approve such decisions, but it does require the state to respect them.
>
> A woman's decision to terminate her pregnancy falls within this class of protected decisions. It is one that will have profound psychological, economic and social consequences for her ... It is not just a medical decision; it is a profound social and ethical one as well.

The Supreme Court decision did leave the door open to some future possible legislation to protect a potentially viable fetus in the advanced stages of pregnancy, but it made it clear that any interference in a woman's abortion decision during the early stages of a pregnancy would violate her rights.

Subsequently, Canadians were subjected to a spectacle of indecision, political cowardice, and irresponsibility as the government and the House of Commons scrambled to respond to the Court's decision. The outcome was a proposed abortion law that pleased no one and continued to violate women's rights and freedoms. The law put abortion back in the Criminal Code, made it illegal unless a woman's health, very broadly and liberally defined, was threatened. A doctor performing an abortion was liable to imprisonment if he or she performed an abortion for reasons other than a threat to physical or mental health.

Although an improvement on the old law, the new law neither guaranteed access nor forced provinces to cover the procedure under medicare. Further, a woman who wanted an abortion still had to shop around for a willing doctor, and the old degrading charade would have had to recommence; women who weren't mentally or physically threatened by the pregnancy would have had to pretend to be so. And doctors performing the service would have been constantly looking over their shoulders, fearing lawsuits from anti-choice groups and estranged biological fathers. A mature, healthy, emotionally stable woman could have been legally denied an abortion, and a physician who respected her right to make the decision faced two years in prison. This rendered the new law as constitutionally invalid as the old and for the very same reasons. The law ultimately would have been struck down by the Supreme Court.

Thankfully, the Senate, in a rare moment of useful assertion, refused to approve the new law. Faced with the prospect of another divisive debate to override the Senate, the federal government wisely let matters rest. The Criminal Code is now silent on abortion, as it should be. This has not prevented a continuing crusade against women's right to reproductive choice. A series of court cases to protect the unborn from abortion, or from the irresponsible

lifestyles of pregnant women, or to give the unborn fetus the legal
status of person under the Criminal Code, have so far been unsuccessful in challenging the constitutional right of a woman to
reproductive choice. As well, efforts by some provinces to remove
abortion procedures from coverage under medicare have failed to
be sustained in court, or have been checkmated by Ottawa through
the *Canada Health Act*. The anti-choice movement has had more
success in denying access to abortion services through political
means — pressure on hospital boards to ban the procedure, pressure on provincial governments to limit funding and locations for
abortion procedures, harassment and pressure, including violence
and threats of violence, directed at doctors performing abortions.
All these measures have severely restricted the practical access of
women to abortion, despite their clear constitutional right to such
access and to coverage of the procedure under medicare.

The "rights of the unborn" are a matter for theology, not for the
state and the law. They concern personal religious conscience.
Some believe that human life starts at conception, others at "quick-
ening," others at birth. The right to unfettered reproductive choice
for women does not mean that a woman who believes that human
life starts at conception would be forced to have an abortion. The
fact that the Supreme Court did recognize the possibility of fetal
rights of some sort in the later stages of pregnancy — presumably
when a fetus is theoretically viable — does not enunciate a legal
principle of the right to life of the unborn. It simply says that the
state *may* have a reasonable and arguable case for deliberately vio-
lating a woman's rights in such circumstances. So far, the state in
Canada, through the House of Commons, has decided not to go in
that direction.

The best solution is to leave the situation as it now rests. Those
opposed to abortions can decline to have them and even continue their aggressive proselytizing efforts to win others to their
views. But those women who want abortions can obtain them,
provided the service is accessible.

New and unsuccessful abortion laws, and the rearguard actions
to protect the fetus through court challenges of a woman's right to
abortion, were among the last gasps of the legally constituted patri-

archal family. They constitute efforts to control women, to make them something less than full legal persons, and to intervene in their personal lives in ways that men would never tolerate. It is probably true that most women who wanted abortions — assuming fair geographical access and medicare funding — would have gotten them under this new law. Yet to do so they would have had to present themselves as flawed, troubled, and less than whole persons before the throne of legal patriarchy.

Economic Equality

The reasons for women's persisting economic inequality are complex. Partly it has to do with women's recent entry into the labour force and the legacy of inferior education and training. Partly it has to do with the ghettoization of women into low-paying jobs. Partly it has to do with women's own lower labour market aspirations. Partly it has to do with women's primary responsibility for home and family. And finally, it has to do with outright sexual discrimination. Taken together, these reasons reinforce a structure of sexual discrimination in the economy. Equality before the law and laws demanding equal pay for equal work have proven inadequate to ensure women economic equality.

As a result, the argument that the only way forward was through programs of pay equity and affirmative action was accepted. Equal pay for the same work will only protect those women who manage to break into traditional male occupations. Women in traditional female occupations will continue to suffer pay discrimination. The solution is pay equity — or equal pay for work of equal value. Affirmative action programs would help women to obtain access to traditional male occupations and to advance within them. Taken together, these two policies could begin to attack the structures of sexual discrimination in the job market. But pay equity and affirmative action programs require real structural changes, cost real dollars, and take away real male privileges.

The Retail Council of Canada, representing most of the country's largest retailers and comprising one of the most notoriously underpaid female job ghettoes, has long complained that pay equity for women would hurt the economy by driving labour costs up. Many among the business lobby oppose pay equity because it would allegedly close businesses and drive people out of work. The Canadian Chamber of Commerce has repeatedly declared its opposition to equal pay for work of equal value.

The campaign against pay equity and affirmative action suffered a serious blow after the release of Judge Abella's report of her Royal Commission on Equality in Employment.[2] Although it focussed on four structurally disadvantaged groups — women, native people, the disabled, and visible minorities — by far the greatest significance of the report was its impact on the debate about pay equity and affirmative action programs as necessary means to achieve equality for women. The judge insisted that only tough interventionist measures could successfully combat discrimination in the work world. Women particularly needed barriers removed by means of programs involving daycare, affirmative action, equal pay for work of equal value, and educational leave. She argued forcefully that only positive action would remove the barriers and that not to act to remove them was to "tolerate prejudice and discrimination." She concluded,

> It is not that individuals in the designated groups are inherently unable to achieve equality on their own, it is that the obstacles in their way are so formidable and self-perpetuating that they cannot be overcome without intervention.[3]

In the aftermath of the Abella Report, the 1980s witnessed the emergence of a near-complete political consensus on the need to implement an effective pay equity program. The move was bitterly and loudly resisted by the business lobby, which claimed that the program would lead to closed businesses and lost jobs, and hurt the entire economy by making it less competitive. The small business lobby — the Chambers of Commerce and the Canadian Federation of Independent Business — was particularly virulent in its opposition, claiming that pay equity was totally unworkable for small businesses. This was understandable — effective pay equity could deprive the business community of its largest single pool of cheap

labour, women. Even as Ottawa and many provinces passed carefully circumscribed pay equity laws — targeted at the public sector
and excluding small businesses — the noise from the business
lobby increased, condemning pay equity "as costly, ineffective ...
a threat to women's jobs" and "a massive intrusion in the free market."[4] The president of the Ontario Chamber of Commerce argued
that the legislation would actually hurt women:

> Once you raise the salaries, it forces employers to look at those
> jobs which were paying $15,000 a year and ask if they still need
> them at $20,000 a year ... There will be fewer jobs — because
> employers will eliminate them ... The guy working under the
> truck in the cold may now decide he would rather be inside
> answering the telephone. He will compete for a job once held by
> a woman.

Business protest notwithstanding, by 1988 pay equity programs
had become well-established across Canada.[5] All provinces, with
the predictable exceptions of Alberta, Saskatchewan, and the federal government, had put in place, or had promised quickly to put
in place, pay equity programs for the public service. Ontario was
the only province to extend the program into the private sector. The
debates became increasingly about how to determine and compare
the value of jobs to an employer and just how much of the sex pay
gap is clearly the result of sexual discrimination. Ontario's program
established four criteria for assessing the value of jobs: skills,
effort, responsibility, and working conditions. The government
also provided advice on assessment procedures. Disputes were ultimately to be settled by a Pay Equity Commission. Time, research,
experience, and continuing argument, many believed, would allow
that issue to work itself out.

   The question of how much of the pay gap between men and
women specifically results from sex discrimination is potentially
controversial. Phillips and Phillips argued that studies generally
suggest that about half of the sex pay gap results from forms of
sexual discrimination, the other half from women's inferior training and experience.[6] In 1988, Ontario's Pay Equity Commissioner

presented a much more modest figure, arguing that about one-third
of Ontario's 36 per cent sex-pay gap is the result of "genuine male-
female wage discrimination ... the rest can be attributed to
experience, education and non-gender-based employment equity
issues."[7] Feminists and their supporters argue for a much wider
conception of sex discrimination. Government and business tend
to argue for a very narrow one. To what extent is a woman's lack
of training and experience a result of forms of sex discrimination?
Does a woman's required absence from the labour market to bear
and raise children, and the subsequent negative economic consequences of that, constitute sex discrimination? For the first time as
a society, after 1988 and for a brief period, we were legally committed to a close scrutiny of job value and sexual discrimination
in pay.

In the 1990s, the pay equity gains came under increasingly successful attack by the persistent and well-financed business lobby
and their allies in government. Provincial governments that had not
yet passed such laws continued to drag their feet. Those that had,
while publicly affirming a continuing commitment to pay equity in
principle, slowed the implementation process to a snail's pace.
Ontario, with the most advanced program in the early 1990s, began
to dismantle the entire program after the defeat of the Rae government. In the context of debt and deficit hysteria, neo-conservative
governments were able to put implementation on hold, to slow
it down, or to reverse the entire process both for ideological, anti-
feminist reasons and for fiscal reasons. Ideologically, it was argued,
pay equity programs discriminate in favour of women at the expense
of men, and therefore contradict basic principles of fairness. Fiscally,
it was argued, pay equity, though perhaps a laudable idea and perhaps necessary in the long run in a perfect world, was just too
expensive. The costs to the public treasury, and to general economic competitiveness, were not sustainable in the new, ruthlessly
competitive global economy.

Assuming a serious commitment to achieving economic justice for women, pay equity programs are easier to assess more or
less objectively than affirmative action programs. In matters of
value of work, clear criteria can be established, jobs compared,

and pay levels codified. Effective affirmative action programs are more difficult to put in place and to monitor. Gaining access for women to traditional male occupations is difficult, because the gatekeepers jealously and zealously guard the portals and have endless good reasons for their choices. A university hiring committee will always have good, sound academic reasons for why they chose the man over the woman. Even in cases where, on paper, the woman is manifestly superior, defensible if vague reasons can always be found. Reasons for hiring and promoting people are notoriously subjective, and most of them have to do with the biases of those making the initial recommendation or decision. That is why the board and administration of a corporation, or a university, or a civil service bureaucracy, can elaborate the most elegant and impressive sounding affirmative action plan for women and find later that it isn't working. Voluntary affirmative action programs have been around for almost three decades, yet they have made very little overall difference in the occupational discrimination women face.

In response to that reality, in June 1986 Ottawa passed the Employment Equity Act, and in October 1986 established the Federal Contractors' Program.[8] The act applied to federal crown corporations and corporations operating in areas of federal jurisdiction. They were given two years to come up with an affirmative action plan to eliminate discriminatory employment barriers against women, native people, the disabled, and visible minorities. The plan had to provide positive opportunities for employment, and for advancement. The Contractors' Program imposed similar requirements on all companies doing business with, or having contracts with, the federal government or its agencies exceeding $200,000. Strict reporting requirements were also put in place to allow the monitoring of achievement of the stated goals. Such corporations had to sign an undertaking to adhere to the program in order to continue to be eligible for government business.

The legislation sounded good on paper. But a 1990 report declared that the employment equity law was failing miserably.[9] An assessment of the reports of 372 affected corporations and companies, employing over 600,000 workers, found that women had made few gains — the pay gap between men and women in the companies had closed by only one-half of 1 cent over a year, and promotions going to women had not increased significantly. There are no clear enforcement mechanisms, nor a clear set of sanctions to be applied against those who do not comply. Granted Ottawa can refuse contracts, but that has only been used against those who fail to sign up; it has not been suggested that such sanctions will be applied against those companies that go through the motions, continue to claim to be trying, and promise to try harder. Nor are there any clear sanctions to ensure that federal agencies, crown corporations, departments, or companies active in federally regulated sectors will comply seriously.

The only clear sanctions are via the federal Human Rights Commission. The Commission does indeed have the authority to impose strict affirmative action requirements, including hiring quotas, on offenders. In the famous CN case, the Commission ruled that CN would have to hire women in one in four job vacancies until women had 13 per cent of the total jobs, a percentage equal to the average of blue collar jobs held by Canadian women at that time. But this puts the onus for enforcing the affirmative action law on women — or the other disadvantaged groups — rather than on the federal government. And when enforcement depends not just on a victim's complaint, but on a victim's having the willingness and resources to mount an effective prosecution, then enforcement becomes a bad joke. Voluntary affirmative action programs are now widely seen as scandalously ineffective. The necessity for mandatory affirmative action programs is now widely accepted, and even embodied in a federal law, however inadequately. What is now needed is the will to make mandatory affirmative action programs effective through diligent enforcement and the establishment of precise and compulsory objectives, as well as to extend them to both the provinces and the private sector generally. But Ottawa, like most provinces, has moved in the opposite direction. A 2001 report concludes that Ottawa's Federal Contractors' Program has had "no substantial positive effects." The program was effectively killed in the mid-1990s due to staff cuts and a moratorium on enforcement.

What is clearly happening in the struggle for women's economic equality is that, as a society, we are now trying to make the painful structural transition from words to action. From the 1960s to the 1980s, rhetoric on women's economic equality was codified into impressive policies and laws designed to grant women economic justice. They did not work, or at least failed to work as quickly as expected for as many women as hoped. But the words and laws symbolized a move to a deepening political acceptance that the injustices faced by women had to be rectified. The words and laws tracked a reshaping of the society's political will and the establishment of a new consensus. Having committed ourselves to the words of equality, we could not forever avoid the required actions. The 1980s witnessed the commencement of the process of translating those words into action. The 1990s witnessed a neo-conservative and business lobby backlash, as the concrete gains made in the 1980s came under serious, relentless, and largely effective attack. Now the battle is joined on the practical terrain of implementation, and whether we have the political will as a society to do what must be done, however difficult and painful, to achieve real, tangible economic equality between men and women. Systems of privilege are rarely easy to dismantle, and the system of male economic privilege will not be an exception. If we succeed, we will emerge in a better place to live as men and women.

Afterword:
A Joyous Funeral

The human species invented the family somewhere in its dark prehistory. It proved the secret of our evolutionary success as a species. But like all human inventions, the family has had to be continuously reinvented.

During the Neolithic Revolution, some ten to fifteen thousand years ago, the human family went through a major reinvention as it developed agriculture and learned how to domesticate animals. The old hunting and gathering family, in which the two sexes enjoyed rough equality as a result of mutual economic interdependence, was replaced by patriarchal family forms. Women were enslaved and consigned to the home and hearth under the control of men. The simple and complementary sexual division of labour was replaced by a separation of human life into the public economic sphere, dominated by men, and the domestic sphere, where women were subordinated.

During the Industrial Revolution, two to three hundred years ago, the human family had to be reinvented again in fundamental ways. The patriarchal family form was reinforced, and the separation between the public sphere and the private domestic sphere increased. Initially women were more deeply enslaved and became more deeply dependent. But the Industrial Revolution also set the stage for the increasing liberation of women, both politically and economically. As women achieved more recognition of their rights as persons, conceptions of the family changed. The modern industrial nuclear family emerged based on a new family ideology in which men and women married for love and carried out their obligations to each other and to their children as wives and husbands. Woman's place was in the home. Man's place was outside the home in the public economic sphere where he earned the family's daily bread. But even as women continued to win legal recognition as persons and more complete civil and political rights, their economic dependence on men in the patriarchal nuclear family still enslaved them. But this reality was cloaked by the happy myth of the nuclear family where men and women lovingly lived out their ordained roles.

After World War II, and particularly since the 1960s, the reality of the family again changed fundamentally. As women moved into the labour force, achieving unprecedented degrees of economic independence, the structural hold of patriarchy on women began to erode. As women successfully demanded relief from forms of sexual oppression, it was inevitable that the traditional patriarchal family would have to change radically. During the four decades of the 1960s to the 1990s, the speed of change in the family was so rapid and so fundamental that people found themselves swept up into a crisis of the family, and new family forms emerged. Old certainties were replaced by new uncertainties. Children, women, and men were confronted with the always difficult need to adapt to a major structural change. Traditional notions of masculinity and femininity were increasingly out of step, and new notions had not yet fully developed. Old core sexual identities found little confirmation in the new reality, and new core sexual identities were only tentatively evolving. The costs, economically and emotionally, were great, but the rewards of the changes were potentially enormous.

In retrospect it is now clear that patriarchy, and the traditional male-dominated family it rested on, was in final decline. As women struggled against patriarchal privilege, it became clear that the foundation of male privilege was rooted in women's economic dependence. Increasingly it became clear that women could achieve their fullest liberation only as the patriarchal family declined. And it has. But it has not been easy. And the crisis is not yet over.

Today, therefore, we are in the final stages of yet another major reinvention of the family. This time we are striving to create a family based on true equality between men and women, a family form that neither requires nor insists on the oppression of women. There is no doubt that the new human family will emerge stronger and happier than its predecessors. But it will be a very different family than those of the past. Men, women, and children, together, should openly celebrate its birth, while joining together in the burial of the remnants of the traditional patriarchal family. That will be a joyous funeral.

Epilogue 2003: Canada's New Family Forms

The family underwent a fundamental reconstruction over the past 40 years. Two generations of Canadians — and we're now well into the third — have lived through difficult times of loss and rebuilding touching the most intimate aspects of their lives and self-concepts. The children who pioneered adjustments to the epidemic of divorce and family breakdown in the 1960s and 1970s are now in their 30s and 40s, and divorce has become a routine event. The sharp, often harsh, debates about the family, particularly in the 1980s and 1990s, have tempered somewhat. The traditional family lobby no longer typically insists we have to go back to the good old family, and when members of that lobby make such proposals today they are greeted with incredulity and ridicule. As a result, traditionalists satisfy themselves with worrying around the edges of the new family forms. The evidence of the family's resiliency and persistence has silenced those who briefly predicted the death of the family in the 1960s and 1970s. Surely the "crisis of the family," as such, is largely over and we have emerged on the terrain of the freshly socially reconstructed family.

In one important sense the crisis is over. At a social structural level the character of the new family forms is clear. Few deny the new reality. The traditional patriarchal family — dad and husband out working; mom and wife at home — is dying and there are few mourners. Many, perhaps most, celebrate the demise and only regret that the death seems to be overly long and lingering. Final acceptance of the new family forms, after 30 years and more of resistance, has been incredibly rapid. Indeed, Canadians now accept without pause the common-law family, increasingly the family form of choice among young Canadian adults. The gay or lesbian family has come out of the closet, is now counted as part of the census, and enjoys the tolerant acceptance of a majority of Canadians. In a word, the family in its various reconstructed forms has been largely accepted, even embraced by Canadians. So where is the crisis?

The crisis is still very much there at the individual level. To note that the first generation of children of divorce is in its 40s, and that divorce has become routine, provides little comfort to the thousands of men, women and children who go through divorce and separation each year. Each episode of divorce is a crisis in the personal lives of those involved. In 2000 there were over 155,000 marriages in Canada. But there were over 70,000 divorces — over 70,000 individual crises. Each family suffering from domestic violence lives through the same horrors as did those when the issue first came out of the family attic, intruded into our daily consciousness and provoked agitated public debate. The tens of thousands of children who run away each year are still out there, alone and victimized. The very fact that the problem of runaway children has become an accepted part of our awareness does not lessen the crisis — it just lessens the shock and horror of first awareness. When the suffering of the casualties of the process of family reconstruction becomes a common element of our public awareness, the atmosphere of public crisis recedes. Yet those individuals who live through episodes of personal crisis feel them no less intensely. Indeed, the very public ordinariness of their plight further isolates them, perhaps conveying to them a sense that they are in this alone, without support or sympathy. Therefore, the grinding routine crises in the individual lives of many Canadians are not over, but the urgent public atmosphere of crisis is in danger of slipping into resignation and benign neglect.

The new family forms have emerged, and most now accept they are here to stay. The foundation is laid, the frame erected and, though incomplete, the new family edifice is unmistakeable in its design and dimensions.

The dominant family form remains the wife/husband family — 84 per cent of all families. Two in three of these are dual-earner families. Indeed, the dual-earner family is now the "typical" or "average" family, comprising 54 per cent of all families. Sixteen per cent of wife/husband families are now common law — double the number in the 1980s — and most of these (about three in four) will eventually opt for legal marriage. The rise of the common-law family is one of the most dramatic developments of the family's reconstruction. More and more young Canadians are very wisely opting for a period of experimental marriage — a process of reality testing of commitment, compatibility, and gender identity negotiation — before taking the final legal plunge.

The dual-earner family signals the most important social structural change since it reflects the increasing economic independence of women. The old patriarchal, traditional nuclear family was premised on the economic dependence of women — that nexus of control over women has been largely shattered. This move by women to economic independence as part of the paid labour force resulted from two forces. As the economic foundation of the traditional patriarchal family, the so-called "family wage" for men, disappeared, women were "pushed" by the family's needs into the paid labour force. As important, however, was the drive of women towards real emancipation, an emancipation that could only be achieved by some degree of economic independence outside the family. Therefore, the "pull" from women demanding a place in the paid labour force was of equal if not greater importance. Further, as women have struggled to close the gender pay gap, they have begun to gain a certain rough equality in the economic partnership with their husbands. The contribution of women's earnings to family income has increased dramatically, in more than one in four dual-earner families the woman is the bigger earner, over eight in 10 families in the top income quintile are dual-earner, and a new growing husband/wife family has emerged — in an estimated five per cent of such families the woman is the sole earner.

The traditional male-headed, patriarchal single-earner husband/wife family has declined sharply to 18 per cent of husband/wife families in 2001 (comprising only 16 per cent of all families). The fall has been precipitous. This family form is obviously the one the "death of the family" theorists were talking about. It is doubtful if it will be more than a social curiosity within two generations. Few lament its passing, though some men, deeply encumbered by traditional masculinity, continue to try to hold back the tide, often with tragic results for themselves and the women and children they claim to love.

Perhaps most remarkable among new family forms is the single-parent family, growing from eight per cent of all families in 1966 to almost 16 per cent in 2001. In 1966, 85 per cent were headed by women, 15 per cent by men; in 2001 the share shifted to 81 per cent and 19 per cent. In fact, not only is the single-parent family growing dramatically, but also those headed by men are projected to grow phenomenally throughout this millennium. Caution is necessary here, however. The single-parent family is a temporary family form for most, an episode in the lives of those affected that ends with the establishment of a husband/wife family. Yet it is estimated that one in two children will experience such an episode. The duration of single parenthood episodes varies by age and the number of children — the older the parent at the start of the episode, the longer the duration. The duration of episodes increases with the number of children involved. Durations for single-parent women typically range between four to six years, and often affect children during their younger years when developmental foundations and potentials are established. Single-parent fathers, on average, face durations of about half of that.

The gay or lesbian family — referred to as the "same-sex-couple" in the census — was first counted in 2001, provoking headlines and controversy. While the number was tiny — just over 34,000 or 0.5 per cent of all couples — the event was symbolically important for two reasons. First, it reflected the growing tolerance of diversity among Canadians, since this official count was preceded by legal and constitutional victories that largely won such couples the right to enjoy similar marital benefits to those enjoyed by heterosexual couples. Further, public opinion polls revealed that a majority of Canadians agreed that same-sex couples deserved recognition and ought not to face discrimination.

The second reason is more general. Canadian attitudes have finally caught up with the reality that the new post-industrial family's most important functions are emotional and psychological — to give family members emotional support, love and affection, psychological security, and rootedness of identity. The family no longer serves any vital economic function, nor has it for many years. Canadians' lagging attitudes and values appear to be catching up with the structural changes that have been long in place. Debates about the family, and family policy, will never be the same again.

Two additional features of the new family reality are significant, indeed demographically ominous. First, there are fewer children in Canadian families. In 1966 there was an average of 1.9 children per family, in 2001 that fell to 1.1. In 1961, 29 per cent of families had no children, in 2001 almost 42 per cent had none. More and more married couples are opting for a life without children. Second, more and more Canadians are living alone. In 1961 only four per cent of Canadians lived alone, rising to 10 per cent in 2001. In 2001, one in four households in Canada counted by the census was a "non-family" household. Clearly, part of this phenomenon can only be attributed to a rising number of Canadians who opt for a life alone, without an intimate partner.

Finally, there's the "blended" family, bringing together men, women and children into a new family subsequent to family breakdown. In 1967 only 12 per cent of marriages were remarriages. In 1997 this figure reached one in four. Given the high divorce rate and the growth in common-law unions, it is arguable that a majority of families today are based on remarriage.

Such is the new family reality in Canada. Perhaps it can be said that the crisis of birth has passed, but there continue the many crises of adjustment and psychological repair. The burden of the family's crisis has fallen on the individual shoulders of those who struggle through it, and each of us has done so in our private lives. The burden fell heaviest on those who were, and are, the casualties of the changes — those who suffered through divorce, loneliness, domestic violence, abuse, neglect, and soul-destroying poverty. The heaviest burdens were, and are, borne by children and women.

Canada still has no comprehensive family policy, no systematic array of social programs to nurture the new families through the stress of birth to stable maturity, no reliable social safety net to catch those who fall victim to the structural changes. Indeed, at the height of the crisis Canada's political leaders — led particularly by Brian Mulroney and his neo-conservative wrecking crew after the 1984 election — had nothing to offer to help the family's crisis, meanly opting instead for cancellations and cutbacks of the few existing social support programs established by the welfare state from World War II to the early 1980s. Even Jean Chrétien's February 2003 $25-billion legacy budget, which raised program spending by 20 per cent over the 2003-06 period, hardly began to repair the damage of the previous 20 years of cuts.[1] The items directly related to family supports were a pittance: the funds for daycare will hardly dent the gap between need and available spaces; the increased child benefit will not significantly lower child poverty rates. Despite the propaganda and headlines, and the political smoke and mirrors, the facts are clear. Even with the jump in spending proposed by Chrétien's retirement gift to the Canadian people, program spending by the federal government in 2003 constitutes just over 12 per cent of Gross Domestic Product (GDP) compared to 19 per cent two decades ago. Indeed, federal spending as a percentage of GDP, even with the increase, is the lowest since 1950. Under neo-conservative governments since 1984, assessed in terms of a commitment to use the government as a tool of social policy and economic justice, Canada marched resolutely back to the past, where we remain mired. Chrétien's legacy money is perhaps best seen as salve for the conscience of a once committed social Liberal who oversaw a dismantling of Canada's social support infrastructure that went far beyond Mulroney's initial hopes. Ottawa — and the provinces — continue to evade their responsibility to devise and implement the family support programs so essential to the viability and robust health of Canada's new array of families. We are no closer to Eichler's social responsibility model of family policy than we were 20 years ago. Indeed, we remain further from it than we were in the early 1980s before the neo-conservative social vandalism began.

The serious flashpoints of crisis documented in this book remain, and some are worsening with little sign of amelioration. These cluster around four areas: economic injustice and poverty; children of divorce; domestic violence; and the anti-feminist backlash.

Economic injustice and poverty

Small gains in closing the gender pay gap seem to have stalled at women earning between 70 and 75 per cent of men (full-time work). Growing resistance from governments and the business lobby to aggressive pay equity and affirmative action programs has slowed women's gains to a snail's pace. The gender pay gap was 62 per cent in 1977 and 72 per cent in 1998 — a 10 per cent gain in over 20 years. At this rate women will have to wait until 2060 in order to achieve full income equality with men. As a society, we have declared this to be a monumental injustice. As part of our political consensus and new political culture, we declare that this gap must be closed. It violates our laws and our *Charter of Rights and Freedoms*. Yet the structure of male privilege remains deeply embedded, while our political and economic leaders play a cynical game of deception by pretending public outrage at this injustice, while privately exercising their powers to protect male privilege by failing to do what is necessary to end it. And despite modest gains, women continue to face discriminatory barriers to fairness in access to, and promotion and advancement within, good careers. In 2003, according to a study done for the Women's Executive Network, 69 per cent of women executives in Canada still meet resistance to advancement from "the old boys" at the top.[2] These women reported that the two major barriers remain: first, the discriminatory attitudes of male executives, especially those at the top; and second, the difficulties women face, given their child-bearing and -rearing responsibilities, reconciling demands of career and family. Women in the executive suite still complain they have to work much harder to succeed than equivalent men.

This deeply rooted economic injustice faced by women — and inevitably by their children — is no where more clear than in the risk factors related to the incidence of poverty. The juvenescence and feminization of poverty continues, alleviated only slightly during good economic times. In 1999, almost one in five Canadian children were poor (18.7 per cent), including over 51 per cent of all children in single-parent families headed by women.[3] Almost 52 per cent of female single-parent families were poor, seven times the poverty rate of dual-earner families (7.5 per cent), almost four times the rate of traditional one-earner families (14.3 per cent), five times the rate of husband/wife families with children (10.5 per cent), and almost three times the rate of families headed by single fathers (18 per cent). Comparing women to men, only women and men aged 45 to 54 suffered similar levels of poverty, in all other age groups women suffered higher rates (for example, the women to men ratio for those 25 to 34 was 1.36; for those 65 to 74 it was 1.9).

The National Council of Welfare examined the depth of poverty in 1999. In terms of depth of poverty, defined as the gap between the income available to the poor and the official poverty line, poor single-parent families, both male and female, were the deepest in poverty (excluding unattached individuals), followed closely by poor husband/wife families with children. Those in "abject poverty," defined as those at 50 per cent or less of the official poverty line, included 62,000 single-parent families headed by women and 45,000 husband/wife families with children.

In 1993, Statistics Canada began a longitudinal study that for the first time permits systematic research on the duration of poverty episodes. For most of the 7 million Canadians touched by poverty between 1993 and 1998, poverty was a revolving door, and people who fall into poverty typically move quickly out as their circumstances improve. Data on the first six year period, 1993–1998, were released in 1999. The results were not surprising. The gender, age, and family poverty categories at greatest risk of suffering the longest durations — and most likely to have been poor during all six years — were, in rank order, children under six, single-parent mothers, women, single-parent fathers, and young husband/wife families with children.

Ottawa has further confused the debates around the politics of poverty by acceding to right-wing pressure, led largely by Fraser Institute ideologues, by introducing a third measure of poverty into the mix.[4] Up until 2003, Statistics Canada provided two measures of poverty. The low-income cutoff (LICO), the most commonly used and widely accepted, involves a calculation of how much an average family spends, as a percentage of after-tax income, on the basic necessities and then sets the official poverty line 20 percentage points above that level. Thus the LICO varies — in the 1970s it was 62 per cent; in the 1980s, 58.5 per cent; in the 1990s, 56.2 per cent; in 2000, 64 per cent. All families in 2000 who spent 64 per cent or more of their incomes on the basics were counted as officially poor. The second measure of poverty was simply set at one-half the median income — this allowed international comparisons since such a measure is often used by other nations.

Statistics Canada's new measure of poverty, the "market basket measure" (MBM), was introduced in 2003 as a response to pressure from the right wing. Beginning in 1994, the Fraser Institute, supported by the Canadian Alliance party and conservative elements in other parties, pushed for the MBM. The argument was that the LICO is too generous and therefore grossly exaggerates the real extent of poverty, defined conservatively as those who fail to have sufficient means to exist on the barest of essentials. Only those without the means to buy a "market basket" of basic life necessities should be counted as poor. Such a proposal struck a chord among all Canadian governments, federal and provincial, embarrassed by the fact that basic welfare rates and full-time work on the minimum wage fail to come anywhere near the LICO. Therefore, poverty advocacy groups and trade unions routinely demanded welfare rates and minimum wages that at least matched the LICO. The MBM solves this embarrassing political problem. With the wave of a statistical magic wand, an estimated 30 to 50 per cent of the Canadian poor under the LICO will not qualify as poor under the MBM. Indeed, by adjusting what is in the "market basket" of bare necessities, governments can raise or lower poverty rates to suit immediate public relations requirements.

Future debates on poverty in Canada will become even more confusing, as groups bandy around markedly different "official" poverty rates. The business lobby, the right wing, and incumbent governments will chose the measure that gives the lowest poverty rate. Reformers and poverty advocacy groups will chose the figure that strengthens their case. The Canadian public will be swept up into a rhetorical cloud, losing sight of the real plight of Canada's poor and the programs needed to help them. In the 1960s Lester Pearson declared a war on poverty. In 2003, Ottawa, most provincial governments, and their allies in the business lobby and the Fraser Institute have declared a war on the poor, commencing with a statistical cleansing process to make many of the poor simply disappear from the official count.

Children of divorce

The negative impacts of divorce on children continue to be a controversial concern. The consensus that has emerged seems widely accepted and sensible — divorce is bad for children, but living with unhappy, conflicting and angry parents is worse; the best situation for children is to be raised by two parents in a reasonably happy relationship. Yet there continues to be disagreement. For example, Judith Wallerstein, who first alerted experts and the public to the negative impacts of divorce on children, has more recently painted such a deeply ominous picture that she became an icon of the conservative traditional family lobby. Wallerstein followed a clinical sample of 131 children of divorce beginning in 1971 and provided solid evidence on the emotional difficulties of divorced children. She has now reported on her sample after 25 years, and the children of divorce now range from their late 20s to early 30s.[5] Wallerstein concludes that the most calamitous consequences of divorce appear in young adults and that the negative effects are cumulative, increasing in negative force as the child matures. While Wallterstein's early work was credited with alerting us to the problems faced by children of divorce, her report on the children as teens in 1989 and now as adults in 2000 has provoked the criticism that she has allowed her bias in favour of the traditional, permanent, two-parent family to exaggerate the situation beyond reason. Scientific critics note that the sample of children originated in Wallerstein's private psychotherapy practice, she followed and assessed them herself, and therefore independent confirmation of her findings is not possible. Furthermore, the sample is far too small to sustain the sweeping generalizations Wallerstein makes.

Obviously divorce is not about to be prohibited, nor are we about to pass laws imposing compulsory permanence on marriage relationships that produce children. An estimated 50,000 children are touched by divorce each year in Canada. Previous studies have thoroughly documented the problems they face and have been discussed in this volume. More recent studies confirm the measures that will help. For example, a recent U.S. study found that when divorced parents received counselling after marriage breakup there was a major reduction in problems among their children as they moved into adolescence.[6] Among the children of divorced parents who received counselling, compared to a control group of parents who did not, there were significant reductions in rates of drug and alcohol abuse, in rates of psychological and behavioural problems, and in rates of promiscuity. Clearly, simple early interventions in the immediate post-divorce period can have enormously positive long-term outcomes.

Further, the research that earlier confirmed the serious emotional consequences for children if one parent, usually the father, simply disappeared from their lives, or became a rare presence, has led to important changes. Joint custody appears to be working well, and the redefinition of custody in ways to encourage co-parenting after divorce is working reasonably well. A Montreal study in the mid-1990s found that only 30 per cent of fathers who had access to children in the mother's sole custody saw their children each week, whereas 40 per cent saw their children rarely or never. New approaches, and a new law, presume co-parenting after divorce unless there is a good reason for sole custody (domestic violence, drug or alcohol abuse, etc.). Even before the new law, however, the courts were moving in the same direction. For example, in 2000 the woman got sole custody in Canada in about 54 per cent of cases (compared to almost 76 per cent in 1988), joint custody was granted in 37 per cent of cases, and men received sole custody in nine per cent of cases.[7]

Clearly Canada is moving in a more sensible direction in response to the post-divorce problems encountered by children and their parents. Yet resources are not sufficient. There is no routine access to post-divorce counselling for Canadians (unless you can afford to pay privately or have private insurance); there are not enough counsellors; nor are there sufficient support programs to help parents embark on an effective co-parenting strategy after divorce. In a sense, as a society we now know what needs to be done, but we are as yet unwilling to devote the resources necessary to do it.

Domestic violence

Home and hearth remain places of terror for thousands of Canadian women and children. Controversies continue about whether rates of child abuse and wife assault have increased with the family's crisis, or whether it is merely a matter of increased awareness and willingness to report such cases. In this book it is argued that there appears to have been an increase in domestic violence as a result of problems associated with the family's reconstruction. The evidence of dramatic rises in such violence cannot be simply explained away by increased awareness and reporting, and that claiming such violence was kept secret and unreported in the past. Despite years of increasing public awareness, and more systematic enforcement of legal penalties on abusers, the rates continue to increase. The facts are clear — domestic violence has been a growing epidemic during the period of the family's crisis and reconstruction.

Recent evidence is not without room for some hope. In 2002 the Status of Women Canada reported, based on police data from 1993 to 1998, that spousal homicide and abuse rates were falling slightly.[8] Twenty six per cent fewer wives were killed by husbands, and 39 per cent fewer husbands were killed by wives in that period, and there has been a slight decline over the last 20 years. The gender ratio remains unchanged; wives were three times as likely to be murdered as husbands from 1979 to 1998. The "Lépine syndrome" continues to afflict many troubled men. Further, there was a very small reduction in the occurrence of the most serious and severe assaults on wives (beating, choking and sexual assault) in 1993 — 50 per cent of total victims compared to 43 per cent in 1999. The risk factors remained the same. Women who were pregnant, or young, or poor, or involved with an abuser of alcohol, or who were previous victims of psychological abuse, were at greatest risk of violence. And, of course, women seeking separation and/or divorce faced the highest risk of violence of all groups. Although it is too early to tell if these data reflect a continuing pattern of decline, there is some hope that recent more aggressive policies of intervention, support and prosecution may be having positive impacts.

Regrettably this slightly optimistic report on wife assault is contradicted by evidence of an increase in child abuse. A 2002 Ontario study reported that confirmed cases of child abuse in that province doubled between 1993 and 1998 — from just over 12,000 to just over 24,000.[9] Among these, the number of cases of physical abuse rose from just over 4,000 to 8,000, while cases of emotional abuse increased by almost nine times. Further, 58 per cent of reported cases had had previous incidents reported, suggesting serious failures in our response to child abuse and measures for the protection of children. Researchers in Ontario attributed this dramatic rise to increased reporting by professionals, like teachers, as well as to changes in Ontario law in 2000 placing an onus to report cases of abuse upon all citizens.

Nevertheless, it seems incredible that such dramatic increases can be entirely explained by increased reporting. They could also be attributed to increases in events of abuse. Doubtless both factors are at work. But, as argued earlier, we can never know for certain. We will never know for sure how many cases of abuse and neglect remained unreported in the past, and remain unreported today. What we do know is that there is a dramatic increase in confirmed cases of abuse, and this increase can arguably be attributed either to increased reporting or to an increase in incidents, or a mixture of both. What we do know is that as the family entered into crisis and reconstruction, reported cases of child abuse became apparently epidemic and seem to have increased over the past 30 or 40 years. A significant proportion of that abuse can only be understood in the context of family breakdown and the resulting emotional and economic stress. This becomes even more obvious when the known risk factors for child abuse are factored into the equation, since many are clearly related to the crisis and reconstruction of the family. Such risk factors include, most importantly, poverty, marital discord, family instability and breakdown, and emotional and economic stress on parents, particularly on men.

Just as Ottawa's decision to add the more parsimonious MBM poverty line to the mix will confuse debates about the incidence of poverty and poverty policy, so too has Ottawa's decision to provide an allegedly "gender-neutral" study of domestic violence. And just as the MBM poverty measure resulted from political pressure from the business lobby and the right wing, so too has the "gender neutral" study of domestic violence resulted from pressure from the anti-feminist men's movement comprised largely of aggrieved and angry ex-husbands. In 1999 Statistics Canada released its new "gender-neutral" survey, reporting on the incidence of domestic violence over the previous five years. The data was re-released in Statistics Canada's annual report on domestic violence in 2002.[10]

The study reported that eight per cent of women and seven per cent of men experienced violence at the hands of their partners. As one would expect, the large headline in the 27 June 2002 edition of *The Globe and Mail* declaimed, "Men as likely to face abuse from partner, Statscan says." This was a clear political victory for the anti-feminist men's movement, which has argued consistently that claims about violence against women in the home have been greatly exaggerated by a radical feminist conspiracy with the help of the guilt-ridden liberal men who dominate government and the legal system. Since 1999 the numbers have been quoted again and again to prove that violence in the family has nothing to do with gender.

There is, of course, a small truth here. Men are indeed victims of domestic violence. But this is not news, despite the headlines. Studies have documented this truth repeatedly for many years. An archetypal image of our popular culture, especially in cartoons and comedy, at least until the very recent past, was the large, ugly woman with a frying pan or rolling pin mercilessly abusing her tiny, timid and pathetic henpecked husband. (Interestingly, images of violence against women were rarely incorporated into cartoons, and in the movies the only men who were allowed to hit women were either nasty gangsters or gallant men trying to reason with a hysterical woman). The fact is that male victims of domestic violence have been studied, and such violence against men has been well-documented in the literature.

This small truth, however, becomes a big lie when we fail to take the next step and look closely at the nature, the frequency, the context, and the outcomes of episodes of domestic violence.[11] If we stop and just conclude, for example, as the anti-feminist men's movement has, that domestic violence is equally distributed in the family and it is not a gender issue, we perpetuate a big lie by clinging to this small truth. Just a few examples will suffice. Both mothers and fathers commit child abuse. But the evidence is clear, 85 to 95 per cent of child abusers, depending on the study examined, are men. In 1994–95, 88 children in Canada were murdered by their parents, 59 by the father and 29 by the mother. From 1974 to 1992 there were 65 familicides in Canada (one parent murders his or her partner and all the children, and then typically commits suicide), 94 per cent of these were committed by the father/husband. Three times as many husbands kill wives as wives kill husbands. Police data reveal that in 52 per cent of husband-victim domestic homicides, the violent episode was initiated by the victim. This was true in only six per cent of wife-victim domestic homicides. A Canadian woman is nine times more likely to be murdered by her husband than by a stranger. The most common, and therefore typical, pattern of spousal homicide against men was a woman-victim lashing back at her abuser. Women seeking separation and divorce face a dramatically elevated risk of violence at the hands of the estranged partner. This is very rare in the case of men seeking separation and divorce. For example, young women going through separation faced a risk of homicide 26 times that of all men and 18 times that of all women. Research on domestic violence has been very clear and consistent: women face an epidemic of domestic violence, often very serious life-threatening violence, whereas men face relatively minor events which only rarely become serious and life threatening. Further, male domestic violence is most frequently of the calculating and controlling sort, whereas female domestic violence is most commonly an outburst in the midst of a heated quarrel. Gender, therefore, and patriarchy, remain the central context in understanding and remedying domestic violence.

To their credit, the Statistics Canada researchers addressed the gender issue carefully, but it is buried deep in the report beyond the immediate view of anti-feminist men or headline writers. Their findings tend to confirm the already known patterns. Men typically reported more minor episodes — slapping, biting, hitting with a thrown object, etc. — compared to women — sexual assault, beatings, choking, threats with a gun or knife, injuries by a weapon. Fifteen per cent of women victims needed medical help compared to three per cent of men victims. Just over one in four women victims reported 10 or more episodes of violence compared to one in eight men victims. The study concluded, as previous studies have, that women victims suffer more serious violence, more frequent violence, and the consequences for the victims are more serious and likely to be life threatening. Gender is quite relevant after all, though the small truth of almost equal numbers will be used by some to suppress and to dismiss this larger and more significant truth.

Domestic violence is real and it is terrible. If we are to deal with it effectively we must face the facts frankly and fully. Men and women — and children — need help. The victims need protection and the perpetrators need to be exposed, stopped, punished and ultimately rehabilitated. We need to know as much as we can about the origins and deeper causes of domestic violence, and we need to identify those at risk if we are to prevent this scourge of Canadian family life. We will not be assisted in these tasks by the anti-feminist men's movement and the traditional family lobby who have used this "gender neutral" study to deny present realities in a desperate effort to reconstruct a long dead past family ideal. It is hoped that Statistics Canada, and their political masters in Ottawa, will resist future pressure to participate in studies that mask or dilute the truth. Studies of domestic violence against men and women need to be carried out, but they are different studies, best done separately, since the nature of the domestic violence each gender faces is quite distinctive.

The anti-feminist backlash

Foes of women's gains continue to campaign for rollbacks of those gains, so far with only marginal success. The anti-feminist men's movement has won some victories, but they have not been total.

In the area of the demand for forced joint custody after divorce, the movement won the legitimate point that fathers who wish to do so should be able to continue co-parenting their children after divorce. But the movement failed to win the imposition of compulsory joint custody. The evidence has been clear for some time that some form of joint custody, co-parenting arrangement is best for the children of divorce, and we are clearly moving in that direction. However, joint custody must be assessed on a case-by-case basis and situations of marriage breakdown that include domestic violence, addictions to drugs and/or alcohol, and psychological abuse ought not to involve joint custody, co-parenting provisions.

As noted above, pressure from the anti-feminist men's movement was key to Statistics Canada's "gender-neutral" domestic violence survey. And, inevitably, the movement has used these data to attack findings by experts on domestic violence that demonstrate the much heavier burden of violence borne by women. As Earl Silverman, a leader of Calgary's Family of Men Support Society, declared upon the study's release, "It demonstrates that there has been a severe bias against men in the past in not considering them victims."[12] The effect is to break the previous consensus on the urgency of the problems of domestic violence against women by deflecting us into futile ideological debates between feminist supporters and feminist bashers. The urgent necessity of pressing forward with timely and effective policy initiatives becomes somewhat lost in the gender wars provoked by the anti-feminist men's movement.

The gains made by women on the economic front face serious resistance. Pay equity and affirmative action programs for women are under attack from a variety of divergent interests: the anti-feminist men's movement; the business lobby; those on the political right, most notably the Canadian Alliance party but also including right-wing elements of all parties. As a result, these programs have largely stalled. In the absence of compulsory targets and timelines, external monitoring and policing, and sufficient resources for aggressive enforcement, these programs become mere window dressing and expressions of ultimate good intent. It is not therefore surprising that, despite significant improvements in the last decade and more, the gender wage gap remains indefensibly large and the discriminatory barriers women face in the world of work remain, doubtless somewhat weakened, but still in place. Systems of privilege which are deeply rooted in social structures are never easy to dismantle, witness the legacy of slavery for black Americans or the legacy of conquest and colonization for Aboriginal Canadians. The system of male privilege is proving no exception.

The right to reproductive choice remains one of the most significant gains of women in their struggle against patriarchy. Forced pregnancy and control of women's reproductive function were key aspects of men's control of women and embodied a central feature in the oppression of women. After a long and bitter struggle women finally won control of their reproductive function, first by the legalization of birth control (a criminal act in Canada until 1969). In the 1973 Roe v. Wade decision the U.S. Supreme Court declared that women had a constitutional right to make their own decisions regarding reproduction, including the decision to have an abortion. Canada's Supreme Court finally agreed in 1988 when it found that efforts by the state, through criminal laws, to control a woman's reproductive choice were a violation of her rights under the *Charter of Rights and Freedoms* in the Canadian constitution. These victories were complete in the legal sense, but incomplete in the practical sense as anti-choice activists pressured hospital boards not to provide abortion services, harassed individual doctors to convince them to cease doing the procedure, and harassed abortion clinics to intimidate both staff and clients. Some anti-choice fanatics have even gone to the extreme of murdering and attempting to murder doctors providing abortion services and, in the U.S., to plant bombs in clinics. As a result, though women in Canada have a legal right to abortion, that right is routinely denied to many women as a result of lack of access.

Furthermore, there is continuing pressure from the anti-choice movement to convince politicians to recriminalize abortion or, alternatively, to have the fetus declared a person under the law and the constitution. In January 2003, Manitoba Judge Linda Giesbrecht called on governments to contemplate laws to protect fetuses from substance abuse by mothers.[13] Any such law would involve a compulsory limitation of the woman's rights in the interests of the fetus. The growing debate about the alleged epidemic of Fetal Alcohol Syndrome (FAS) and Fetal Alcohol Effect (FAE) children has provoked such a consideration. The problem here, of course, is that once you have passed a law to protect the fetus from FAS or FAE by compelling a women to do certain things, you have given the fetus a legal and constitutional existence that trumps the rights of the mother as a person under the Charter. For anti-choice activists, eager to impose their religious doctrines on all Canadians, it would be a small step to extend such a fetal right to protection from abortion (or, as they prefer to term it, "the murder of the unborn"). Such laws would be unlikely to pass the scrutiny of the Supreme Court. The 1988 decision made it clear that the sole area in which such laws might pass a Charter test would be laws to protect a potentially viable fetus in the advanced stages of pregnancy, i.e., a fetus which could successfully live outside the woman's womb.

The anti-feminist backlash has been relatively moderate in Canada, and its gains, though significant, have been far from dramatic. It is a different story in the U.S. With Republicans in control of both Houses of Congress and the White House, the assault on women's gains, strong since the days of Reagan, has intensified. The whole elaborate edifice of affirmative action programs are under relentless attack and have been largely successfully dismantled or rendered ineffective at the federal level and in many states. Recently the U.S. Supreme Court, now much move conservative than the liberal court of 1973 and Roe v. Wade, overturned an earlier ruling by declaring that anti-choice activists cannot be prohibited from blocking entrances to abortion clinics. (In Canada, police routinely impose buffer zones to keep anti-choice demonstrators a reasonable distance from clinics). This decision was seen by many as a license to resume the campaign of violence that had led to the earlier Court's decision to prohibit such actions. As the head of Operation Rescue, a militant anti-choice organization in the U.S., said of the decision, "This is a great win for Christ and his unborn children."[14] Members of the pro-choice movement see this as the opening salvo in a new effort by the Republicans to overturn the freedom of reproductive choice by granting the unborn fetus the legal and constitutional status of person. Regrettably, certain Canadian politicians, most notably the Canadian Alliance party, have a tendency to seek inspiration from the initiatives taken by conservative Republicans and the religious right in the U.S. Hence events in the U.S. tend to spill over into Canadian political debates, and the excesses of the anti-feminist crusade in the U.S. will find inevitable articulation in Canada.

We should perhaps be grateful that the anti-feminist backlash in Canada has not yet gone as far as that in the U.S. And the backlash in Canada and the U.S. has not yet gone as far as that in Australia. There the self-proclaimed vanguard of the anti-feminist men's movement call themselves the Blackshirts.[15] Largely composed of ex-husbands angry at their treatment by their former wives and the courts, the Blackshirts, dressed all in black and wearing face masks and sunglasses, regularly picket family courts and have begun picketing the homes of targeted ex-wives. Besides complaining about the usual list of grievances of such groups worldwide, the Blackshirts have gained notoriety for supporting what they call "the sanctity of marriage" and the death penalty for adulterers (which appear only to include women). They have threatened to begin lynching adulterers. While few take the movement literally or seriously, their violent language and violent symbolism resonate with many very angry men. What the Blackshirts are proposing is little different from what far too many ex-husbands and ex-boyfriends actually do when they beat and often murder their estranged wives and girlfriends.

The reconstruction of the Canadian family and the crisis of birth of the new family forms together constitute a profound and revolutionary social structural change. The new "typical" family, the two-earner family, is the location of the continuing renegotiation between men and women of new definitions of gender identity, new notions of emotional commitment and responsibility, and new strategies of parenting. The evidence so far is overwhelmingly positive. Women and men are successfully negotiating a family form, and a redefinition of masculinity and femininity, that strives to reconcile the family and sexual intimacy with the liberation and independence of women. There are problems. The process is painful and difficult. The dynamics of change and adjustment are far from over. But the fact remains that Canadian women and men are together reconstructing a set of family forms and family strategies that will make our social world a better place than before.

At both a personal and social structural level, the struggle involves a long and painful process of negotiating and reconstructing male and female gender identities. In a sense, besides reconstructing the new family, we are reconstructing the "new woman" and the "new man." What the ultimate content of these new gender identities will be is as yet not fully known. Hence, there is a great deal of anxiety and confusion in the conversations between men and women, both in public and in private. We are all aware that we are in the midst of constructing an equal gender partnership in the family, in sexual intimacy, and in the world of work. And we are all pretty much aware of what we reject from the past — the traditional, domineering, patriarchal male; the traditional dependent, submissive, ever-accommodating female. Beyond that the agreement is not so easy to come by.

For the "new woman" the process of gender reconstruction is largely positive, as new possibilities and opportunities, formerly forbidden and closed to women, open up in a panorama of positive growth and choice. Therefore, for women the last few decades, though difficult, have involved a certain exultation and excitement. But there is doubt and confusion. To what extent must the new woman embody elements of traditional masculinity? Obviously, given growing independence and autonomy, there will be some transfer. But what are the elements to be embraced? to be avoided? Women in the executive suite complain that they are expected to imitate some of the worst aspects of the old masculinity — toughness, aggressivity, insensitivity, selfishness — in order to succeed. Many young women seem to have the view that to be equal with men they have to be equally nasty and violent, and to engage in irresponsible and risky behaviour. Nevertheless, the reconstruction of a new gender identity for women is overwhelmingly positive.

For the "new man" the process is more confusing and difficult. There is the very real loss of male privilege, and this is hitting younger men hardest, since affirmative action and pay equity programs tend to redress historical grievances by imposing the greatest cost on young men just starting out. Men complain that women want both kinds of men — aggressive sexual initiators and emotionally sensitive "new age guys" — and they never know for sure what is expected of them in interactions with women. The gains of women in educational achievement and advancement have been phenomenal in the past 20 years, but now we face a new gender inequity — young men are falling behind women in all academic subjects. Young men complain that they are expected to co-parent, and most want to do so, but women continue to assert primary authority over child rearing and continue to exclude men from equal parenting after separation and divorce.

Out of all this confusion and uncertainty the trends are becoming clear. The "new man" will be constructed from the best of the old — responsible, loyal, compassionate, strong, courageous, hard-working, devoted to his family and so on — with elements of a new realm of masculinity involving emotional expressivity and tenderness, a capacity for nurturing and parenting, and a sensitivity to the feelings of others. The "new woman" will be constructed from the best of the old — tender, loving, sensitive to others, nurturing and so on — with elements of a new femininity involving independence, assertiveness, strength, and discipline. Clearly the process we are undergoing involves a blurring of the sharp edges that formerly defined and divided "real men" and "real women" into two solitudes.

Simone de Beauvoir once commented that the old gender dialogues about relationships between men and women involved complaints from women of expectations that they will give up everything for husband and family, while men complained that women and the family took everything from them. Today the renegotiation revolves around what each can be expected to give, and can expect to receive, in intimate relationships and in the new family. This is a whole new dialogue and, given it is now increasingly a dialogue of equals, the outcome remains uncertain and probably always will be. After all, it is only in relationships of clear domination and subordination that humans can be certain about what the rules and expectations are. Once you enter the realm of human relationships among equals the outcome is constantly open to renegotiation and there are, finally, no real certainties.

Endnotes

Preface

1. In the 1990s the marriage rate ranged between 5 and 7 per 1000 population. The divorce rate was in the 2.5 to 3 per 1000 range. Throughout the 1980s and 1990s, the divorce rate hovered near one-half the level of the marriage rate (see Statistics Canada, *Canadian Social Trends*, Winter 1988 to Winter 2002). In 2000 there were almost 153,000 marriages and just under 72,000 divorces. Between 1971 and 1996, the percentage of Canadians who were divorced grew by 6 times, while the percentage of Canadians who were married fell by over 10 per cent.

2. Owen Adams, "Divorce Rates in Canada," Statistics Canada, *Canadian Social Trends* (Winter 1988): 18-19. In 1969 the median duration of marriage before divorce was 15 years. In 1986 it was just over nine years. Since divorce rates from 1986 to 1991 remained high (2.9 to 3.4 per 1000 population), while marriage rates remained steady (6.9 to 7.3 per 1000 population), the duration of marriage before divorce in all likelihood continued to decrease. See "Social Indicators," Statistics Canada, *Canadian Social Trends* (Autumn 1992): 32, and "Family Indicators for Canada: Trends and Projections," *Canadian Social Trends* (Summer 1996): 32-33. However, given the remarkable growth in common-law marriages, combined with the rise in age of first marriage among both men and women, both documented in the 1991 Census, some moderation in these trends in legal marriage resulting in legal divorce occurred (both marriage and divorce rates fell slightly in the 1990s).

3. Statistics Canada, "Changes in Living Arrangements," *Canadian Social Trends* (Spring 1989): 27-29.

4. Regina *Leader Post*, 14 December 1986.

5. Robert S. Lynd, *Knowledge for What?* (New York: Grove Press, 1964 [1939]).

6. C. Wright Mills, *The Sociological*

Imagination (New York: Oxford University Press, 1959).

Part I: The Changing Nature of the Family
Chapter 1: Families Past

1. See S. Freud, *Totem and Taboo* (New York: Standard Edition, vol. 13, 1950 [1913]), and S. Freud, *Moses and Monotheism* (New York: Standard Edition, vol. 23, 1939).

2. S. Freud, *Civilization and Its Discontents* (London: Lewis, 1963 [1930]).

3. F. Engels, *The Origin of the Family, Private Property and the State* (New York: International, 1972 [1884]).

4. Marshall D. Sahlins, "The Origin of Society," *Scientific American*, 203, no. 31 (1960): 76-86.

5. Jane B. Lancaster and Phillip Whitten, "Family Matters," *Sciences* (January 1980): 10-15.

6. *Ibid.*, 14.

7. Kathleen Gough, "The Origin of the Family," in *Toward an Anthropology of Women*, ed. R. Reiter Rayna (New York: Monthly Review, 1975): 52.

8. *Ibid.*, 53.

9. Karen L. Anderson, "Historical Perspectives on the Family," in *Family Matters*, ed. Karen L. Anderson *et. al.* (Toronto: Methuen, 1987): 21-39.

10. Paul Phillips and Erin Phillips, *Women and Work*, rev. ed. (Toronto: Lorimer, 1993): 33-34.

11. All statistics quoted are taken from the Census of the year indicated, unless otherwise noted.

12. P. Armstrong and H. Armstrong, *The Double Ghetto*, 3rd ed. (Toronto: McClelland and Stewart, 1994): 15-19.

13. F. H. Leacy, ed., *Historical Statistics of Canada* (Ottawa: Statistics Canada, 1983): Series D8-85. [Hereafter cited as *HSC*.]

14. *HSC*, Series E60-68.

15. *The Gallup Report*, 23 March 1987.

16. *HSC*, Series B1-14.

17. *HSC*, Series B51-58.

18. Simone de Beauvoir, *The Second Sex* (New York: Bantam, 1961).

19. Betty Friedan, *The Feminine Mystique* (New York: Norton, 1963).

20. Canada, *Report of the Royal Commission on the Status of Women in Canada* (Ottawa: Information Canada, 1970).
21. Phillips and Phillips, *Women and Work*, 1983 edition: viii.
22. *HSC*, Series A110-24.
23. Owen Adams, "Divorce Rates in Canada," Statistics Canada, *Canadian Social Trends* (Winter 1988): 18-19.
24. *HSC*, Series D431-48.
25. *The Gallup Report*, 23 March 1987.
26. Statistics Canada, *Women in Canada: A Statistical Report* (Ottawa, 1984), the data are compiled from tables provided throughout the publication.
27. Maureen Moore, "Women Parenting Alone," Statistics Canada, *Canadian Social Trends* (Winter 1987): 31-46.
28. Margrit Eichler, *Families in Canada Today* (Toronto: Gage, 1983): 236.

Chapter 2: Families Present

1. Statistics Canada, *Projections of Households and Families for Canada, Provinces and Territories, 1994-2016* (Ottawa: Ministry of Industry, 1995); T. Chui, "Canada's Population: Charting into the 21st Century," Statistics Canada, *Canadian Social Trends* (Autumn 1996): 3-7; Census 91, *Families: Number, Type and Structure*, Catalogue # 93-312 (Ottawa: Statistics Canada, 1993); Statistics Canada, "Changes in Living Arrangements," *Canadian Social Trends* (Spring 1989): 27-29. 2001 census data.
2. M. Moore, "Dual-Earner Families: The New Norm," Statistics Canada, *Canadian Social Trends* (Spring 1989): 24-26; R. Chawla, "The Changing Profile of Dual-Earner Families," *Perspectives on Labour and Income* (Summer 1992): 22-29; J. Oderkirk et. al., "Traditional Earner Families," Statistics Canada, *Canadian Social Trends* (Spring 1994): 19-25.
3. R. Logan and J.-A. Belliveau, "Working Mothers," Statistics Canada, *Canadian Social Trends* (Spring 1995): 24-28; P. Best, "Men, Women and Work," Statistics Canada, *Canadian Social Trends* (Spring 1995): 30-33; Census 91, *Labour Force Activity*

by *Presence of Children*, Catalogue # 93-325 (Ottawa: Statistics Canada, 1993); J.-A. Parliament, "Women Employed Outside the Home," Statistics Canada, *Canadian Social Trends* (Summer 1989): 3-6.
4. A. Rashid, "Changes in Real Wages," Statistics Canada, *Canadian Social Trends* (Spring 1994): 16-18; A. Rashid, "Seven Decades of Wage Change," *Perspectives on Labour and Income*, Summer 1993; C. Lindsay, "The Decline of Real Family Income, 1980-1984," Statistics Canada, *Canadian Social Trends* (Winter 1986): 15-17.
5. B. J. Wylie, *All in the Family: A Survival Guide for Family Living and Loving in a Changing World* (Toronto: Key Porter, 1988).
6. G. S. Lowe, "Canadians and Retirement," Statistics Canada, *Canadian Social Trends* (Autumn 1992): 18-21; M. Monette, "Retirement in the 90s," Statistics Canada, *Canadian Social Trends* (Autumn 1996): 8-11; C. Lindsay, "The Decline in Employment Among Men Aged 55-64, 1975-1985," Statistics Canada, *Canadian Social Trends* (Spring 1987): 12-15; C. Lindsay and C. McKie, "Annual Review of Labour Force Trends," Statistics Canada, *Canadian Social Trends* (Autumn 1986): 2-6.
7. E. L. Lipman et. al., "The Problems of Children in Lone-Mother Families," Statistics Canada, *Canadian Social Trends* (Spring 1997):7-8; J. Oderkirk and C. Lochhead, "Lone Parenthood: Gender Differences," Statistics Canada, *Canadian Social Trends* (Winter 1992): 16-19; M. Moore, "Women Parenting Alone," Statistics Canada, *Canadian Social Trends* (Winter 1987): 31-46.
8. C. F. Grindstaff, "Canadian Fertility, 1951 to 1993," Statistics Canada, *Canadian Social Trends* (Winter 1995): 12-16; M. Belle and K. McQuillan, "Births Outside Marriage: A Growing Alternative," Statistics Canada, *Canadian Social Trends* (Summer 1994): 14-17; M. S. Deveraux, "Decline in the Number of Children," Statistics Canada, *Canadian Social Trends* (Autumn 1990): 32-34.
9. B. Arnoti, "Children in Low-income

Families," Statistics Canada, *Canadian Social Trends* (Winter 1986): 18-20; National Council of Welfare, *Poverty Profile 1995*; Census 91, *Labour Force Activity by Presence of Children*, Catalogue #93-325 (Ottawa: Statistics Canada, 1993).

10. M. Moore, "Female Lone Parenthood: The Duration of Episodes," Statistics Canada, *Canadian Social Trends* (Autumn 1988): 40-42.

11. K. Rodgers, "Wife Assault," Statistics Canada, *Canadian Social Trends* (Autumn 1994): 3-8; H. Johnson, "Wife Abuse," Statistics Canada, *Canadian Social Trends* (Spring 1988): 17-20.

12. E. M. Nett, *Canadian Families: Past and Present* (Toronto: Butterworths, 1988): 147.

13. M. Boyd, "Canadian Family Forms: Issues for Women," in *Reconstructing the Canadian Family: Feminist Perspectives*, eds. N. Mandell and A. Duffy (Toronto: Butterworths, 1988): 85-109; J. Oderkirk and C. Lochhead, "Lone Parenthood: Gender Differences," Statistics Canada, *Canadian Social Trends* (Winter 1992): 16-19.

14. S. Methot, "Low Income in Canada," Statistics Canada, *Canadian Social Trends* (Spring 1987): 2-7; National Council of Welfare, *Poverty Profile 1995 and 1998*.

15. R. A. Stebbins, "Men, Husbands and Fathers: Beyond Patriarchal Relations," in *Reconstructing the Canadian Family*, eds. Mandell and Duffy: 27-47.

16. C. Stout, "Common Law: A Growing Alternative," Statistics Canada, *Canadian Social Trends* (Winter 1991): 18-20; C. McKie, "Common-Law: Living Together as Husband and Wife," Statistics Canada, *Canadian Social Trends* (Autumn 1986): 39-41; P. Turcotte, "Common-Law Unions: Nearly Half a Million in 1986," Statistics Canada, *Canadian Social Trends* (Autumn 1988): 35-39.

17. *Globe and Mail*, 27 and 28 July 1989.

18. *Globe and Mail*, 27 December 1984.

19. *Globe and Mail*, 11 January 1989.

20. Boyd, "Canadian Family Forms," 89; M. Eichler, *Families in Canada Today* (Toronto: Gage, 1983): 236; Vanier Institute of the Family, *Profiling Canadian Families* (Ottawa, 1994).

21. A. Clubb Neuman, *Love in the Blended Family* (Toronto: NC Press, 1988).

22. Nett, *Canadian Families*: 161; Eichler, *Families in Canada*: 235; C. J. Richardson, "Children of Divorce," in *Family Matters*, eds. Anderson et. al.: 193; A.-M. Ambert and M. Baker, "Marriage Dissolution," in *Family Bonds and Gender Divisions*, ed. B. Fox (Toronto: Canadian Scholars' Press, 1988): 453-75, 469, 475.

23. Regina *Leader Post*, 26 August 1985.

24. Regina *Leader Post*, 8 June 1988.

25. *Globe and Mail*, 18 May 1988.

26. Regina *Leader Post*, 5 April 1989.

27. In 1988, the parliament of Denmark legalized homosexual marriages granting them the same rights enjoyed by married heterosexual couples. Sweden also passed a similar law in 1988 (Regina *Leader Post*, 26 May 1989). In 1990, New York's highest state court ruled that a partner of a long-standing gay relationship can retain the lease on an apartment when the holder of a lease dies. The court found that the legal definition of "family members" should include adults who show long-term financial and emotional commitment. In Canada, the controversy remains largely unresolved, though it is moving in the same direction. In 1992, an Ontario board of inquiry under the Human Rights Code ordered pension survivor benefits to be paid to same sex couples. Courts of Appeal and the Supreme Court have ruled that discrimination on the basis of sexual orientation is contrary to the Charter. But whether that should extend to a re-definition of the family to include gay couples remains unclear. In February 1993 the Supreme Court ruled 4 to 3 that Brian Mossop was properly denied bereavement leave to attend the funeral of his partner's father on the grounds that, in the absence of a specific Charter challenge, the meaning of "family status" does not include same sex couples if Parliament clearly excludes such couples from such benefits. This leaves the door open to a Charter challenge on the right of gay couples to claim family status. See

Globe and Mail, 5 July 1990; 3 June 1992; 8 June 1992; 8 August 1992; 2 September 1992; 3 February 1993. For a recent favourable ruling see *Globe and Mail*, 19 December 1996; 10 February 1996. For a summary of the status of same-sex couples' rights see *Globe and Mail*, 12 October 1996. See the *Gallup Reports*, 11 October 1996 and 4 November 1996. For further analysis, see K. R. Allen and D. H. Demo, "The families of lesbians and gay men," *Journal of Marriage and the Family*, 57 (1995): 111-27; P. Rush, "Same-sex spousal benefits and the evolving conception of family," *University of Toronto Law Review*, 53 (1993): 170-85.

Chapter 3: Families Future

1. *Globe and Mail*, 8 March 1983.
2. B. Rabkin, *Loving and Leaving: Why Women Are Walking Out of Marriage* (Toronto: McClelland and Stewart, 1985).
3. B. Ehrenrich, *Hearts of Men: American Dreams and the Flight from Commitment* (Garden City, N.J.: Anchor, 1983).
4. Y. A. Cohen, *Social Structure and Personality* (New York: Holt, 1961): 459ff.
5. B. Saraceno and C. Barbui, "Poverty and Mental Illness," *Canadian Journal of Psychiatry*, 42:3 (April 1997): 285-90; H. Hafner and W. an der Heiden, "Epidemiology of Schizophrenia," *Canadian Journal of Psychiatry*, 42:2 (March 1997): 139-51; B. P. Dohrenwend et. al., "Socioeconomic status and psychiatric disorders: the causation-selection issue," *Science*, 255 (1992): 946-52; J. Paris, "Social Risk Factors for Borderline Personality Disorders: A Review and Hypothesis," *Canadian Journal of Psychiatry*, 37:7 (September 1992): 510-15; L. R. Robins, B. Z. Locher and D. A. Reiger, *An Overview of Psychiatric Disorders in America* (New York: Free Press, 1991); L. R. Robins and D. A. Reiger, *Psychiatric Disorders in America* (New York: Free Press, 1991); B. P. Dohrenwend, "Socioeconomic status (SES) and psychiatric disorders: are the issues still com-

pelling?" *Social Psychiatry and Psychiatric Epidemiology*, 25 (1990): 41-7; B. J. Gallagher, The Sociology of Mental Illness (Englewood Cliffs, N. J.: Prentice-Hall, 1987): 266ff; W. W. Eaton, *The Sociology of Mental Disorders* (New York: Praeger, 1986); C. P. Holzer et. al., "The increased risk for specific psychiatric disorders among persons of low socioeconomic status," *American Journal of Social Psychology*, 4 (1986): 259-71; J. J. Schwab and M. E. Schwab, *Sociocultural Roots of Mental Illness: An Epidemiological Survey* (New York: Plenum, 1978); G. W. Brown and T. Harris, *Social Origins of Depression: A Study of Psychiatric Disorder in Women* (London: Tavistock, 1978); L. Strole, T. S. Langer et. al. *Mental Health in the Metropolis: The Midtown Manhattan Study* (New York: Harper, 1975); M. H. Brenner, *Mental Illness and the Economy* (Cambridge, Mass.: Harvard, 1973); B. P. Dohrenwend and B. S. Dohrenwend, *Social Status and Psychological Disorders* (New York: Wiley, 1969); A. H. Leighton et. al. *My Name is Legion*, vol. I, Stirling County Study (New York: Basic, 1959); C. C. Hughes et. al. *People of Cove and Woodlot*, vol. II, Stirling County Study (New York: Basic, 1960); D. C. Leighton et. al. *The Character of Danger*, vol. III, Stirling County Study (New York: Basic, 1963); A. B. Hollingshead and F. C. Redlich, *Social Class and Mental Illness* (New York: Wiley, 1958); Y. A. Cohen, *Social Structure and Personality* (New York: Holt, 1961): 457ff.
6. Regina *Leader Post*, 24 March 1986.
7. M. C. Mahood, "Depression in Women," unpublished paper, 1986.
8. Brenner, *Mental Illness and the Economy*.
9. C. M. Renzetti and D. J. Curran, *Women, Men and Society* (Boston: Allyn and Bacon, 1992); C. F. Epstein, *Deceptive Distinctions: Sex, Gender, and the Social Order* (New Haven: Yale, 1988); R. J. Hafner, *Marriage and Mental Illness: A Sex-Roles Perspective* (New York: Guilford, 1986).
10. *Toronto Star*, 26 February 1987.

Part II: Victims of the Crisis: Children
Introduction: Who Cares for the Children?

1. *UN Declaration of the Rights of the Child* (New York: United Nations, 1960); *The Universal Declaration of Human Rights* (New York: United Nations, 1949); *Globe and Mail*, 25 November 1995.
2. See S. Brody and S. Axelrod, *Mothers, Fathers and Children: Explorations in the Formation of Character in the First Seven Years* (New York: International University Press, 1978); M. S. Maher, *et. al. The Psychological Birth of the Human Infant* (New York: Basic, 1975); R. A. Spitz, *The First Year of Life* (New York: International University Press, 1968); and G. H. Mead, *Mind, Self and Society* (Chicago: University of Chicago, 1973 [1934]).
3. A. Leibowitz, "Home Investments in Children," *Journal of Political Economy* (March/April 1974): 111-31; A. Leibowitz, "Parental Inputs and Children's Achievement," *Journal of Human Resources* (Spring 1977): 242-51; both cited in L. Osberg, *Economic Inequality in Canada* (Toronto: Butterworths, 1981).
4. N. Mandell, "The Child Question: Links Between Women and Children in the Family," in *Reconstructing the Canadian Family: Feminist Perspectives*, eds. N. Mandell and A. Duffy (Toronto: Butterworths, 1988): 51.
5. *The Gallup Report*, 14 August 1989.
6. R. Logan and J.-A. Belliveau, "Working Mothers," *Canadian Social Trends*, Statistics Canada (Spring 1995): 24-28; K. Marshall, "Balancing Work and Family Responsibilities," *Perspectives on Labour and Income*, Statistics Canada (Spring 1994); N. Z. Ghalam, "Women in the Workplace," *Canadian Social Trends*, Statistics Canada (Spring 1993): 2-6; M. A. Burke et. al., "Caring for Children," Statistics Canada, *Canadian Social Trends* (Autumn 1991): 12-15; S. Crompton, "Who's Looking After the Kids? Child Care Arrangements of Working Mothers," *Perspectives on Labour and Income*, Statistics Canada (Summer 1991).
7. House of Commons, *Sharing the Responsibility: Report of the Special Committee on Childcare* (Ottawa: Queen's Printer, 1987): 8, 34-36, 44, 151, 154; for the 1996 figure see *Globe and Mail*, 8 April 1996.
8. *Globe and Mail*, 14 January 1987.
9. *Ibid.*, 15 January 1987.
10. *Globe and Mail, Report on Business*, 2 December 1988.
11. C. E. Ross and J. Mirowsky, "Child Care and Emotional Adjustment to Wives' Employment," *Journal of Health and Social Behaviour*, 29:2, (June 1988): 127-38; see also J. E. Fast and J. A. Frederick, "Working Arrangements and Time Stress," Statistics Canada, *Canadian Social Trends* (Winter 1996): 14-19; E. B. Akyeanpong, "Absenteeism at Work," Statistics Canada, *Canadian Social Trends* (Summer 1992): 26-28; L. Geran, "Occupational Stress," Statistics Canada, *Canadian Social Trends* (Autumn 1992): 14-17.
12. *Globe and Mail, Report on Business*, 23 May 1988; *Globe and Mail*, 7 December 1996.
13. Mandell, "The Child Question," pp. 75-76.

Chapter 4: The Economic Insecurity of Children

1. Statistics Canada, *Charting Canadian Incomes, 1951-81* (Ottawa: Supply and Services, 1984); W. I. Gillespie, *The Redistribution of Income in Canada* (Ottawa: Carleton University, 1980); *Globe and Mail, Report on Business*, 5 February 1991; Statistics Canada, *Income Distribution by Size in Canada, 1991* (Ottawa 1993); Canada, Department of Finance, *Economic Reference Tables*, Reference Table 14, "Structural Change in the Sources and Disposition of Personal Income, 1947-1991" (Ottawa, August 1993); Statistics Canada, *Income After Tax: Distribution by Size in Canada, 1995* (Ottawa 1997). As a result of the cuts in social spending of the past decade, redistribution of income has in fact increasingly favoured the rich, who are getting richer while the poor are getting

poorer. This is largely a result of the decline in the amounts expended, and in the narrowing of eligibility criteria, for government income transfers to individuals, most importantly employment insurance and social assistance payments.

2. C. Sarlo, *Poverty in Canada - 1994* (Vancouver: Fraser Institute, 1994); A. Spector, "Measuring Low Incomes in Canada," Statistics Canada, *Canadian Social Trends* (Summer 1992): 8-11; Economic Council of Canada, *The New Face of Poverty: Income Security Needs of Canadian Families* (Ottawa 1992); G. Swimmer (ed.), *How Ottawa Spends, 1996-97: Life Under the Knife* (Ottawa: Carleton University, 1996).

3. D. P. Ross, *The Canadian Fact Book on Poverty -1983* (Toronto: Lorimer, 1983); D. P. Ross et. al. *The Canadian Fact Book on Poverty - 1994* (Ottawa: Canadian Council on Social Development, 1995); A. Frizzel and J. H. Pammett, eds. *Social Inequality in Canada* (Ottawa: Carleton University, 1996).

4. National Council of Welfare, *Poverty Profile 1988; Poverty Profile 1990; Poverty Profile 1994; Poverty Profile 1995* (Ottawa: Supply and Services, 1989, 1991, 1995, 1996).

5. *Globe and Mail*, 11 July 1985.

6. National Council of Welfare, *Welfare Incomes 1995* (Ottawa: Supply and Services, 1997).

7. National Council of Welfare, *1988 Poverty Lines* (Ottawa: Supply and Services, 1988).

8. Cited in R. H. de Lone, *Small Futures: Children, Inequality and the Limits of Liberal Reform* (New York: Harcourt Brace Jovanovich, 1970): 20.

9. National Council of Welfare, *Poor Kids* (Ottawa: Supply and Services, 1975): 1.

10. I. Adams et. al. *The Real Poverty Report* (Edmonton: Hurtig, 1971): 22.

11. J. Oderkirk, "Food Banks," Statistics Canada, *Canadian Social Trends* (Spring 1992): 6.14; T. Peressini, *Disadvantage, Drift and Despair: Homelessness in Canada*, PhD dissertation, Department of Sociology, University of Waterloo, 1995.

12. For what follows, see: *Globe and Mail*, 22 December 1983; 22 July 1987; 2 August 1987; 8 April 1987; 3 October 1987; 30 October 1987; 24 May 1988; 16 June 1989; Regina *Leader Post*, 4 November 1986.

13. G. Riches, *Food Banks and the Welfare Crisis* (Ottawa: Canadian Council on Social Development, 1986).

14. This was the charge made by B.C. Premier Bill Vander Zalm in 1988 (*Globe and Mail*, 12 May 1988). In 1996 Ontario Premier Mike Harris attributed it to "certain lifestyle changes," most notably working mothers (*Globe and Mail*, 7 November 1996).

15. G. D. Smith et. al., "Lifetime socioeconomic position and mortality," *British Medical Journal*, 314 (22 February 1997): 547-52; A. Haines, "Working together to reduce poverty's damage," *British Medical Journal*, 314 (22 February 1997): 529-30; G. D. Smith, "Income inequality and mortality: why are they related?" *British Medical Journal*, 312 (20 April 1996): 987-88; W. Millar and M. P. Beaudet, "Health Facts from the 1994 National Population Health Survey," Statistics Canada, *Canadian Social Trends* (Spring 1996): 24-27; G. Picot and J. Myles, "Children in Low-income Families," Statistics Canada, *Canadian Social Trends* (Autumn 1996): 15-19; S. Davidson and I. G. Manion, "Facing the challenge: mental health and illness in Canadian youth," *Psychology, Health and Medicine*, 1:1, 1996: 41-56; G. A. Kaplan et. al., "Inequality in income and mortality in the United States," *British Medical Journal*, 312 (20 April 1996): 999-1003; G. D. Smith et. al., "Socioeconomic differentials in mortality risk among men screened for the multiple risk factor intervention trial: results for 300,685 white men," *American Journal of Public Health*, 86, 1996: 486-96; R. Roberge et. al., "Health and socio-economic inequalities," Statistics Canada, *Canadian Social Trends* (Summer 1995): 15-19; J. W. Lynch et. al., "Childhood and adult socioeconomic status as predictors of mortality in Finland," *Lancet*, 343, 1994: 524-27;

D. Vagero and D. Leon, "Effect of social class in childhood and adulthood on adult mortality," *Lancet*, 343, 1994: 1224-25; W. J. Millar et. al., "Trends in Low Birth Weight," Statistics Canada, *Canadian Social Trends* (Spring 1993): 26-29; C. A. Schoenborn, "Trends in Health Status and Practices: Canada and the United States," Statistics Canada, *Canadian Social Trends* (Winter 1993): 16-21; M. Wolfson et. al., "Career earnings and death: a longitudinal analysis of older Canadian men," *Journal of Gerontology: Social Sciences*, 48, 1993: 5167-79; P. L. Menchik, "Economic status as a determinant of mortality among black and white older men: does poverty kill?" *Population Studies*, 47, 1993: 427-36; R. J. Waldman, "Income distribution and infant mortality," *Quarterly Journal of Economics*, 107, 1992: 1283-1302; J. Oderkirk, "Parents and Children Living with Low Income," Statistics Canada, *Canadian Social Trends* (Winter 1992): 11-15; J. Oderkirk and C. Lochhead, "Lone Parenthood: Gender Differences," Statistics Canada, *Canadian Social Trends* (Winter 1992): 16-19; I. T. Elo and S. H. Preston, "Effects of early-life conditions on adult mortality," *Population Index*, 58, 1992: 186-212; V. Carstairs and R. Morris, *Deprivation and Health in Scotland* (Aberdeen: University of Aberdeen, 1991); R. Alter and J. Riley, "Frailty, sickness and death: models of morbidity and mortality in historical populations," *Population Studies*, 43, 1989: 25-46; F. Aitken and A. Mitchell, "The relationship between poverty and child health," *Canadian Review of Social Policy*, 35 (1995): 19-36.

16. National Council of Welfare, *Poor Kids* (Ottawa 1975); Canadian Council on Social Development, *The Progress of Canada's Children*, 1996 (Ottawa 1996).

17. *Globe and Mail*, 16 October 1987.

18. These estimates of poor children for whom marriage breakdown was a significant factor in precipitating a fall below the poverty line were arrived at by multiplying the total number of poor children in single parent categories by the percentage of such families resulting from separation or divorce.

19. Ross, *Fact Book on Canadian Poverty - 1983*: 60-61.

20. National Council of Welfare, *Poverty Profile 1999*. Ottawa, 2002, pp. 107-24.

21. Regina *Leader Post*, 5 May 1986.

22. *Globe and Mail*, 21 April, 4 July and 22 July 1980.

23. Y. Lamontagne et. al., "Les jeunes itinérants de Montréal: une enquête transversale," *Canadian Journal of Psychiatry*, 33:8 (November 1988): 716-22.

24. *Globe and Mail*, 14 July 1984 and 11 July 1985.

25. T. S. Parish and G. K. Nunn, "The Importance of the Family in Forming Life Values and Personal Values," *Journal of Psychology*, 122:5 (September 1988): 519-21.

26. J. H. Kashani et. al., "Characteristics of Well-Adjusted Adolescents," *Canadian Journal of Psychiatry*, 32:6 (August 1987): 418-22.

Chapter 5: The Emotional Insecurity of Children

1. For reviews of some of the sociological literature, see the following: A.-M. Ambert and M. Baker, "Marriage Dissolution," in *Family Bonds and Gender Divisions*, ed. B. Fox (Toronto: Canadian Scholars Press, 1988): 453ff.; E. M. Nett, *Canadian Families: Past and Present* (Toronto: Butterworths, 1988): 160-61, 260-61; C. J. Richardson, "Children of Divorce," in *Family Matters*, eds. K. L. Anderson et. al. (Toronto: Methuen, 1987): 163ff.; M. Eichler, *Families in Canada Today* (Toronto: Gage, 1983): chs. 7-9, 201ff; M. Eichler, *Family Shifts* (Toronto: Oxford, 1997): 112-13.

2. Eichler, *Families in Canada Today*, 216-18, emphasis added.

3. Ambert and Baker, "Marriage Dissolution," 466-67.

4. B. D. Whitehead, *The Divorce Culture* (New York: Knopf, 1996); Richardson, "Children of Divorce;" J. F. Peter, "Changing Perspectives on Divorce," in *Family Matters*, ed. K. L. Anderson et. al., 141ff.

5. Richardson, "Children of Divorce," 166.

6. Richardson, *ibid.*, 165.

7. S. Davidson and I. G. Manion, "Facing the challenge: mental health and illness in Canadian youth," *Psychology, Health and Medicine*, 1:1 (1996): 41-56; D. R. Orford, "Child pyschiatric epidemiology," *Canadian Journal of Psychiatry*, 40 (1995): 284-88; L. H. Harvey *et. al.*, *The Health of Canada's Children* (Ottawa: Canadian Institute on Child Health, 1994); Ontario, Premier's Council on Health, Well-Being and Social Justice, *Yours, mine and ours: Ontario children and youth* (Toronto: Queen's Printer for Ontario, 1994); R. Tonkin *et. al.*, *Adolescent Health Survey: Province of British Columbia* (Vancouver: McCreary Centre Society, 1993).

8. Regina *Leader Post*, 29 October 1979.

9. R. Sutherland and M. J. Fulton, *Health Care in Canada* (Ottawa: Health Group, 1988): 16-18, 30; S. Davidson and I. G. Manion, "Facing the challenge: mental health and illness in Canadian youth," *Psychology, Health and Medicine*, 1:1 (1996): 41-56.

10. R. Beneteau, "Trends in Suicide," Statistics Canada, *Canadian Social Trends* (Winter 1988); K. Williams, "Causes of Death: How the Sexes Differ," Statistics Canada, *Canadian Social Trends* (Summer 1996): 11-17; Statistics Canada, *Suicide in Canada* (Ottawa, 1994); Statistics Canada, *Deaths, 1990* (Ottawa, 1992).

11. M. Greenblatt *et. al.*, "Social Networks and Mental Health: An Overview," *American Journal of Psychiatry*, 139 (1982):977-84; G. Caplan, *Support Systems and Community Mental Health* (New York: Behavioural Publications, 1974); M. Barley *et. al.*, "Health and life course: why safety nets matter," *British Medical Journal*, 314 (April 1997): 1194-96; M. E. J. Wadsworth, *The imprint of time: childhood, history and adult life* (Oxford: Oxford University, 1991).

12. *Globe and Mail*, 15 October 1982.

13. *Ibid.*, 24 March 1986.

14. S. Fine, "Children in Divorce, Custody and Access Situations: An Update," *Journal of Child Psychology*, 28:3 (May 1987): 361-64; B. E. Robson, "The Impact of Divorce and Separation on Children," *Contemporary Pediatrics*, 2 (1986): 6-21; F. Furstenberg et. al., "The life course of children of divorce," *American Sociological Review*, 48 (1983): 656-68.

15. R. Bolgar *et. al.*, "Childhood Antecedents of Interpersonal Problems in Young Adult Children of Divorce," *Journal of the American Academy of Child and Adolescent Psychiatry*, 34:2 (1995): 143-50; A. P. Derdeyn, "Parental Separation, Adolescent Psychopathology and Problem Behaviours," *Journal of the American Academy of Child and Adolescent Psychiatry*, 33:8 (1994): 1131-33; U. Palosaari and H. Aro, "Effect of Timing of Parental Divorce on the Vulnerability of Children to Depression in Young Adulthood," *Adolescence*, 19:115 (1994): 681-88; A. Breier et. al., "Early Parental Loss and Development of Adult Psychopathology," *Archives of General Psychiatry*, 45 (November 1988): 987-93.

16. Q. Rae-Grant and G. Awad, "The Effects of Marital Breakdown," in *Psychological Problems of the Child in the Family*, eds. P. D. Steinhauer and Q. Rae-Grant (New York: Basic, 1983).

17. S. McLanahan and L. Bumpass, "Intergenerational Consequences of Family Disruption," *American Journal of Sociology*, 94:1 (June 1988): 130-52.

18. E. Papthomopoulos *et. al.*, "Suicidal Attempts by Ingestion of Various Substances in 2050 Children and Adolescents in Greece," *Canadian Journal of Psychiatry*, 34:3 (April 1989): 205-10.

19. B. D. Garfinkel, "Suicidal Behaviour in a Pediatric Population," *Proceedings*, Congress on Suicide Prevention and Crisis Intervention, Ottawa, 1979.

20. H. S. Merskey and G. T. Swart, "Family Background and Physical Health of Adolescents Admitted to an Inpatient Psychiatric Unit, I: Principal Caregivers," *Canadian Journal of*

Psychiatry, 34:2 (March 1989): 79-83.

21. B. J. Fidler and E. B. Saunders, "Children's Adjustment During Custody/Access Disputes: Relation to Custody Arrangement, Gender and Age of Child," *Canadian Journal of Psychiatry*, 33:6 (August 1988): 517-23.

22. E. M Hetherington *et. al.*, "The Aftermath of Divorce," in *Mother-child/Father-child Relations*, eds. J. H. Stevens and M. Matthews (Washington: National Association for the Education of Children, 1978); E. M. Hetherington *et. al.*, "Family Interactions and the Social, Emotional and Cognitive Development of Children Following Divorce," in *The Family: Setting Priorities*, eds. J. C. Vaughan and J. B. Brazelton (New York: Science and Medicine Publishers, 1979); E. M. Hetherington, "Play and Social Interaction in Children Following Divorce," *Journal of Social Issues*, 35:4 (1979): 26-49; E. M. Hetherington et. al.,"Long-term Effects of Divorce and Re-marriage on the Adjustment of Children," *Journal of the American Academy of Child Psychiatry*, 24 (1965): 518-30. E. M. Hetherington, *Stress, Coping and Resiliency in Children and Families* (Mahwah, N. J.: Erlbaum, 1996); E. M. Hetherington, *Family Transitions* (Hillsdale, N. J.: Erlbaum, 1991); E. M. Hetherington, *Impact of Divorce, Single Parenting and Stepparenting on Children* (Hillsdale, N. J.: Erlbaum, 1988). See also, M. Fine and L. A. Kurdek, "The adjustment of adolescents in stepfather and stepmother families," *Journal of Marriage and the Family*, 54 (1992): 725-46; G. Kitson and L. Morgan, "The multiple consequences of divorce," *Journal of Marriage and the Family*, 52 (1990): 913-24; I. N. Sandler *et. al.*, "Coping, Stress and the Psychological Symptoms of Children of Divorce: A Cross-Sectional and Longitudinal Study," *Canadian Journal of Child Development*, 65 (1994): 1744-63; M. Wadsby and C. Svedin, "Parental Divorce: From the Children's Viewpoint," *Nordic Journal of Psychiatry*, 48:2 (1994): 107-16; F. Furstenberg and J. Teitler, "Re-considering the effects of marital disruption: what happens to children of divorce in early adulthood?" *Journal of Family Issues*, 15:32 (1994): 173-90; W. Clark, "School Leavers Revisited," Statistics Canada, *Canadian Social Trends* (Spring 1997): 10-12.

23. For a brief review of this literature, see Q. Rae-Grant and B. Robson, "Moderating the Morbidity of Divorce," *Canadian Journal of Psychiatry*, 33:6 (August 1988): 443-52.

24. E. D. Dubo et. al., "Childhood antecedents of self-destructiveness in borderline personality disorders," *Canadian Journal of Psychiatry*, 42:1 (February 1997): 63-9; E. L. Lipman et. al., "The Problems of Children in Lone-Mother Families," Statistics Canada, *Canadian Social Trends* (Spring 1997): 7-8; J. H. Beitchman, "Prediction of adjustment from preschool to middle childhood," *Canadian Journal of Psychiatry*, 38:9 (November 1993): 622-27; N. Grizenko and C. Fisher, "Review of studies of risk and protective factors for psychopathology in children," *Canadian Journal of Psychiatry*, 37:10 (December 1992): 711-21; J. M. Beitchman et. al., "Child psychiatry and early intervention: II. The internalizing disorders," *Canadian Journal of Psychiatry*, 37:4 (May 1992): 234-39; J. M. Beitchman et. al., "Child psychiatry and early intervention: I. The aggregate burden of suffering," *Canadian Journal of Psychiatry*, 37:4 (May 1992): 230-33; J. H. Beitchman et. al., "Child psychiatry and early intervention: III. The developmental disorders," *Canadian Journal of Psychiatry*, 37:4 (May 1992): 240-4; J. H. Beitchman *et. al.*, "Child psychiatry and early intervention: III. The externalizing disorders," *Canadian Journal of Psychiatry*, 37:4 (May 1992): 245-9; S. B. Patten, "The loss of a parent during childhood as a risk factor for depression," *Canadian Journal of Psychiatry*, 36:10 (December 1991): 706-11; P. S. Jensen *et. al.*, "Children at risk: I. Risk factors and child symptomatology," *Journal of the American Academy of Child and Adolescent Psychiatry*, 29 (1990): 51-9; J. M. Jenkins

and M. A. Smith, "Factors protecting children living in disharmonious homes: maternal reports," *Journal of the American Academy of Child and Adolescent Psychiatry*, 29 (1990): 60-9; R. Stirtzinger and L. Cholvat, "Preschool age children of divorce: transitional phenomena and the mourning process," *Canadian Journal of Psychiatry*, 35:6 (August 1990): 506-13; J. E. Fleming et. al., "Epidemiology of childhood depressive disorders: a critical review," *Journal of the American Academy of Child and Adolescent Psychiatry*, 29 (1990): 571-80; B. Robson, "Changing Family Patterns: Developmental Impacts on Children," *Journal of Counselling and Human Development*, 19:6 (1987): 2-12; T. M. Cooney et. al., "Parental Divorce in Young Adulthood: Some Preliminary Findings," *American Journal of Orthopsychiatry*, 56 (1986): 470-77; J. S. Wallerstein, "Children of Divorce: Stress and Developmental Tasks," in *Stress, Coping and Development in Children*, eds. N. Garmenzy and M. Rutter (New York: McGraw-Hill, 1983); B. Robson, "Marriage Concepts of Older Adolescents," *Canadian Journal of Psychiatry*, 28:8 (1983): 646-49; J. S. Wallerstein and J. B. Kelly, *Surviving the Breakup: How Children and Parents Cope with Divorce* (New York: Basic, 1980).

25. B. A. Stein et. al., "The relationship between life events during adolescence and affect and personality functioning," *Canadian Journal of Psychiatry*, 39:6 (August 1994): 354-7; R. Forehand et. al., "The role of family stressors and parent relationships on adolescent functioning," *Journal of the American Academy of Child and Adolescent Psychiatry*, 30 (1991): 316-22; C. Z. Garrison et. al., "A longitudinal study of depressive symptomatology in young adolescents," *Journal of the American Academy of Child and Adolescent Psychiatry*, 29 (1990): 581-85; E. E. Werner, "High-risk children in young adulthood: a longitudinal study from birth to 32 years," *American Journal of Orthopsychiatry*, 59:1 (1989): 72-81; B. E. Compas et. al., "Risk fac-

tors for emotional/behavioural problems in young adolescents: a prospective analysis of adolescent and parental stress and symptoms," *Journal of Consulting and Clinical Psychology*, 57 (1989): 732-40; J. Saucier and A. Ambert, "Adolescents' Perception of Self and of Immediate Environment by Parental Marital Status: A Controlled Study," *Canadian Journal of Psychiatry*, 31:6 (1986): 505-12.

26. Rae-Grant and Robson, "Moderating the Morbidity of Divorce": 446.

27. Richardson, "Children of Divorce": 171.

Chapter 6: The Physical Insecurity of Children

1. *Globe and Mail*, 1 February 1996; 8 June 1987.

2. CTV News Report, 29 September 1989.

3. *Globe and Mail*, 4 March 1988.

4. When the word "more" is used, it is understood to mean a larger proportion of children rather than necessarily more in absolute numbers.

5. *Globe and Mail*, 20 June 1980.

6. *Globe and Mail*, 8 July 1988; *Regina Leader Post*, 5 September 1980.

7. K. S. Joseph and M. S. Kramer, "Recent trends in Canadian Infant Mortality Rates," *Canadian Medical Association Journal*, 155:8 (October 15, 1996): 1047-52, update of article, *Canadian Medical Association Journal*, 156:2 (January 15, 1997): 161-63; *Globe and Mail*, 2 June 1995. Low birth weight is commonly associated with a higher risk of infant mortality. Both Toronto and Alberta, where cuts to health care and social services have been deepest, have reported an alarming increase in low birth weight babies. The most common factors associated with such babies are poverty, poor nutrition, and stress. Alberta also had the highest infant mortality rate in Canada in 1993 and 1995. See *Globe and Mail*, 14 March 1996 and 25 November 1996.

8. L. Lapierre and H. Aylwin, *Canadian Youth: Perspectives on Their Health* (Ottawa: Supply and Services, 1985): 80-81; K. Wilkins, "Causes of Death:

How the Sexes Differ," Statistics
Canada, *Canadian Social Trends*
(Summer 1996): 11-17.
9. *Toronto Star*, 9 September 1989.
10. R. Beneteau, "Trends in Suicide,"
Statistics Canada, *Canadian Social
Trends* (Winter 1988): 22-24; Statistics Canada, *Suicide in Canada*, Ottawa, 1994.
11. According to psychiatrist and suicide
specialist Barry Garfinkel, *Globe and
Mail*, 15 October 1982. See also
Globe and Mail, 17 July 1996.
12. All data on mortality are taken from
the following: Dominion Bureau of
Statistics, *Vital Statistics*, 1966 (Ottawa 1966); Vital Statistics, vol. III,
Deaths (Ottawa: Information Canada,
1974); Vital Statistics, vol. III, *Mortality: Summary List of Causes* (Ottawa: Supply and Services, 1983);
Statistics Canada, *Deaths*, 1990 (Ottawa: Supply and Services, 1992);
Statistics Canada, *Mortality: Summary List of Causes* (Ottawa: Supply
and Services, 1988); and Statistics
Canada, *Mortality: Summary List of
Causes* (Ottawa: Supply and Services, 1996).
13. See C. R. Pfeffer, *The Suicidal Child*
(New York: Guilford, 1986).
14. B. Rabkin, *Growing Up Dead: A
Hard Look at Why Adolescents Commit Suicide* (Toronto: McClelland
and Stewart, 1978): 13.
15. B. D. Garfinkel, "Suicidal Behaviour
in a Pediatric Population," *Proceedings* (Congress for Suicide Prevention and Crisis Intervention, Ottawa,
1979); B. D. Garfinkel and H.
Golombek, "Suicidal Behaviour in
Adolescents," in *The Adolescent and
Mood Disturbance*, eds. B. D.
Garfinkel and H. Golombek (New
York: International University, 1983):
189-217; H. M. Hoberman and B. D.
Garfinkel, "Completed Suicide in
Youth," *Canadian Journal of Psychiatry*, 33:6 (August 1988): 494-502; G.
F. G. Moens et. al., "Epidemiological
Aspects of Suicide Among the Young
in Selected European Countries,"
*Journal of Epidemiology and Com-
munity Health* 42 (1988): 279-85; F.
Nelson et. al., "Youth Suicide in Cal-
ifornia: A Comparative Study of Per-
ceived Causes and Interventions,"

Community Mental Health Journal,
24:1 (1988): 31-42; J. Pettifor et. al.,
"Risk Factors Predicting Childhood
and Adolescent Suicides," *Journal of
Child Care*, 1 (1983): 17-49; D. J. Po-
teet, "Adolescent Suicide," *American
Journal of Forensic Medical Pathology*, 8 (1987): 12-17; D. Shaffer and
P. Fisher, "The Epidemiology of Suicide in Children and Young Adolescents," *Journal of the American
Academy of Child Psychiatry*, 20
(1981): 545-65; N. Shaffi et. al.,
"Psychological Autopsy of Completed Suicide in Children and Adolescents," *American Journal of Psychiatry*, 142 (1985): 1061-64; H. S. Sudak
et. al., "Adolescent Suicide: An
Overview," *American Journal of
Psychotherapy* (1984): 350-63; T. R.
Thompson, "Childhood and Adolescent Suicide in Manitoba," *Canadian
Journal of Psychiatry*, 32:4 (1987):
264-69; E. Sigurdson et. al., "A five
year review of youth suicide in Manitoba," *Canadian Journal of Psychiatry*, 39:8 (October 1994): 397-403.
16. Thompson, "Childhood and Adolescent Suicide in Manitoba": 265, 267.
17. The Popen Case: *Globe and Mail*, 10
and 11 November 1982. The Turner
Case: *Globe and Mail*, 9 June and 5
December 1995; 10 April, 5 June, 21
June, 10 October and 11 October
1996. The Podniewicz Case: *Globe
and Mail*, 15 May and 19 September
1996. The Schmidt Case: *Globe and
Mail*, 25 January 1997. The Vaudreuil
Case: *Globe and Mail*, 30 November,
1 December, 4 December, 5 December 1995; 24 July and 24 September
1996; 3 August 1997.
18. D. P. Ross et. al., "National Longitudinal Survey of Children and Youth,
Canadian Children in the 1990s: Selected Findings," Statistics Canada,
Canadian Social Trends (Spring
1997): 2-9; Statistics Canada, Family
Violence in Canada (Ottawa: Supply
and Services, 1994); M. Mian et. al.,
"Familial risk factors associated with
intrafamilial and extrafamilial sexual
abuse of three to five year old girls,"
Canadian Journal of Psychiatry,
39:6 (August 1994): 348-53; W. A.
Cole and J. M. Bradford, "Abduction
during custody and access disputes,"

Canadian Journal of Psychiatry, 37:4 (May 1992): 264-6; P. G. Ney *et. al.*, "Causes of child abuse and neglect," *Canadian Journal of Psychiatry*, 37:7 (August 1992): 401-5; D. Carson et. al., "Intrafamilial sexual abuse: family-of-origin and family-of-procreation characteristics of female adult victims," *Journal of Psychology*, 125 (1991): 579-97; J. Drakich and C. Guberman, "Violence in the Family," in *Family Matters*, ed. K. Anderson et. al. (Toronto: Methuen, 1987); S. Cole, "Child Battery," in *No Safe Place: Violence Against Women and Children*, eds. C. Guberman and M. Wolfe (Toronto: Women's Press, 1985), also in *Family Bonds and Gender Divisions* ed. B. Fox (Toronto: Canadian Scholars' Press, 1988); B. Pressman, *Family Violence: Origins and Treatment* (Guelph: University of Guelph, 1984); Canada, *Report of the Committee on Sexual Offences against Children and Youth* (Ottawa: Supply and Services, 1984, The Badgely Report); Ontario Legislature, Social Development Standing Committee, *Second Report on Family Violence: Child Abuse* (Toronto: Government of Ontario, 1983); E. Bass and L. Thornton, eds. *I Never Told Anyone: Writings by Women Survivors of Child Sexual Abuse* (New York: Harper and Row, 1983); R. Finkelhor et. al. eds. *The Dark Side of Families: Current Family Violence Research* (Beverley Hills: Sage, 1983); G. Gerbner *et. al.* eds. *Child Abuse* (New York: Oxford, 1980); R. Helfner, ed. *The Battered Child* (Chicago: University of Chicago, 1980); Senate of Canada, *Child At Risk* (Ottawa: Supply and Services, 1980); M. A. B. Gammon, ed. *Violence in Canada* (Toronto: Methuen, 1978); N. Von Stolk, *The Battered Child in Canada* (Toronto: McClelland and Stewart, 1978).

19. Regina *Leader Post*, 18 September 1989.
20. *The Gallup Report*, 6 June 1991.
21. *Globe and Mail*, 10 March 1983.
22. L. MacLeod, *Battered But Not Beaten...Preventing Wife Battering in Canada* (Ottawa: Canadian Advisory Committee on the Status of Women, 1987): 32-3.
23. A. E. Walker et. al. "Childhood Injury Deaths: National Analysis and Geographic Variations," *American Journal of Public Health*, 79:3 (March 1989): 310-15. The quotation is from the *Globe and Mail*, 1 March 1989.
24. P. Resnick, "Murder of the Newborn: A Psychiatric Review of Neonaticide," *American Journal of Psychiatry*, 126:10 (1970): 1414-20.
25. E. Cherland and P. C. Matthews, "Attempted Murder of a Newborn: A Case History," *Canadian Journal of Psychiatry*, 34:4 (May 1989): 337-39.
26. H. Johnson and P. Chisolm, "Family Homicide," Statistics Canada, *Canadian Social Trends* (Autumn 1989): 17-18.
27. H. Johnson, "Homicide in Canada" Statistics Canada, *Canadian Social Trends* (Winter 1987): 2-6.
28. O. Fedorowycz, "Homicide in Canada - 1995," *Juristat*, 16:11 (Canadian Centre for Justice Statistics, Statistics Canada, Ottawa, July 1996); J. Buteau et. al., "Homicide followed by suicide: a Quebec case series, 1988-1990," *Canadian Journal of Psychiatry*, 38:8 (October 1993): 552-6; A. Labelle *et. al.*, "Adolescent murderers," *Canadian Journal of Psychiatry*, 36:8 (October 1991): 583-7.
29. National Council of Welfare, *In the Best Interests of the Child* (Ottawa, 1979). Estimates of the number of children in care in Canada on any particular day vary, but usually range from 50,000 to 100,000.
30. *Ibid.*: 22.
31. Interview with Trevor Williams, Family Service of Canada, Ottawa.
32. J. H. Maher, *Report in the Matter of a Royal Commission Appointed by the Lieutenant Governor of the Province of Saskatchewan under the Public Inquiries Act to Inquire into the Wilderness Challenge Camps as Proposed and Operated by the Ranch Ehrlo Society* (Regina, 1977).
33. *Globe and Mail*, 8 March 1980.
34. *Ibid.*, 30 September 1989.
35. D. Tickell, *The Protection of Children, The Rights of Children: The Urgent Need to Improve a System in*

Crisis (Regina: Saskatchewan Ombudsman, 1986).

36. For more on the crisis in Ontario provoked by the death of 100 children in 1994-95 while under the care and protection of the publicly funded system of child protection, see the following: *Globe and Mail*, 5 December 1995; 26 August 1996; 19 September 1996; 26 March 1997; 18 March 1997. For more on the controversy in Manitoba involving six abuse related murders in 1996 where the victims had previously come to the attention of child protection officials, see *Globe and Mail*, 25 January 1997. For more on the crisis in British Columbia created by 49 deaths, including 5 murders, of children under the protection and care of official agencies assigned the responsibility for the care and protection of children at risk, see *Globe and Mail*, 30 November 1995; 1, 4, and 5 December 1995; 24 and 26 July 1996; 3 August 1996; 24 September 1996.

37. For example, see some details on scandals involving the physical and sexual abuse of children in care that have become public recently in the following: *Globe and Mail*, 9 June 1995 (Kingsclear Reform School near Fredericton, New Brunswick); *Globe and Mail*, 26 June 1996 (St. John's and St. Joseph's reform schools in Ontario); *Globe and Mail*, 13 November 1996 (Fort Francis Indian School in Ontario); *Globe and Mail*, 21 October 1996 (St. Anne's Residential School in Fort Albany, Ontario); *Globe and Mail*, 4 May 1996 (Shellburne School for Boys and Nova Scotia Youth Training Centre, Nova Scotia School for Girls); Regina *Leader Post*, 6 and 7 December 1996, 10 February 1997 (Gordon Indian Residential School in Punichy, Saskatchewan); Regina *Leader Post*, 29 January 1997 (Beleveduere Orphanage in St. John's, Newfoundland). The most infamous and most widely known case, of course, is the Mount Cashel orphanage scandal in St. John's, Newfoundland. For more details on native residential schools in Canada, see J. Miller, *Singwaulk's Vision: A History of Native Residen-*

tial Schools in Canada (Toronto: University of Toronto, 1996).

38. Montreal *Gazette*, 20 October 1986.

Part III: Victims of the Crisis: Women
Introduction: The Oppression of Women

1. *Globe and Mail, Report on Business*, 6 December 1988; 12 August 1985.
2. *Globe and Mail*, 7 July 1989.
3. *Globe and Mail*, Report on Business, 5 September 1996; *Globe and Mail*, 17 July 1996.
4. Regina *Leader Post*, 20 January 1986; *Globe and Mail*, 12 August and 27 September 1996.
5. *Globe and Mail*, 17 March and 23 May 1985; 18 April 1996; 1 and 2 January 1997.
6. See P. Armstrong and H. Armstrong, *The Double Ghetto: Canadian Women and Their Segregated Work*, 3rd ed. (Toronto: McClelland and Stewart, 1994); A. Duffy *et. al.*, eds. *Few Choices: Women, Work and Family* (Toronto: Garamond, 1989); N. Mandell and A. Duffy, eds. *Reconstructing the Canadian Family: Feminist Perspectives* (Toronto: Butterworths, 1988); J. Lewis, ed. *Labour and Love: Women's Experience of Home and Family* (London: Blackwell, 1986); P. Armstrong and H. Armstrong, *A Working Majority: What Women Must Do For Pay* (Ottawa: Canadian Advisory Committee on the Status of Women, 1983); M. Luxton, *More Than A Labour of Love: Three Generations of Women's Work in the Home* (Toronto: Women's Press, 1980); M. Meissner et. al., "No Exit for Wives: Sexual Division of Labour and the Cumulation of Household Demands," *Canadian Review of Sociology and Anthropology*, 12:4 (November 1975): 424-39; A. Oakley, *The Sociology of Housework* (New York: Pantheon, 1974).
7. D. Dinnerstein, *The Mermaid and The Minotaur: Sexual Arrangements and Human Malaise* (New York: Harper and Row, 1976).
8. S. Hewlett, *A Lesser Life: The Myth of Women's Liberation in America* (New York: Morrow, 1986).

9. Regina *Leader Post*, 4 April 1985.
10. *Globe and Mail*, 28 September 1985.
11. *Ibid.*, 8 September 1989; 5 September 1995.
12. *The Gallup Report*, 8 March 1993; 23 December 1993; 24 January 1993; 25 June 1992; 16 October 1989.
13. *Globe and Mail*, 19 August 1987. The report, *The More Things Change, the More They Stay the Same*, refused to recommend a single one of 12 readers approved by the Ontario Ministry of Education. The following is based on a summary and analysis by the *Globe and Mail*'s Margaret Polanyi.
14. M. Baker, *What Will Tomorrow Bring?... A Study of the Aspirations of Adolescent Women* (Ottawa: Canadian Advisory Committee on the Status of Women, 1985). In addition to reporting on data collected in 1983 and 1984, Baker also provides a review of earlier studies on the question. For a more impressionistic and personal account, based on interviews with "fifty or so" adolescent girls, see M. Kostash, *No Kidding: Inside the World of Teenage Girls* (Toronto: McClelland and Steward, 1987).
15. Baker, *What Will Tomorrow Bring?*: 3-4.
16. *Ibid.*: 113-14.
17. M. Pipher, *Reviving Ophelia: Saving the Selves of Adolescent Girls* (New York: Ballantine, 1994): 11-13; *Globe and Mail*, 5 October 1995; 12 June and 24 August 1996; Regina *Leader Post*, 30 August and 16 September 1996.
18. Regina *Leader Post*, 27 December 1988 and 21 November 1996; *Globe and Mail*, 1 July 1996.
19. H. MacKay and C. Austin, *Single Adolescent Mothers in Ontario* (Ottawa: Canadian Council on Social Development, 1983). The figure 17,000 is taken from this report, p. vii.
20. R. E. Culp *et. al.*, "Adolescent and Older Mothers: Comparison Between Prenatal Maternal Variables and New-born Interaction Measures," *Infant Behaviour and Development*, 11:3 (1987): 353-62.
21. S. Freud, *Civilization and Its Discontents* (London: Hogarth, 1972

[1930]): 61.
22. S. Brownmiller, *Femininity* (New York: Simon and Schuster, 1984): 14, 236.

Chapter 7: The Double Burden

1. For much of what follows and a good review of the literature, see P. Armstrong and H. Armstrong, *The Double Ghetto: Canadian Women and Their Segregated Work*, 3rd ed. (Toronto: McClelland and Stewart, 1994): 77ff.
2. Armstrong and Armstrong, *The Double Ghetto*: 13.
3. C. Jackson, "Measuring and Valuing Households' Unpaid Work," Statistics Canada, *Canadian Social Trends* (Autumn 1996): 25-29. For earlier estimates see, Statistics Canada, "The Value of Household Work in Canada," *Canadian Social Trends* (Autumn 1986): 42. For the complete explanation of the calculations involved, see J. L. Swinamen, "The Value of Household Work in Canada, 1981," Statistics Canada, *Canadian Statistical Review*, 60:3 (Ottawa 1986).
4. M. S. Devereaux, "The New Necessities: Popular Household Appliances," Statistics Canada, *Canadian Social Trends* (Autumn 1988): 31-34.
5. L. Robbins, "Eating Out," Statistics Canada, *Canadian Social Trends* (Summer 1989): 7-9.
6. Regina *Leader Post*, 1 November 1989.
7. N. Zukewich Ghalam, "Women in the Workplace," Statistics Canada, *Canadian Social Trends* (Spring 1993): 2-6; Regina *Leader Post*, 2 November 1989; *Globe and Mail*, 15 August 1996.
8. R. A. Stebbins, "Men, Husbands and Fathers: Beyond Patriarchal Relations," in *Reconstructing the Canadian Family*, eds. N. Mandell and A. Duffy (Toronto: Butterworths, 1988): 31.
9. Regina *Leader Post*, 7 November 1985; *Globe and Mail*, 2 April 1988.
10. A. Hochschild and A. Machung, *The Second Shift: Inside the Two-Job Marriage* (New York: Penguin, 1989). According to a report in the *Globe and Mail* (10 May 1997)

Hochschild's follow-up research in 1994-97 found the situation to be even more stressful for working wives and mothers, and their partners had not changed significantly in sharing domestic work.

11. K. Marshall, "Dual Earners: Who's Responsible For the Housework?" Statistics Canada, *Canadian Social Trends* (Winter 1993): 11-14; L. Duxbury et. al., "Work-family conflict: a comparison by gender, family type and perceived control," *Journal of Family Issues*, 15:3 (1994): 449-66.

12. Armstrong and Armstrong, *The Double Ghetto*: 114.

13. S. N. Lewis and C. L. Cooper, "The Transition to Parenthood in Dual-earner Couples," *Psychological Medicine*, 18:12 (May 1988): 477-86.

14. C. E. Ross and J. Mirowsky, "Child Care and Emotional Adjustment to Wives' Employment," *Journal of Health and Social Behaviour*, 29:2 (June 1988): 127-38.

15. *Globe and Mail, Report on Business*, 2 December 1988.

16. Regina *Leader Post*, 14 July 1989.

17. *Ibid.*, 23 September 1989.

18. *Globe and Mail*, 8 March 1989.

19. J. Frederick, "Tempus Fugit: Are You Time Crunched?" Statistics Canada, *Canadian Social Trends* (Winter 1993): 6-9; *Globe and Mail*, 23 December 1994 and 8 January 1997; *Globe and Mail, Report on Business*, 8 January 1997.

20. P. L. Kotler, *Having It All: Multiple Roles and Mortality* (New York: Columbia University, 1989).

21. *Globe and Mail*, 8 June 1989.

22. The following statements are taken from A. Duffy *et. al.*, ed. *Few Choices: Women, Work and Family* (Toronto: Garamond, 1989): 32, 39; P. Armstrong and H. Armstrong, *A Working Majority* (Ottawa: Canadian Advisory Council on the Status of Women, 1983): 203ff; and *Globe and Mail*, 7 January 1989.

Chapter 8: Women's Economic Oppression

1. P. Phillips and E. Phillips, *Women and Work: Inequality in the Canadian Labour Market* (Toronto: Lorimer, 1993): 1, 15ff.

2. Regina *Leader Post*, 20 March 1987.

3. *Globe and Mail*, 18 June 1988; 11 March 1989; 15 January 1993; 20 December 1995; 28 January 1997; Regina *Leader Post*, 21 December 1995.

4. J.-A. Boule and L Lavallee, *The Changing Economic Status of Women* (Ottawa: Supply and Services, 1984): 27ff.; J. Normand, "Education of Women in Canada," Statistics Canada, *Canadian Social Trends* (Winter 1995): 17-21.

5. Statistics Canada, *Earnings of Men and Women* (Ottawa, 1997); P. Best, "Women, Men and Work," Statistics Canada, *Canadian Social Trends* (Spring 1995): 30-33; Saskatchewan, "The Wage Gap," *The Source*, 1:2 (Regina: Women's Secretariat, 1997).

6. All figures are taken from data in the 1980s and 1990s, and percentages are rounded. See P. Armstrong and H. Armstrong, *The Double Ghetto*, 3rd ed. (Toronto: McClelland and Stewart, 1994); K. Kendall, *Profiling Women in the Saskatchewan Economy* (Saskatoon: Community Educators for Women, 1989); Statistics Canada, *Women in Canada: A Statistical Report* (Ottawa: Supply and Services, 1995); Boule and Lavallee, *The Changing Economic Status of Women*; *Globe and Mail*, 22 March 1985, 13 and 20 March 1987, 11 March 1989; Regina *Leader Post*, 23 January 1989.

7. Phillips and Phillips, *Women and Work*: 1.

8. Armstrong and Armstrong, *The Double Ghetto*: 33-36 (1984 ed.).

9. Census 91, *Occupations* (Ottawa: Statistics Canada, 1993); *Globe and Mail, Report on Business*, 18 August 1988.

10. Armstrong and Armstrong, *The Double Ghetto*: 43 (1994 ed.).

11. Phillips and Phillips, *Women and Work*: 55.

12. Cited in *ibid.*: 55.

13. Statistics Canada, *Women in Canada: A Statistical Report* (Ottawa: Supply and Services, 1995): 95.

14. *Globe and Mail, Report on Business*, 30 June 1992 and 3 October 1985.

15. K. Marshall, "Women in Male-Dominated Professions," Statistics Canada, *Canadian Social Trends* (Winter 1987): 7-10; K. Marshall, "Women in Professional Occupations: Progress in the 1980s," Statistics Canada, *Canadian Social Trends* (Spring 1989): 13-16.
16. *Globe and Mail*, 18 September 1995; K. Hughes, "Women in non-traditional occupations," Perspectives on Labour and Income, Autumn 1995.
17. C. McKie, "The Law: A Changing Profession," Statistics Canada, *Canadian Social Trends* (Summer 1986): 18-24; Statistics Canada, *Women in Canada: A Statistical Report, 1995*: 116; Armstrong and Armstrong, *The Double Ghetto*: 46.
18. *Globe and Mail*, 11 August 1988.
19. K. Zarzour, "Women in Medicine: Making Healthy Gains in the Medical World," *Toronto Star*, 13 November 1987. The figures below are largely from this source, which used data from the Association of Canadian Medical Colleges and the Canadian Medical Association. The figures for the 1990s are from Armstrong and Armstrong, *The Double Ghetto*: 46.
20. J. Hollands, "Women Teaching at Canadian Universities," Statistics Canada, *Canadian Social Trends* (Summer 1988): 5-7; J. Lee, "Women in academia - a growing minority," *Perspectives on Labour and Income* (Spring 1993).
21. G. Wheeler, "Employment of Humanities and Sciences Graduates," Statistics Canada, *Canadian Social Trends* (Summer 1989): 28-30.
22. *Globe and Mail*, 19 September 1980.
23. *Ibid.*, 20 August 1988.
24. *Ibid.*, 11 September 1987.
25. *Globe and Mail*, Report on Business, 7 November 1989.
26. *Ibid.*, 11 August 1988.
27. A. I. Dagg and P. Thompson, *Miseducation, Women and Canadian Universities* (Toronto: OISE Press, 1988).
28. *Globe and Mail*, 2 May 1988.
29. *Ibid.*, 18 June 1988.
30. *Ibid.*, 22 October 1988.
31. *Globe and Mail, Report on Business*, 17 November 1988; Armstrong and Armstrong, *The Double Ghetto*,

1994; Phillips and Phillips, *Women and Work*, 1993.
32. National Council of Welfare, *Poverty Profile 1988* (Ottawa: Supply and Services, 1989); D. P. Ross and R. Shillington, *The Canadian Fact Book on Poverty 1988* (Ottawa: Canadian Council on Social Development, 1989); National Council of Welfare, *Poverty Profile 1995* (Ottawa: Supply and Services, 1996); D. P. Ross et. al., *The Canadian Fact Book on Poverty 1994* (Ottawa: Canadian Council on Social Development, 1995); National Council of Welfare, *Welfare Incomes 1995* (Ottawa: Supply and Services, 1997); Economic Council of Canada, *The New Face of Poverty: Income Security and the Needs of Canadian Families* (Ottawa: 1992).
33. Phillips and Phillips, *Women and Work*: 36ff.
34. A. Rashid, "Changes in Real Wages," Statistics Canada, *Canadian Social Trends* (Spring 1994): 16-18; J. Oderkirk et. al., "Traditional Earner Families," Statistics Canada, *Canadian Social Trends* (Spring 1994): 19-25; *Globe and Mail, Report on Business*, 12 December 1992 and 5 December 1989.
35. J.-A. Parliament, "Women Employed Outside the Home," Statistics Canada, *Canadian Social Trends* (Summer 1989): 3-6; M. A. Burke, "The Growth of Part-Time Work," Statistics Canada, *Canadian Social Trends* (Autumn 1986): 9-14; P. Best, "Women, Men and Work," Statistics Canada, *Canadian Social Trends* (Spring 1995): 30-33.
36. M. Boyd et. al., *Ascription and Achievement: Studies in Mobility and Status Attainment in Canada* (Ottawa: Carleton University, 1985): 516-17.
37. Statistics Canada, *Women in Canada: A Statistical Report, 1995*: 59-62; Regina *Leader Post*, 16 February 1987.
38. Boyd et. al., *Ascription and Achievement*: 519. A 1992 study estimated that interruptions in a woman's career for family reasons cost a woman an average of $80,000 in lost earning potential (*Globe and Mail*, 7 July 1992).

39. L. Stone *et. al., Dimensions of Job-Family Tensions* (Ottawa: Statistics Canada, 1994); J. E. Fast and J. A. Frederick, "Working Arrangements and Time Stress," Statistics Canada, *Canadian Social Trends* (Winter 1996): 14-19.
40. *Globe and Mail*, 15 January 1993 and 11 March 1989.
41. Statistics Canada, *Women in Canada: A Statistical Report*, 1995: 87; K. Marshall, "Women in Male-Dominated Professions,": 11; K. Marshall, "Women in Professional Occupations: Progress in the 1980s."
42. *Globe and Mail*, 11 August 1988.
43. *Financial Post*, 13 October 1979.
44. E. Gilson (with S. Kane), *Unnecessary Choices: The Hidden Life of the Executive Woman* (Toronto: Macmillan, 1987).
45. J. B. White and C. Hymowitz, "Women Climbing Past the Glass Ceiling," *Wall Street Journal*, reprinted in the *Globe and Mail, Report on Business*, 10 February 1997; *Globe and Mail, Report on Business*, 21 August 1996.
46. M. Gibb-Clark, "Sex Differences Show in Behaviour at the Workplace," *Globe and Mail, Report on Business*, 8 August 1987.
47. *Globe and Mail, Report on Business*, 4 May 1996; Regina *Leader Post*, 19 September 1996; *Globe and Mail*, 5 April 1989.
48. R. S. Abella, *Report of the Commission on Equality in Employment* (Ottawa: Supply and Services, 1984). The report examined the employment problems faced by women, native people, disabled persons, and visible minorities.
49. Statistics Canada, Women in Canada: A Statistical Report, 1995: 21ff; Regina Leader Post, 16 November 1988.
50. Parliament, "Women Employed Outside the Home": 4; M. Devereaux and C. Lindsay, "Female lone parents in the labour market," *Perspectives on Labour and Income* (Spring 1993).
51. Regina *Leader Post*, 14 March 1986.
52. *Ibid.*, 27 March 1981.
53. *Ibid.*, 5 May 1986.
54. *Globe and Mail*, 21 November 1989.
55. Regina *Leader Post*, 9 July 1996; *Globe and Mail*, 7 and 9 March 1996, 19 July 1996.
56. *Globe and Mail*, 10 April 1997, a report based on the recently released Statistics Canada report, *Family Income After Separation* (Ottawa, 1997).
57. National Council of Welfare, *Poverty Profile 1988; Poverty Profile 1990; Poverty Profile 1994.*

Chapter 9: Women's Emotional Oppression

1. See P. Armstrong and H. Armstrong, *The Double Ghetto* 3rd ed. (Toronto: McClelland and Stewart, 1995): 77ff. The Parons quote is on page 125.
2. C. Degler, *At Odds: Women and the Family in America from the Revolution to the Present* (New York: Oxford, 1980); P. Armstrong, *Labour Pains: Women's Work in Crisis* (Toronto: Women's Press, 1984); B. Fox, ed. *Hidden in the Household* (Toronto: Women's Press, 1980); P. Kome, *Somebody Has to Do It* (Toronto: McClelland and Stewart, 1982); M. Luxton, *More Than a Labour of Love* (Toronto: Women's Press, 1980); A. Oakley, *The Sociology of Housework* (New York: Pantheon, 1974).
3. J. M. Lewis *et.al., No Single Thread: Psychological Health in Family Systems* (New York: Brunner and Mazel, 1976).
4. D. A. Luepnitz, *The Family Interpreted: Feminist Theory in Clinical Practice* (New York: Basic, 1988).
5. C. M. Anderson and D. P. Holder, "Women and Serious Mental Disorders," in *Women in Families: A Framework for Family Therapy*, eds. M. McGoldrick *et. al.* (New York: Norton, 1989).
6. *Globe and Mail*, 7 November 1987.
7. P. S. Penfold, "Family Therapy: Critique from a Feminist Perspective," *Canadian Journal of Psychiatry*, 34:4 (May 1989): 311-15.
8. J. H. Gold and E. Gold, "The Belittled Wife: Social, Legal and Psychotherapeutic Considerations," *Canadian Journal of Psychiatry*, 26:6 (October 1981): 402-05.

9. P. Caplan and I. Hall-McCorquodale, "Mother-Blaming in Major Clinical Journals," *American Journal of Orthopsychiatry*, 55 (1985): 345-53; J. Holten, "When Do We Stop Mother-Blaming?" *Journal of Feminist Family Therapy*, 2:1 (1990): 53-60; E. McCollum and C. Russell, "Mother-Blaming in Family Therapy: An Empirical Investigation," *American Journal of Family Therapy*, 20:1 (1992): 71-76; J. Harrower, "The Dubious Nature of Mrs. Doubtfire - Yet Another Case of Mal de Mere?" *Feminism and Psychology*, 5:3 (1995): 419-25.

10. K. Chernin, *The Obsession: Reflections on the Tyranny of Slenderness* (New York: Harper and Row, 1981); M. Pipher, *Hunger Pains: The Modern Woman's Tragic Quest for Thinness* (New York: Ballantine, 1995).

11. Luepnitz, *The Family Interpreted*: 13-17, 144; S. Hays, *The Cultural Contradictions of Motherhood* (New Haven: Yale University, 1996); D. Eyer, *Motherguilt: How Our Culture Blames Mothers For What's Wrong With Society* (New York: Random, 1996).

12. See D. Eyer, *Motherguilt; The Gallup Report*, 29 January 1993; Regina *Leader Post*, 7 November 1996.

13. For this and what follows, see: J. Bernard, *The Future of Marriage* (New York: Bantam, 1972); W. R. Gove, "The Relationship between Sex Roles, Marital Status and Mental Illness," *Social Forces*, 51 (1972): 34-44; P. Chesler, *Women and Madness* (Garden City, N.Y.: Doubleday, 1972); W. R. Gove and J. F. Tudor, "Adult Sex Roles and Mental Illness," *American Journal of Sociology*, 78 (1973): 812-35; M. M. Wiseman and E. S. Paykel, *The Depressed Woman: A Study of Social Relationships* (Chicago: University of Chicago, 1974); G. W. Brown and M. W. Brolchain, "Social Class and Psychiatric Disturbance among Women in an Urban Population," *Sociology*, 9 (1975): 225-54; A. Rich, *Of Woman Born: Motherhood as Experience and Institution* (New York: Norton, 1976); S. Bothwell and M. M. Weissman, "Social Impairments Four Years

after an Acute Depressive Epidode," *American Journal of Orthopsychiatry*, 47 (1977): 231-37; G. E. Brown and T. Harris, *Social Origins of Depression* (London: Tavistock, 1978); L. S. Radloff , "Depression and the Empty Nest," *Sex Roles*, 6 (1980): 775-81; C. Tennant *et. al.*, "Female Vulnerability to Neurosis: The Influence of Social Roles," *Australian and New Zealand Journal of Psychiatry*, 16 (1982): 135-40; S. Penfold and G. Walker, *Women and the Psychiatric Paradox* (Toronto: Eden, 1983); M. Kaplan, "A Woman's View of DSM-III," *American Psychologist*, (July 1983): 786-814; K. R. Merikangas et. al., "Marital Adjustment in Major Depression," *Journal of Affective Disorders*, 9 (1985): 5-11; R. J. Hafner, *Marriage and Mental Illness* (New York: Guilford, 1986); B. J. Gallagher, *The Sociology of Mental Illness* (Englewood Cliffs, N.J.: Prentice-Hall, 1987); E. Schaefer and C. Burnett, "Stability and Predictability of Quality of Women's Marital Relationships and Demoralization," *Journal of Personality and Social Psychology*, 53 (1987): 1129-36; C. E. Ross and J. Mirowsky, "Child Care and Emotional Adjustment to Wives' Employment," *Journal of Health and Social Behaviour*, 29:2 (1988): 127-38; C. Chamberlain *et. al.*, "The Role of Intimacy in Psychiatric Help-Seeking," *Canadian Journal of Psychiatry*, 34:1 (February 1989); G. Kitson and L. Morgan, "The multiple consequences of divorce," *Journal of Marriage and the Family*, 52 (1990): 913-24; M. Eliany, "Alcohol and Drug Use," Statistics Canada, *Canadian Social Trends* (Spring 1991): 19-26; H. Tait, "Sleep Problems: Who Do They Affect?" Statistics Canada, *Canadian Social Trends* (Winter 1992): 8-10; A. Sev'er, *Women and Divorce in Canada: a sociological analysis* (Toronto: Canadian Scholars Press, 1992); Statistics Canada, *Women in Canada: A Statistical Report*, Ottawa (1995): 37, 45, 47, 52; W. Millar and M. P. Beaudet, "Health Facts from the 1994 National Population Health Survey," Statistics Canada, *Canadian Social Trends* (Spring

1996): 24-27; J. M. Murphy *et. al.*, "Depression and anxiety in relation to social status: a prospective epidemiological study," *Archives of General Psychiatry*, 48 (1991): 223-30; J. Birtchnell, "Negative modes of relating, marital quality and depression," *British Journal of Psychiatry*, 158 (1991): 648-57; E. M. Waring *et. al.*, "The etiology of non-psychotic emotional illness," *Canadian Journal of Psychiatry*, 35:1 (1990): 50-57.

14. Anderson and Holder, "Women and Serious Mental Disorders": 389.
15. *Globe and Mail*, 12 June 1996.
16. Regina *Leader Post*, 7 May 1980 and 7 March 1983; *Globe and Mail*, 1 and 15 November 1985 and 7 November 1987; Statistics Canada, Women in Canada: A Statistical Report, 1995: 52.
17. *Globe and Mail*, 8 July 1989 and 1 January 1997.
18. *The Gallup Report*, 11 February 1989.
19. See the studies noted in endnotes 14 to 24 in Chapter 5. A good summary of the literature is provided in Q. Rae-Grant and B. E. Robson, "Moderating the Morbidity of Divorce," *Canadian Journal of Psychiatry*, 33:6 (August 1988): 443-52. See also, J. M. Murphy, "Depression and anxiety in relation to social status: a prospective epidemiological study," *Archives of General Psychiatry*, 48 (1991): 223-30; J. Wallerstein, *Second Chances: men, women and children a decade after divorce* (New York: Ticknor and Fields, 1989); S. B. Patten, "The Loss of a Parent During Childhood as a Risk Factor for Depression," *Canadian Journal of Psychiatry*, 36:10 (December 1991): 706-11; E. E. Werner, "High-risk Children in Young Adulthood: a longitudinal study from birth to 32 years," *American Journal of Orthopsychiatry*, 59:1 (1989): 72-81.
20. Rae-Grant and Robson, *ibid.*: 445.
21. A. D'Ercole, "Single Mothers: Stress, Coping and Social Support," *Journal of Community Psychology*, 16:1 (January 1988): 41-54; L. Hechtman, "Teenage Mothers and Their Children: Risks and Problems: A Review," *Canadian Journal of Psychiatry*, 34:6 (August 1989): 569-75.
22. J. Essen, "Living in One-Parent Families: Attainment at School," *Child: Care, Health and Development*, 5:3 (1979): 189-200; A. M. Morton and P. S. Glick, "Marital Instability in America," in *Divorce and Separation*, eds. G. Levingen and O. C. Moles (New York: Basic, 1979); K. Morrison and A. Thompson-Guppy, *Stepmothers: Exploring the Myth* (Ottawa: Canadian Council on Social Development, 1985); C. Hobart and D. Brown, "Effects of Prior Marriage Children on Adjustment in Re-Marriage: A Canadian Study," *Journal of Comparative Family Studies*, 19:3 (Fall 1988): 381-96.

Chapter 10: The Physical and Sexual Oppression of Women

1. J. Boswell, *The Kindness of Strangers: The Abandonment of Children in Western Europe from Late Antiquity to the Renaissance* (New York: Pantheon, 1988): 4-5.
2. *Globe and Mail*, 16 February 1985.
3. L. MacLeod, *The City for Women: No Safe Place* (Ottawa: Secretary of State, 1989).
4. L. W. Kennedy and D. G. Dutton, *The Incidence of Wife Assault in Alberta* (Edmonton: University of Alberta, Population Research Laboratory, 1987).
5. Solicitor General of Canada, "Family Violence," *Liaison*, 15:3 (March 1989): 4-13.
6. H. Johnson, "Wife Abuse," Statistics Canada, *Canadian Social Trends* (Spring 1988): 17-22.
7. K. Rodgers, "Wife Assault in Canada," Statistics Canada, *Canadian Social Trends* (Autumn 1994): 3-8; K. Rodgers, "Wife Assault: The Findings of a National Survey," Statistics Canada, Canadian Centre for Justice Statistics, *Juristat*, 14:9 (March 1994); C. Strike, "Women Assaulted by Strangers," Statistics Canada, *Canadian Social Trends* (Spring 1995): 2-6.
8. *Globe and Mail*, 23 October 1980 and 30 June 1988.
9. *The Gallup Report*, 30 May 1991.
10. *Globe and Mail*, 30 June 1988.
11. *Ibid.*, 16 February 1985.
12. *Ibid.*, 12 August 1985.

13. *Ibid.*, 13 August 1985 and 31 May 1995.
14. *Ibid.*, 13 January 1988.
15. *Ibid.*, 9 and 13 December, 1995; 5 and 6 March, 4 April, 4 and 5 July, 1996.
16. *Ibid.*, 19 August 1989.
17. *Ibid.*, 20 January and 3 September, 1989.
18. Regina *Leader Post*, 23 September 1985.
19. *Globe and Mail*, 3 May 1988.
20. M. H. Gagne, F. Lavoie and M. Hèbert, "La violence sexuelle dans les fréquentations chez un group d'adolescents et d'adolescentes," *Revue sexologique*, 2:1 (1994): 145-59; M. Poitras and F. Lavoie, *A Preliminary Study of the Prevalence of Sexual Violence in Adolescent Dating Relationships in a Quebec Sample* (Quebec: Groupe de recherche sur l'appropriation psychosociale, Ecole de psychologie, Université Laval, 1994). See also W. DeKeseredy and K.I. Kelly, *The Incidence and Prevalence of Woman Abuse in Canadian University and College Dating Relationships: Results from a National Survery* (Ottawa: Carleton University, 1993), also published in *Canadian Journal of Sociology*, 18:2 (1993): 137-60; M. Paludi, ed. *Ivory Power: Sexual Harassment on Campus* (Albany: SUNY, 1990); P. R. Sanday, *Double Jeopardy, A Woman Scorned: Acquaintance Rape on Trial* (New York: Doubleday, 1996).
21. H. Johnson, "Work-related Sexual Harassment," *Perspectives on Labour and Income,* Statistics Canada (Winter 1994); *Globe and Mail, Report on Business,* 16 March 1987.
22. *Globe and Mail, Report on Business*, 6 December 1988.
23. For the examples below see: *Globe and Mail*, 30 July 1987, 11 August 1988, 12 August 1989, 16 January 1988, 8 November 1989; *Globe and Mail, Report on Business*, 6 December 1988, 16 March 1987; Montreal *Gazette*, 22 October 1989.
24. *Globe and Mail*, 8 November 1989.
25. *Ibid.*, 16 June 1988.
26. *Ibid.*, 11 October 1985.
27. *The Gallup Report*, various dates, 1991 to 1997.
28. Regina *Leader Post*, 26 December 1989.
29. See *Globe and Mail* and Regina *Leader Post*, 7 to 11 December 1989; *Maclean's*, 18 December 1989; *CAUT Bulletin*, 37:1 (Janaury 1990); and *Le Devoir*, 7 to 12 December 1989.
30. Letter to editor, Regina *Leader Post*, 18 January 1990.
31. For an overview and background on wife battering, see: T. Davidson, *Conjugal Crime: Understanding and Changing the Wife Beating Pattern* (New York: Hawthorn, 1970); R. J. Gelles, *The Violent Home* (Beverley Hills: Sage, 1972); S. K. Steinmetz, *The Cycle of Violence* (New York: Praeger, 1977); M. Roy, ed. *Battered Women: A Psychosocial Study of Domestic Violence* (New York: Van Nostrand and Reinhold, 1977); J. M. Eekelaar and S. N. Katz, eds. *Family Violence* (Toronto: Butterworths, 1978); J. P. Martin, ed. *Violence and the Family* (New York: Wiley, 1978); R. E. Dobash and R. Dobash, *Violence Against Wives* (New York: Free Press, 1979); L. E. Walker, *The Battered Woman* (New York: Harper and Row, 1979); M. A. Straus and G. T. Hotaling, eds. *The Social Causes of Husband-Wife Violence* (Minneapolis: University of Minnesota, 1980); M. Roy, *The Abusive Partner* (New York: Van Nostrand Reinhold, 1982); D. Findelhor et. al., eds. *The Dark Side of Families* (Beverley Hills: Sage, 1983); W. A. Stacey and A. Shupe, *The Family Secret* (Boston: Beacon, 1983); L. E. Walker, *The Battered Woman Syndrome* (New York: Spring, 1984); G. Hotaling and D. Sugarman, "An Analysis of Risk Markers in Husband to Wife Violence," *Journal of Family Violence*, 1:1 (1986): 101-24; for an excellent, selective review of both feminist and non-feminist approaches to wife battering, see D. Scott, *Theoretical Approaches to the Problem of Wife Assault: A Critique and Modest Reformulation* (Regina: University of Regina, M.A. thesis, Social Studies, 1988): chs., 2 and 3, pp. 9 ff; D. G. Dutton, *The Domestic Assault of Women: Psychological and Criminal*

Perspectives (Toronto: Allyn and Bacon, 1988); Church Council on Justice and Corrections and the Canadian Council on Social Development, *Family Violence in a Patriarchal Culture: A Challenge to Our Way of Living* (Ottawa: Canadian Council on Social Development, 1989); M. D. Smith, "Sociodemographic risk factors in wife abuse: results from a survey of Toronto Women," *Canadian Journal of Sociology*, 15:1 (1990): 38-58; M. A. Straus and G. T. Hotaling, eds. *Physical Violence in American Families: Risk Factors and Adaptations to Violence in 8145 Families*, (New Brunswick, N. J.: Transaction, 1990); D. Carson *et. al.*, "Intrafamilial sexual abuse: family-of-origin and family-of-procreation characteristics of female adult victims," *Journal of Psychology*, 125 (1991): 579-97; W. S. DeKeseredy and R. Hinch, *Woman Abuse* (Toronto: Thompson, 1991); R. Dobash and R. E. Dobash, *Women, Violence and Social Change* (London: Routledge, 1992); D. A. Counts *et. al.*, *Sanctions and Sanctuary: Cultural Perspectives on the Beating of Wives* (Boulder: Westview, 1992); E. Buzawa and C. Buzawa eds., *Domestic Violence: the changing criminal justice system response* (Westport, Conn.: Greenwood, 1993); L. L. Heise *et. al.*, *Violence Against Women: The Hidden Health Burden* (Washington, D. C.: World Bank, 1994); J. Roberts and R. Mohr, eds. *Confronting Sexual Assault: A Decade of Legal and Social Change* (Toronto: University of Toronto, 1994); C. Regeher and G. Glaney, "Battered woman syndrome defense in Canadian courts," *Canadian Journal of Psychiatry*, 40:3 (April 1995): 130-35; D. Ellis and N. Stuckless, *Mediating and negotiating marital conflicts* (Beverley Hills: Sage, 1996).

32. L. MacLeod, *Wife Battering in Canada: The Vicious Circle* (Ottawa: Canadian Advisory Council on the Status of Women, 1980); L. MacLeod, *Battered But Not Beaten...Preventing Wife Battering in Canada* (Ottawa: Canadian Advisory Council on the Status of Women, 1987).

33. H. Johnson, "Wife Abuse."

34. E. Lupri, "Male Violence in the Home," Statistics Canada, *Canadian Social Trends* (Autumn 1989): 19-21.

35. K. Rodgers, "Wife Assault."

36. K. Rodgers and G. MacDonald, "Canada's Shelters for Abused Women," Statistics Canada, *Canadian Social Trends* (Autumn 1994): 10-14.

37. L. MacLeod, *Battered But Not Beaten*: 16.

38. H. Johnson, "Homicide in Canada," Statistics Canada, *Canadian Social Trends* (Winter 1987): 2-6; H. Johnson and P. Chisholm, "Family Homicide," Statistics Canada, *Canadian Social Trends* (Autumn 1989); Statistics Canada, *Homicide in Canada: A Statistical Perspective* (Ottawa: Supply and Services, 1989); O. Fedorowycz, "Homicide in Canada - 1995," Statistics Canada, Canadian Centre for Justice Statistics, *Juristat*, 16:1 (July 1996); M. Wilson and M. Daly, "Spousal Homicide," Statistics Canada, Canadian Centre for Justice Statistics, *Juristat*, 14:8 (March 1994); J. Buteau *et. al.*, "Homicide followed by suicide: a Quebec case series, 1988-1990," *Canadian Journal of Psychiatry*, 38:8 (October 1993): 552-56.

39. J. C. Campbell, "If I can't have you, no one can: issues of power and control in homicide of female partners," in J. Radford and D. E. H. Russell, eds. *Femicide: the politics of woman killing* (New York: Macmillan, 1992); R. P. Dobash *et. al.*, "The myth of sexual symmetry in marital violence," *Social Problems*, 39 (1992): 401-21; A. Browne, *When Battered Women Kill* (New York: Free Press, 1987); P. W. Easteal, *Killing the Beloved: homicide between adult sexual intimates* (New York: Criminal Justice Press, 1993); A. Goetting, "Homicidal Wives," *Journal of Family Issues*, 8 (1989): 322-41.

40. F. McNulty, *The Burning Bed: The True Story of an Abused Wife* (New York: Avon, 1980).

41. *Ibid.*: 279, 283.

42. B. Vallee, *Life with Billy* (Toronto: McClelland and Stewart, 1986).

43. MacLeod, *Battered But Not Beaten*: 19ff.
44. MacLeod, *Wife Battering in Canada*: 14.
45. Kennedy and Dutton, *The Incidence of Wife Assault in Alberta*.
46. Johnson, "Wife Abuse": 17-18.
47. Lupri, "Male Violence in the Home": 20-21.
48. M. Daly and M. Wilson, *Homicide* (Hawthorne, N. Y.: Aldine de Gruyter, 1988); M. Wilson and M. Daly, "Spousal homicide risk and estrangement," *Violence and Victims*, 8 (1993): 3-16; M. Wilson, M. Daly and C. Wright, "Uxoricide in Canada: demographic risk patterns," *Canadian Journal of Criminology*, 35 (1993): 263-91.
49. Statistics Canada, *Homicide in Canada: A Statistical Perspective* (1989): 17, 55, 67; Fedorowycz, "Homicide in Canada - 1995."
50. *Globe and Mail*, 4 December 1982.
51. Regina *Leader Post*, 26 December 1989.
52. *Ibid.*, 19 September 1989.
53. *Globe and Mail*, 19 April 1997.
54. Scott, *Theoretical Approaches to the Problem of Wife Assault*: ch. 5: 116-38.
55. *Ibid.*: 136-37.
56. This was confirmed in a clinical study of 99 identified men who abused their wives. Eighty-seven were found to exhibit evidence of a serious personality disorder including: "schizoidal/borderline," "narcissistic/anti-social," and "passive dependent/compulsive." Reasonably serious psychopathology and wife abuse seem to go together. See L. K. Hamberger and J. E. Hastings, "Personality Correlates of Men Who Abuse Their Partners: A Cross-Validation Study," *Journal of Family Violence*, 1:4 (1986): 323-41. See also E. Gondolf, "Who are these guys? Toward a behavioural typology of batterers," *Violence and Victims*, 3:3 (1988): 187-203; A. Holtzworth-Monroe, "Types of Abusers," *Journal of Clinical and Consulting Psychology*, (July 1994): 13-24.

Part IV: Victims of the Crisis: Men

Introduction: Elusive Masculinity and Patriarchy

1. S. de Beauvoir, *The Second Sex* (New York: Bantam, 1961 [1949]): 678.
2. *Ibid.*: 645.
3. N. Chodorow, *The Reproduction of Mothering* (Berkeley: University of California, 1978); D. Dinnerstein, *The Mermaid and the Minotaur* (New York: Harper and Row, 1976); B. Easlea, *Science and Sexual Oppression: Patriarchy's Confrontation with Women and Nature* (London: Weidenfeld and Nicolson, 1981); R. Horrocks, *Masculinity in Crisis* (New York: St. Martin's, 1994); A. Gorodensky, *Mums the Word: The Mamma's Boy Syndrome Revealed* (New York: Cassell, 1996).
4. S. Oberson, *Finding Our Fathers* (New York: Free Press, 1986); D. Blankenhorn, *Fatherless America: confronting our most urgent social problem* (New York: Harper, 1996).
5. R. T. Hare-Mustin, "The Problem of Gender in Family Therapy Theory," in *Women in Families: A Framework for Family Therapy*, eds. N. McGoldrick et. al. (London: Norton, 1989): 70-71.
6. R. M. Eisler and J. R. Skidmore, "Masculine Gender Role Stress: Scale Development and Component Factors in the Appraisal of Stressful Situations," *Behaviour Modification*, 11:2 (April 1987): 123-36.
7. W. E. Snell et. al., "The Masculine Role as a Moderator of Stress-Distress Relationships," *Sex Roles*, 15:7-8 (1986): 359-66.
8. R. M. Counts and K. Reid, "A Comparison of Men Who Are Divorce Prone with Those Who Are Marriage Phobic," *Journal of Divorce*, 10:1-2 (Fall/Winter 1986): 69-86.
9. Globe and Mail, 24 December 1986.
10. S. Blotnick, *Ambitious Men: Their Drives, Dreams and Delusions* (New York: Penguin, 1988).
11. M. E. Snow et. al., "Sex-of Child Differences in Father-Child Interactions at One Year of Age," *Child Development*, 54 (1983): 227-32.
12. K. Millett, *Sexual Politics* (New

York: Avon, 1969): 33.
13. de Beauvoir, *The Second Sex*: 679.
14. Millett, *Sexual Politics*: 40.
15. de Beauvoir, *The Second Sex*: 639, 641.

Chapter 11: Men and Economic Stress

1. M. Moore, "Dual-Earner Families: The New Norm," Statistics Canada, *Canadian Social Trends* (Spring 1989): 24-26; National Council of Welfare, *Poverty Profile 1990* and *Poverty Profile 1995*; J. Oderkirk et. al., "Traditional-Earner Families," Statistics Canada, *Canadian Social Trends* (Spring 1994): 19-25.
2. *Globe and Mail, Report on Business*, 5 December 1989; A. Rashid, "Changes in Real Wages," Statistics Canada, *Canadian Social Trends* (Spring 1994): 16-18.
3. National Council of Welfare, *Poverty Profile 1990* and *Poverty Profile 1995*.
4. T. Garland, "The Better Half: The Male in the Dual-Career Professional Family," in *Toward a Sociology of Women*, ed. C. Safilios-Rothschild (Lexington: Xerox College Publishing, 1972); S. Hardesty and N. Betz, "The Relationship of Career Salience, Attitudes toward Women, and Demographic and Family Characteristics to Marital Adjustment in Dual-Career Couples," *Journal of Vocational Behaviour*, 17 (1980): 242-50; E. Nettles and J. Lovinger, "Sex Role Expectations and Ego Level in Relation to Problem Marriages," *Journal of Personality and Social Psychology*, 45 (1983): 676-87; B. Gray-Little and N. Burks, "Power and Satisfaction in Marriage," *Psychological Bulletin*, 93 (1983): 513-38; G. I. Bowen and D. K. Orthner, "Sex-role Congruency and Marital Quality," *Journal of Marriage and the Family*, 45 (1983): 223-33; L. A. Gilbert, *Men in Dual-Career Families: Current Realities and Future Prospects* (Hillsdale, N. J.: Lawrence Erlbaum, 1985): ch. 3, "The Husband-Wife Relationship": 22ff.
5. *Globe and Mail*, 6 December 1995, 17 February and 15 August 1996.

Chapter 12: Men and Emotional Stress

1. M. Komarovsky, *Dilemmas of Masculinity* (New York: Norton, 1976): 252-53.
2. *Globe and Mail*, 21 April 1987.
3. *Ibid.*, 25 August 1984.
4. See G. J. Bown and D. K. Orthner, "Sex-Role Congruency and Marital Quality," *Journal of Marriage and the Family*, 45 (1983): 223-33. Bowen and Orthner found "low marriage quality" in relationships between traditional men and liberated women. Marriage quality was best in relationships where the sex-role attitudes of the men and the women were congruent.
5. B. Yeh and D. Lester, "Statewide Divorce Rates and Wives' Participation in the Labour Market," *Journal of Divorce*, 11:1 (Fall 1987): 107-14.
6. Regina *Leader Post* 16 September 1980; H. Goldberg, *The New Male* (New York: New American Library, 1980).
7. See the sources cited in endnotes 12 to 15 in Chapter 9, and endnotes 4, 5, and 10 in Chapter 3.
8. *Globe and Mail*, 23 October 1989. An unpublished study by Statistics Canada and the Canadian Institute for Advanced Research, based on Canada Pension plan data for 500,000 men who turned 65 on 1 September 1979, reports that unmarried men of age 65 experienced a 50 per cent greater chance of dying before the age of 70 than those who were married. The study also found a strong direct positive correlation between the amount of income earned in the last 20 years of a man's working life and life expectancy. Men in the bottom 5 per cent income group faced twice the probability of death by the age of 70 as men in the top 5 per cent income group.
9. J. Kiecolt-Glaser *et. al.*, "Marital Discord and Immunity in Males," *Psychosomatic Medicine*, 50:3 (1988): 213-29.
10. A. Zeiss *et. al.*, "Sex Differences in Initiation of and Adjustment to Divorce," *Journal of Divorce*, 4 (1980): 21-33; W. A. Cole and J. M. Brad-

ford, "Abduction During Custody and Access Disputes," *Canadian Journal of Psychiatry*, 37:4 (May 1992): 264-66.

11. D. S. Huntington, "Fathers: The Forgotten Figures in Divorce," in *Divorce and Fatherhood*, ed. J. Jacobs (Washington, D. C.: American Psychiatric Association, 1986): 53-83, 63-64 (my emphasis). Cited in Q. Rae-Grant and B. Robson, "Moderating the Morbidity of Divorce," *Canadian Journal of Psychiatry*, 33:6 (August 1988): 443-52.

12. E. Goffman, *The Presentation of Self in Everyday Life* (New York: Anchor, 1959).

13. F. Travato, "A Longitudinal Analysis of Divorce and Suicide in Canada," *Journal of Marriage and the Family*, 49:1 (1987): 193-203.

14. O. Adams, "Divorce Rates in Canada," Statistics Canada, *Canadian Social Trends* (Winter 1988): 18-19; K. Wilkins, "Causes of Death: How the Sexes Differ," Statistics Canada, *Canadian Social Trends* (Summer 1996): 11-17; Statistics Canada, *Mortality: Summary List of Causes, 1994* (Ottawa: Ministry of Industry, 1996).

15. E. Durkheim, *Suicide* (New York: Free Press, 1966 [Paris, 1897]): ch. 3, "Egoistic Suicide": 171ff; ch. 5, "Anomic Suicide": 241ff.

16. *Ibid.*: 275-76.

17. J. Bachman *et. al.*, *Smoking, Drinking and Drug Use in Young Adulthood* (Mahwah, N. J.: Erlbaum, 1997).

18. Regina *Leader Post*, 20 October 1984.

19. *Ibid.*, 12 January 1990.

20. W. J. Wilson, *When Work Disappears: the world of the new urban poor* (New York: Knopf, 1996). For further discussion of the crisis men face and some of its impacts, see M. Berger *et. al.*, *Constructing Masculinity* (New York: Routledge, 1995); W. Gaylin, *The Male Ego* (New York: Viking, 1992); and R. Horrocks, *Masculinity in Crisis* (New York: St. Martin's, 1994).

21. M. Siggins, *A Canadian Tragedy: JoAnn and Colin Thatcher: A Story of Love and Hate* (Toronto: Macmillan, 1985).

22. *Globe and Mail*, 28 November 1980.

23. For the following on anti- and pro-women men's groups see the following: *Globe and Mail*, 11 March 1988; 25 February, 15 July, 2 August, and 17 October 1989; 16 March and 3 December 1996; Regina *Leader Post*, 9 December 1996 and 29 January 1997. For an analysis of the fathers' rights movement see, C. Bertoia and J. Drakitch, "The fathers' rights movement: contradictions in rhetoric and practice," *Journal of Family Issues*, 14:4 (1993): 592-615.

24. For a good overview of these shifts and splits see: R. W. Connell, *Masculinities* (Berkeley: University of California, 1995); J. Kaufman and R. L. Timmer, "Searching for the hairy man," *Social Work with Groups*, 6 (1983): 163-75; R. W. Connell, "Drumming up the wrong tree," *Tikkun*, 7 (1992): 31-6; R. W. Connell, "The state, gender and sexual politics," *Theory and Society*, 19 (1990): 507-44. For examples of those men who changed their positions, compare W. Farrell, *The Liberated Man, Beyond Masculinity: Freeing Men and Their Relationship with Women* (New York: Random House, 1974) to both W. Farrell, *Why Men Are the Way They Are: The Male-Female Dynamic* (New York: McGraw-Hill, 1986) and W. Farrell, *The Myth of Male Power: Why Men Are the Disposable Sex* (New York: Simon and Shuster, 1993); compare H. Goldberg, *The Hazards of Being Male: Surviving the Myth of Masculine Privilege* (New York: Nash, 1976) to H. Goldberg, *The Inner Male: Overcoming Roadblocks to Intimacy* (New York: Signet, 1988). Farrell moved from a strongly pro-feminist position in 1974 to a position very hostile to feminism in 1993, while Goldberg's anti-feminism became quite vicious between 1976 and 1988. A good example of early, largely pro-feminist writings by men include, A. Ellis, *Sex and the Liberated Man* (New York: Lyle Stuart, 1976); H. C. Lyon, *Tenderness is Strength* (New York: Harper and Row, 1977). More recent books, directly or indirectly hostile to feminism, besides

those of Farrell and Goldberg, include R. Bly, *Iron John: A Book About Men* (New York: Addison-Wesley, 1990), S. Keen, *Fire in the Belly: On Being a Man* (New York: Bantam, 1991), and A. Kimbrell, *The Masculine Mystique: The Politics of Masculinity* (New York: Ballantine, 1995).

25. A. Kimbrell, *ibid.*: 312. On p. 20 Kimbrell defines misandry as: "the general assumption that masculinity is the source of all our social ills. It is the sexist assumption that it is 'natural' for any male person to be dominating, oppressive, violent, sexually abusive, spiritually immature, and antagonistic to nature. It assigns blame solely to men for humanity's historic evils. It naturally leads to a hatred of men and masculinity."

26. *Globe and Mail*, 25 September 1995.

27. E. Kruk, *Divorce and Disengagement: Patterns of Fatherhood Within and Beyond Marriage* (Halifax: Fernwood, 1993).

28. M. Diamantopolus, "Family Feud: Kids 'R Casualties in Divorce," *Prairie Dog* (April 1997): 8.

29. *The Gallup Report*, 25 June 1992; 24 January 1993; 8 March 1993; 23 December 1993.

30. Komarovsky, *Dilemmas of Masculinity*: 257.

31. de Beauvoir, *The Second Sex*: 689.

32. Ehrenreich, *The Hearts of Men*: 182.

33. Millett, *Sexual Politics*: 363.

Chapter 13: The Double Burden: Men's Version

1. M. Eichler, *Families in Canada Today* (Toronto: Gage, 1983): 75ff.

2. M. Eichler, *Family Shifts: Families, Policies and Gender Equality* (Toronto: Oxford, 1997): 60.

3. J.-A. Parliament, "How Canadians Spend Their Day," Statistics Canada, *Canadian Social Trends* (Winter 1989): 23-27.

4. K. Marshall, "Dual-Earners: Who's Responsible for the Housework," Statistics Canada, *Canadian Social Trends* (Winter 1993): 11-14; K. Marshall, "Employed Parents and the Division of Housework," *Perspectives on Labour and Income, Statistics*

Canada (Autumn 1993); A. A. Brayfield, "Employment Resources and Housework in Canada," *Journal of Marriage and the Family*, 54:1 (February 1992): 19-30.

5. A. Hochschild and A. Machung, *The Second Shift: Inside the Two-Job Marriage* (New York: Penguin, 1989).

6. For what follows, see L. Haas, "Role-sharing in Couples: A Study of Egalitarian Marriages," *Family Relations*, 29 (1980): 289-96; L. Haas, "Domestic Role-sharing in Sweden," *Journal of Marriage and the Family*, 43 (1981): 957-68; S. Model, "Housework by Husbands," in *Two Paychecks: Life in Dual-Career Families*, ed. J. Aldous (Beverley Hills: Sage, 1982); J. Scanzoni, *Sex Roles, Women's Work and Marital Conflict* (Lexington: Heath: 1978); K. Weingarten, "The Employment Pattern of Professional Couples and the Distribution of Involvement in the Family," *Psychology of Women Quarterly*, 3 (1978): 43-53; S. Yogev, "Do Professional Women Have Egalitarian Marital Relationships?" *Journal of Marriage and the Family*, 43 (1981): 865-71; L. Duxbury *et. al.*, "Work-family conflict: a comparison by gender, family type and perceived control," *Journal of Family Issues*, 15:3 (1994): 449-66; R. A. Ward, "Marital happiness and household equity in later life," *Journal of Marriage and the Family*, 55 (1993): 427-38; K. R. Blaisure and K. R. Allen, "Feminists and the ideology and practice of marital equality," *Journal of Marriage and the Family*, 56 (1995): 5-19.

7. L. A. Gilbert, Men in *Dual-Career Families: Current Realities and Future Prospects* (Hillsdale, N. J.: Lawrence Erlbaum, 1985). In this excellent book, Gilbert not only reports on the results of her study, but provides a first-rate review of the pertinent literature. In addition to her research focussing on men in dual-job families, Gilbert has done additional work on this new "normal" family, analyzing the problems, stresses, and adjustments required in the transition, as well as documenting the ultimately positive impacts of this new family

form on men, women and children: L. A. Gilbert, *Sharing It All: The Rewards and Struggles of Two-Career Families* (New York: Plenum, 1988); L. A. Gilbert, *Two Careers, One Family: The Promise of Gender Equality* (Newbury Park, Calif.: Sage, 1993). For further information on dual-job or dual-career families, including problems, controversies, and benefits, see, D. Ehrensaft, *Parenting Together: Men and Women Sharing the Care of Their Children* (New York: Free Press, 1987); F. N. Schwartz, *Breaking with Tradition: Women and Work, The New Facts of Life* (New York: Warner, 1992); L. R. Silberstein, *Dual-Career Marriage: A System in Transition* (Hillsdale, N. J.: Erlbaum, 1992); T. L. Parcel, *Parents' Jobs and Childrens' Lives* (New York: de Gruyter, 1994); R. M. Rose, *Working Wives and Dual-Earner Families* (Westport, Conn.: Praeger, 1994); R. Mahony, *Kidding Ourselves: Breadwinning, Babies, and Bargaining Power* (New York: Basic, 1995).

8. *Globe and Mail, Report on Business*, 2 December 1988.
9. J. Oderkirk and C. Lochhead, "Lone Parenthood: Gender Differences," Statistics Canada, *Canadian Social Trends* (Winter 1992): 16-19.
10. *Globe and Mail, Report on Business*, 7 January 1989.
11. S. Feinman, "Why is Cross-Sex Role Behaviour More Approved for Girls than for Boys?" *Sex Roles*, 7 (1981): 289-300.
12. Cited in R. Maynard, "The New Executive Father," *Report on Business Magazine*, (March 1989): 46.
13. Gilbert, Men in *Dual-Career Families*: 115ff.
14. *Ibid.*: 115.
15. D. H. Bell, "About Men," New York *Times Magazine* (31 July 1983), cited in Gilbert, *Men in Dual-Career Families*: 3, 47.
16. C. Avery-Clark, "Sexual Dysfunction and Disorder Patterns of Husbands of Working and Nonworking Women," *Journal of Sex and Marital Therapy*, 12:4 (1986): 282-96.
17. Gilbert, *Men in Dual-Career Families*: 115ff.
18. *Ibid.*: 85ff.

Part V: Conclusion: Easing the Crisis
Introduction: Toward a New Family Policy

1. M. Eichler, *Families in Canada Today: Recent Changes and Their Policy Consequences* (Toronto: Gage, 1983): ch. 9, "Legal Policies": 272ff ; ch. 10, "Governmental Policies": 306ff, especially 320ff. See also J. Ursel, *Private Lives and Public Policy: One Hundred Years of State Intervention in the Family* (Toronto: Women's Press, 1992).
2. *Ibid.*: 329.
3. *Ibid.*: 330-31.
4. M. Eichler, *Family Shifts: Families, Policies, and Gender Equality* (Toronto: Oxford, 1997).
5. For details on the triumph of the neoconservative consensus and the imposition of deep cuts in social, health, and education spending, see J. Calvert, *Government Limited: The Corporate Takeover of the Public Sector in Canada* (Ottawa: Centre for Policy Alternatives, 1984); W. Magnusson et. al., *The New Reality: The Politics of Restraint in British Columbia* (Vancouver: New Star, 1984); S. Clarkson, *Canada and the Reagan Challenge* (Toronto: Lorimer, 1985); D. Drache and D. Cameron, eds. *The Other Macdonald Report* (Toronto: Lorimer, 1985); D. Cameron, ed. *The Free Trade Papers* (Toronto: Lorimer, 1986); J. Krieger, *Reagan, Thatcher and the Politics of Decline* (New York: Oxford, 1986); J. Laxer, *Leap of Faith: Free Trade and the Future of Canada* (Edmonton: Hurtig, 1986); C. Gonick, *The Great Economic Debate* (Toronto: Lorimer, 1987); L. McQuaig, *Behind Closed Doors* (Toronto: Penguin, 1987); J. W. Warnock, *Free Trade and the New Right Agenda* (Vancouver: New Star, 1988); H. Hardin, *The Privatization Putsch* (Halifax: Institute for Research on Public Policy, 1989); A. Tupper and G. G. Doern, eds. *Privatization, Public Policy and Public Corporations in Canada* (Halifax: Institute for Research on Public Policy, 1989); N. Brooks, *Paying for Civilized Society: The Need for Fair and*

Responsible Tax Reform (Ottawa: Canadian Centre for Policy Alternatives, 1990); D. Savoie, *The Politics of Public Spending in Canada* (Toronto: University of Toronto, 1990); H. Mimoto and P. Cross, "The Growth of the Federal Debt," *Canadian Economic Observer*, Statistics Canada (June 1991); P. M. Marchak, *The Integrated Circus: The New Right and the Restructuring of Global Markets* (Montreal: McGill-Queen's, 1991); M. Watkins, *Madness and Ruin: Politics and the Economy in the Neo-conservative age* (Toronto: Between the Lines, 1992); J. J. Rice and M. J. Prince, "Life of Brian: A social policy legacy," *Perception* (June 1993); L. McQuaig, *The Wealthy Banker's Wife: The Assault on Equality in Canada* (Toronto: Penguin, 1993); S. McBride and J. Sheilds, *Dismantling a Nation: The Canadian Agenda* (Halifax: Fernwood, 1993); L. Martin, *Pledge of Allegiance: The Surrender of Canada During the Mulroney Years* (Toronto: McClelland and Stewart, 1993); J. Laxer, *False God: How the Globalization Myth Impoverished Canada* (Toronto: Lester, 1993); National Forum on Family Security, *Family Security in Insecure Times* (Ottawa: Canadian Council on Social Development, 1993); M. Baker, ed. *Canada's Changing Families: Challenges of Public Policy* (Ottawa: Vanier Institute, 1994); M. Friendly, *Child Care Policy in Canada* (Don Mills: Addison-Wesley, 1994); M. Barlow and B. Campbell, *Straight Through the Heart: How the Liberals Abandoned the Just Society* (Toronto: Harper/Collins, 1996); L. Osberg and P. Fortin, eds. *Unnecessary Debts* (Toronto: Lorimer, 1996); P. Armstrong and H. Armstrong, *Wasting Away: The Undermining of Canadian Health Care* (Toronto: Oxford, 1996). The *CCPA Monitor*, published ten times a year by the Canadian Centre for Policy Alternatives in Ottawa, is a good source of information on the neo-consevative agenda and its implementation in Canada over the last 15 years.

Chapter 14: Proposed Directions in Family Policy

1. *The Gallup Report*, 14 August 1989.
2. For what follows, see *Globe and Mail*, 27 December 1984; 13 April 1988; 11 January, 29 February, 13 April, 14 September, 1 November 1989. See also Canada, Human Resources Development, *Employment Insurance: maternity, parental and sickness benefits* (Ottawa, 1997).
3. *The Gallup Report*, 4 December 1986.
4. Q. Rae-Grant and B. E. Robson, "Moderating the Morbidity of Divorce," *Canadian Journal of Psychiatry*, 33:6 (August 1988): 443-52.
5. N. Rae-Grant, "Primary Prevention: Implications for the Child Psychiatrist," *Canadian Journal of Psychiatry*, 33:6 (August 1988): 433-42.
6. D. Ellis and N. Stuckless, *Mediating and negotiating marital conflicts* (Beverley Hills: Sage, 1996); W. A. Cole and J. M. Bradford, "Abduction During Custody and Access Disputes," *Canadian Journal of Psychiatry*, 37:4 (May 1992): 264-66; E. Lipmen et. al., "The Problems of Children in Lone-Mother Families," Statistics Canada, *Canadian Social Trends* (Spring 1997): 7-8; J. H. Beitchman, "Prediction of Adjustment from Preschool to Middle Childhood," *Canadian Journal of Psychiatry*, 38:9 (November 1993): 622-37; M. E. Lamb, "Effects of non-parental care on child development: an update," *Canadian Journal of Psychiatry*, 41:6 (August 1996): 330-42; A. M. Delorey, "Joint legal custody: a reversion to patriarchal power," *Canadian Journal of Women and the Law*, 3:1 (1989): 33-44; B. J. Fidler et. al., "Joint Custody: Historical, Legal, and Clinical Perspectives with Emphasis on the Situation in Canada," *Canadian Journal of Psychiatry*, 34:6 (August 1989): 561-68; J. A. Arditti and T. Z. Keith, "Visitation frequency, child support payments and the father-child relationship post-divorce," *Journal of Marriage and the Family*, 55 (1993): 699-712; D. R. Meyer and S. Garasky, "Custodial fathers: myths, realities, and child

support policy," *Journal of Marriage and the Family*, 55 (1993): 73-89; N. Grizenko and C. Fisher, "Review of Studies of Risk and Protective Factors for Psychopathology in Children," *Canadian Journal of Psychiatry*, 37:10 (December 1992): 711-21; J. M. Jenkins and M. A. Smith, "Factors protecting children living in disharmonious homes: maternal reports," *Journal of the American Academy of Child and Adolescent Psychiatry*, 29 (1990): 60-69; A. Koel et. al., "Patterns of relitigation in the postdivorce family," *Journal of Marriage and the Family*, 56 (1994): 265-77.

Chapter 15: Proposed Directions in Feminist Policy

1. For what follows see *Globe and Mail*, 28 August 1982: 23 and 29 January, 17 and 21 May, 27 July, 8 and 22 August 1988: 19, 25 and 31 July; 5 August; 4, 6 and 23 November 1989; 24 January and 2 February 1991.
2. R. S. Abella, *Report of the Royal Commission on Equality in Employment* (Ottawa: Supply and Services, 1984).
3. *Ibid.*: 254.
4. *Financial Post*, 22 June 1987.
5. *Financial Post*, 30 May 1988.
6. P. Phillips and E. Phillips, *Women and Work* (Toronto: Lorimer, 1983): 57-58.
7. *Financial Post*, 30 May 1988.
8. *Financial Post*, 9 May 1988.
9. *Globe and Mail*, 17 January 1990.

Epilogue 2003: Canada's New Family Forms

1. *Globe and Mail*, 18 January 2003; 19 January 2003; 24 February 2003.
2. *Globe and Mail, Report on Business*, 25 September 2002.
3. National Council of Welfare. *Poverty Profile 1999*. Ottawa: Public Works and Government Services, 2002. All poverty figures are taken from here.
4. Conway, J. F. "Ottawa Embarks on Poverty Cleansing," Regina *Leader Post*, 21 April 1999. *Globe and Mail*, 9 January 2003; *National Post*, 14 December 1998.

5. Wallerstein, Judith, *et. al. The Unexpected Legacy of Divorce: A 25 Year Landmark Study*. New York: Hyperion, 2000.
6. *Globe and Mail*, 16 October 2002.
7. Ambert, A.-M. *Contemporary Family Trends: Divorce: Facts, Figures and Consequences*. Nepean, ON: Vanier Institute of the Family, 2002; Kronby, Malcolm. *Canadian Family Law*. Toronto: Stoddart, 2001.
8. Status of Women Canada. *Assessing Violence Against Women: A Statistical Profile*. Ottawa, 2002.
9. Trocmé, N., *et. al. 1993 Ontario Incidence Study of Reported Child Abuse And Neglect*. Toronto: Centre of Excellence for Child Welfare, University of Toronto, 1994; Trocmé, N., *et. al. 1998 Ontario Incidence Study of Reported Child Abuse and Neglect*. Toronto: Centre of Excellence for Child Welfare, University of Toronto, 2002. For national incidence figures see: Trocmé, N., *et. al. Child Maltreatment in Canada: Canadian Incidence Study of Reported Child Abuse and Neglect*. Ottawa: Health Canada, 2001.
10. Statistics Canada. *Family Violence in Canada: a statistical profile 1999*. Ottawa, 1999; Statistics Canada. *Family Violence in Canada: a statistical profile 2000*. Ottawa, 2000.
11. Conway, J. F. "The small truth and the large lie, *Briarpatch*, September 2000, pp. See also Flood, Michael, "Claims About Husband Battering," at <http://www.xyonline.net/husband battering.shtml>.
12. *Globe and Mail*, 17 June 2002.
13. *Globe and Mail*, 17 January 2003.
14. *Globe and Mail*, 26 February 2003; 17 February 2003.
15. *The Guardian*, 26 August 2002.

Index

196–97, 200; masculine role,
185–87, 194–96; new identity,
280; reasons for divorce, 75–76;
single-parent fathers, 28–29,
192, 216–17; victims of spousal
homicide, 169–70
men's movement, 203–9; fathers'
rights groups, 205–6; and rights
of non-custodial parents, 209;
right-wing crusade, 207–9;
shifts and splits in, 206–8
mental health. *See also* emotional
health: of adolescent girls, 148;
of children, 70–71; of divorced
men, 197–200; family breakdown and, 41–44, 151–52; of
husbands in dual-income families, 219–20; of married
women, 147–49; poverty and,
60, 66; of stay-at-home mothers, 147; of traditional men,
197–203; working women, 150
Messier, Camille, 99
middle manager/administration
positions, 123
Midtown Manhattan study, 42
military: sexism in, 104, 130
Mill, John Stuart, 14
Miller, Arthur, 190
Millett, Kate, 187, 212
minimum-wage earnings, 57
Mirowsky, J., 117
monogamy, 6, 10, 200
Morgan, Lewis H., 6
Morgentaler, Henry, 245–46
motherhood: middle-class notion
of, 12
Mount Cashel Orphanage, 98
Mulroney government, 228, 264

Nakamura, Alice, 139
National Council of Welfare, 60,

62, 266
National Shared Parenting
Association (NSPA), 209
Naugler, Gail, 175
neglect, parental, 97
neo-conservatism: cuts in social
spending, 55–56, 58, 230–32;
and daycare crisis, 50–51; family policies, 226–27, 228,
229–30; and official poverty
figures, 56; woman-blaming
analyses, 147
Nett, E.M., 35
Neumann, A. Clubb, 34
New Men, Partners in Change, 210
non-government organizations
(NGOs), 243
nuclear family, 11–13
nursing, 123

O'Brien, Dereck, 98
Ontario Federation of Women
Teachers' Association, 108
Ontario Health Survey, 70
Operation Rescue, 278
orphanages. *See* juvenile institu-
tions

Parsons, Talcott, 145
part-time jobs, 133, 134, 135, 140
patriarchy: and child abuse, 91–92;
complicity of women, 183–84;
decline of, 18–22; economic
dependence of women and, 187;
and liberation of women, 212;
traditional families, 186–87; and
wife abuse, 177
pay equity, 218, 249–53, 275–76
pay inequity: extent of, 121–22;
job segregation, 127–29; occupational segregation, 123–26;
and professional advancement,